CRITICAL ISSUES IN SPORT AND SOCIETY

Michael Messner and Douglas Hartmann, Series Editors

Critical Issues in Sport and Society features scholarly books that help expand our understanding of the new and myriad ways in which sport is intertwined with social life in the contemporary world. Using the tools of various scholarly disciplines, including sociology, anthropology, history, media studies and others, books in this series investigate the growing impact of sport and sports-related activities on various aspects of social life as well as key developments and changes in the sporting world and emerging sporting practices. Series authors produce groundbreaking research that brings empirical and applied work together with cultural critique and historical perspectives written in an engaging, accessible format.

Jules Boykoff, *Activism and the Olympics: Dissent at the Games in Vancouver and London*

Kathryn Henne, *Testing for Athlete Citizenship: The Regulation of Doping and Sex in Sport*

Jeffrey Montez de Oca, *Discipline and Indulgence: College Football, Media, and the American Way of Life during the Cold War*

INDIAN SPECTACLE

College Mascots and the Anxiety of Modern America

JENNIFER GUILIANO

RUTGERS UNIVERSITY PRESS
New Brunswick, New Jersey, and London

Library of Congress Cataloging-in-Publication Data

Guiliano, Jennifer.
 Indian spectacle : college mascots and the anxiety of modern America / Jennifer
Guiliano.
  pages cm. — (Critical issues in sport and society)
  Includes bibliographical references and index.
  ISBN 978-0-8135-6555-2 (hardback) — ISBN 978-0-8135-6554-5
(pbk.) — ISBN 978-0-8135-6556-9 (e-book (web pdf))
  1. Indians as mascots. 2. Sports team mascots—Social aspects—United
States. 3. Indians of North America—Social conditions—20th century.
 I. Title.
  GV714.5.G85 2015
  306.4′83—dc23   2014030636

A British Cataloging-in-Publication record for this book is available from the British
Library.

Visit our website: http://rutgerspress.rutgers.edu

Manufactured in the United States of America

In elementary school, my mom taught me to thread a microfiche machine to read nineteenth-century census rolls, and my dad taught me to love sports. I didn't realize then how much those two things would inform the rest of my life. This is dedicated to them, the historian and the coach. Thanks for teaching me everything I know.

CONTENTS

ACKNOWLEDGMENTS

As a student of history and a scholar working at the intersection of history, critical sport studies, and race, I have been honored to have individuals, institutions, and organizations contribute their time, energy, money, and emotional support to this work in its various incarnations. I am deeply thankful for the mentoring and engagement offered by coadvisers, committee members, and faculty during various degrees. Passionate about the field and about my work, Adrian Burgos was a champion adviser, mentor, teacher, and friend, who I am certain made me a better scholar. He was, and continues to be, an influential presence in my academic life. I am proud to have been his doctoral student and can only hope to carry on his legacy of excellence with my own students one day. Dave Roediger offered an incredible breadth of knowledge and enthusiastic support for this project, which greatly shaped this text, its predecessors, and my experience in writing it. Dave's joy at being a scholar and activist continually reminds me that being caring and engaged is just as important in our scholarship as the critical thinking that we are doing. Committee members Frederick Hoxie and Michael Giardina invested their intellectual and emotional energies in guiding my scholarship. Fred introduced me to the incredible field of American Indian studies and has served as an important example of how one can construct a decades-long career that blends advocacy, activism, and historical analysis. I am particularly indebted to Michael for his continual urging to consider and reconsider innovative theoretical and methodological approaches to this book. Michael's incredible range of productivity around critical sport studies serves as a model of how one can be a fan of sports but also a critical theoretician and author. I am honored to call him a colleague and friend. I owe a large measure of thanks to additional scholars who directly and indirectly shaped this project: Daniel A. Nathan, Marguerite S. Shafer, Allan M. Winkler, Andrew R. L. Cayton, Kristin Hoganson, C. L. Cole, O. Vernon Burton, Jean Allman, Antoinette Burton, Susan Sleeper-Smith, Brenda Farnell, Carol Spindel, Norm Denzin, Philip J. Deloria, Eric Lott, Jim Barrett, and the entire Committee on Institutional Cooperation American Indian Studies Consortium (2001–2008).

I am delighted to offer thanks to my former graduate-student colleagues at the University of Illinois and Miami University. A truly brilliant group of academics, they provided valuable insights in coursework through informal discussions and in formal reviews of papers and proposals. Of particular note for their intellectual and personal support are Alexandra "Sasha" Mobley, Amanda Brian, Anita Bravo, April Lindsey, Karlos Hill, Melissa Rohde-Cherullo, Michelle Kleehammer, and Sandra Henderson. All are great scholars in their own right, and I eagerly anticipate every lecture, article, and book that they produce. You should buy their books and go hear them speak. Their scholarship will change your conception of the world and how it came to be. I also offer my thanks to Trevor Muñoz; Kate Parkhurst; Kelsey, Carlos, and Cy Corlett-Rivera; Paz Magat; Tara Rodgers; and Rebecca Appleford. Always willing to have a cocktail, eat dinner, have a chat, or watch a game, they provided a much-needed outlet throughout the revision process.

This project benefited from extensive assistance from the individuals, archivists, and departments that provided access to their collections. At the University of Illinois, I must extend special thanks to former librarian Mary Stuart of the History, Philosophy, and Newspaper Library, as well as the University Archives, the Sousa Archives, and the Center for American Music. Staff at the Florida State University Special Collections and University Archives, the Miami University Archives, the Stanford University Native American Cultural Center, the Stanford University Special Collections and University Archives, the University of North Dakota Department of American Indian Studies, and the Elwyn B. Robinson Department of Special Collections at the University of North Dakota ably assisted and greatly enriched my efforts. A number of university departments and their faculty and staff supported my research by providing funding, leave to complete my work, or unique collaborative opportunities. They include the Department of History at Miami University; the Miami University Archives; the Departments of History and American Indian Studies at the University of Illinois; the Committee on Institutional Cooperation American Indian Studies Consortium; the Institute for Computing in Humanities, Arts, and Social Science at the University of Illinois; and the Maryland Institute for Technology in the Humanities at the University of Maryland.

Various incarnations and portions of material throughout this book were presented at conferences and invited presentations including, but not limited to, the North American Society for Sport History Annual Conference (May 2002); Capitalizing on Sport: America, Democracy, and Everyday Life Conference sponsored by the University of Illinois at Urbana-Champaign and the Center on Democracy in a Multiracial Society (March 14, 2003); the Association for Cultural Studies Annual Conferences (2004, 2007); the Committee on Institutional Cooperation/American Indian Studies Consortium's Annual Graduate Conference sponsored by Indiana University (April 21, 2006); and the Department of History at the University of Maryland (2012). I offer thanks to the attendees of these events for their comments and criticism, with particular appreciation for C. Richard King, whose interest and willingness to provide opportunities for young scholars led directly to the publication of this work. His own scholarship on mascotry and race represents the best of this small but growing field. Along with Richard, I extend my gratitude to series editors Douglas Hartmann and Michael Messner as well as Rutgers University Press editor Peter Mickulas. Thank you for your contributions to the study of sport and society and your support of my work.

Six friends deserve special mention for their tireless support of this book. Simon Appleford, a digital humanist and scholar of American political humor, offered encouragement when I questioned whether I was going to move forward with this work in book form and commented on numerous versions of proposals and drafts. Joseph Genetin-Pilawa and James J. Buss deserve recognition for their contributions to the field of Native American studies and the quality of friendship and collaboration they have given over the years. The depth of knowledge and quality of scholarship each has contributed to our collective knowledge on the lived experiences of Native peoples cannot be understated. Jim, in particular, devoted significant time to commenting on my introduction and encouraged me to not shy away from making claims about the place of American spectacle in middle-class life. Karen Rodriguez'G, a scholar of the British Empire with an emphasis on spatiality and identity, was an influential sounding board in considerations of spatial, postcolonial, and performative theories as well as the practice of doing history. Her theoretical and methodological insights enriched this book at every stage. She always returned my panicked calls and was willing to listen to my professional and personal dramas. Rory Walker-Graham gave me a shoulder to cry on when the writing process grew frustrating and, most important, someone to watch soccer with when I wanted to avoid the book. His emotional support deserves my deepest thanks. Debi Back has served as best friend, therapist, colleague, voice-of-reason, and historian-in-crime throughout the past fourteen years. I lucked into a best friend simply by sitting down in the back row of a Civil War history class in college. She has seen the best and worst of my work throughout the years and, even when I doubt myself, is always there with a kind word and a laugh that will make me feel better. I can only hope that she understands how much I appreciate her love and support. She, and everyone else mentioned here, mean the world to me. Thank you to each of you a thousand times over. I owe you more than one.

For all the intellectual development and collaboration offered by my academic colleagues and friends, this work would not have been completed without the incredible support of my extended family. My parents, to whom this work is dedicated, provided emotional and financial support. They cheered me on through the many trials and tribulations of getting an advanced degree and helped me enjoy the successes that this work represents. My sister, Teri Downing, and brothers, Jay and Sean Guiliano, continually reminded me to enjoy life to the fullest and celebrate every day. They made sure that I felt part of it all even when I had my head buried in books. Significantly, they have shared with me six of the funniest, cutest, and cleverest children. Cullen and Chloe Downing, Isabella and Jonathon Guiliano, and Luca and Ava Guiliano have made me laugh, cry, and smile throughout the long and sometimes rocky road to completing this work.

I can only hope that each of them realizes how much I love being their aunt. Lori and Wes Shipley opened their home during a particularly difficult research trip, while their children, Dillon and Regan, provided a welcome opportunity to enjoy the simple things in life. Marsha and Rick West were my saviors throughout my tenure in Champaign completing the dissertation that preceded this book. From lunches filled with laughter to dinner debates about academic tenure and the Illinois mascot, my aunt and uncle have always made sure I am fed, housed, and loved. Collectively, I am so blessed to have a supportive, funny, and engaged family who do not mind that I spend significant portions of my time arguing with them about sports and their meaning.

Finally, my acknowledgments would not be complete without mentioning my grandparents, Joe and Marge Miller. Although they were not with us through most of the stages of this work, this book would never have been written without their involvement. My grandparents were lifelong Champaign residents who loved the University of Illinois and were consummate fans. Although they would not have agreed with my analysis of the meaning of Chief Illiniwek to their community, they would have loved that I was willing to enter the debate.

All errors within this work are, of course, my own and should not reflect on those acknowledged here.

ABBREVIATIONS

ABA	American Bandmasters Association
AFCA	American Football Coaches Association
BSA	Boy Scouts of America
FSU	Florida State University
IAA	Intercollegiate Athletic Association
Illinois	University of Illinois
Miami	Miami University
NFL	National Football League
Stanford	Stanford University
UC	University of California, Berkeley
UND	University of North Dakota
UPenn	University of Pennsylvania
YMCA	Young Men's Christian Association

INDIAN SPECTACLE

INTRODUCTION

On January 1, 1952, nearly 100,000 college football fans filled the seats of the famed Rose Bowl in Pasadena, California, to watch the Pacific Coast Conference champions of Stanford University compete against a squad from the University of Illinois, champions of the Big Ten Conference.[1] Three days of Pacific storms had cleared the air and left the grass crisp, as football players from both universities took to the field. While the contest had taken place on thirty-seven previous occasions, 1952 marked the first time that it, or any football game for that matter, appeared on nationally broadcast television. Throughout the previous collegiate season, Stanford's "Cinderella" team, coached by Chuck Taylor, won nine of ten games, while the University of Illinois had struggled against the University of Michigan and the University of California, Los Angeles, each of whom Stanford handily defeated. The events surrounding the game were as dramatic as the game itself. Prior to kickoff, fans from Illinois and Stanford welcomed the new year by enjoying the sights and sounds of collegiate marching bands, equestrian teams, and heavily decorated floral floats that ambled down Colorado Boulevard during the Tournament of Roses Parade. The festivities included a performance by "Chief Illiniwek"—portrayed by Illinois student William "Bill" Hug, a twenty-three-year-old white man from the suburban community of Park Ridge, Illinois, outside of Chicago—and Stanford University's unofficial mascot, "Prince Lightfoot"—portrayed by H. D. "Timm" Williams, a twenty-seven-year-old enrolled member of the Yurok tribe from near Sacramento.[2] Hug performed an "Indian Dance" during the parade, and Williams cheered for his school.[3] The Tournament of Roses court waved from their perches while the Stanford band played its spirit songs.

As with most football contests, one team walked away a victor and the other a loser, but this particular Rose Bowl highlights how both schools chose to market themselves—visually, aurally, and athletically—both to game attendees and to a nationally televised audience for the first time. The moment signaled the apex of what college football had been trying to accomplish since the turn of the century: a commercial spectacle that blended athletics, fan participation, and national audiences. From the stopovers en route to the game where the players greeted alumni to the lively tailgating prior to the game and the halftime performance itself, the game of college football had transformed from local matches played on rough fields to a carefully crafted industry that allowed universities to brand themselves. In the case of the University of Illinois and Stanford, that industry employed the performances of a white man dressed as an Indian and an Indian dressed in tribal garb to present an engaging, entertaining spectacle to thrill the audience.

Between the two halves of a lopsided outcome—Illinois won the game 40-7—Illinois's Hug, in the guise of Chief Illiniwek, and Williams, in his adopted character Prince Lightfoot, took to the field to perform with their university bands during halftime.[4] The details of yardage and scoring drives are of little significance to the larger cultural analysis of the 1952 Rose Bowl, because, after all, this particular Rose Bowl was about far more than a game. It was about the bands and fans who flooded the Arroyo Seco area surrounding the stadium, newspaper writers whose articles filled the pages of national newspapers, university presidents and alumni constituencies who used the game as fund-raising opportunities, and spectators who viewed the game as an opportunity to cheer for their favorite team. This was an audience that represented a culmination of roughly fifty years of debate about college football, spectacle, and the role of universities in educating the public.

By the end of the 1930s, football accounted for 20 to 25 percent of all newsreel footage.[5] It was covered in local papers and the weekly magazines the *Saturday Evening Post* and *Collier's*, and was even the subject of a feature film. Many of these stories spoke of warriors and heroes, victors and vanquished, will and triumph. Athletes and coaches, band members and their leaders, spectators, newspaper writers, university presidents, alumni, faculty, students (especially fraternity members), artists, writers, and even American presidents had been engaged with crafting these narratives in the years after football spread from the Northeast to the rest of the country. With television cameras trained on the field, the 1952 contest capped a national spectacle that incorporated aural and visual rituals. And with the spectacle, the eyes of a nation consumed a larger narrative of masculinity, race, and collegiate athletics.

THE WORLD THAT MADE COLLEGIATE FOOTBALL

Individuals of the early twentieth century lived in a world that was an environment in flux. The latter half of the nineteenth century and the early twentieth century were marked by the consequences of rapid industrialization, immigration, migration, political upheaval, and social instability. The rural, agrarian economy where men undertook hard physical labor in the fields and woods of America had transitioned into an increasingly urban society where men worked within factories and in the white-collar world of business. A new class of managers and supervisors who oversaw mechanisms that increased technological efficiency rose to replace the artisans and skilled craftsmen who had carved out a living in the post–Civil War world. Wealth accumulated in the hands of fewer men, primarily industrial titans who were involved in factories, railroads, and steel.[6] Men like Andrew Carnegie, Philip Armour, J. P. Morgan, and John D. Rockefeller enjoyed latitudes that lower- and even middle-class men did not as the nation's economy grew from $16 billion on the eve of the Civil War to over $88 billion by 1900.[7] That growth continued well into the twentieth century, even through cycles of depression.

As they moved away from occupations that tested their physical limits, men sought opportunities to prove themselves through autonomy, self-control, and ownership of one's home and business. While it was entirely appropriate for the lower classes to work for a wage six days a week, men who imagined themselves as part of the rising middle class were leery of the perception that they were physically weak, emotionally effeminate, and fiscally unsound. Working for wages, as Horace Greeley once noted, would place grown men under the yoke of young boys, leading to their humiliation and emasculation.[8] Manhood, a complex interaction of institutional allegiances, ideologies, and daily practice enacted by men, became an obsession of middle-class men in the waning decades of the nineteenth century and the beginning of the twentieth.[9] They feared that they would be supplanted as heads of households unless they could overtly "prove" their masculinity. Gentility, respectability, and character coupled with strength, will, and doing one's duty offered white middle-class men the opportunity to protect family, friends, and even employees.[10] Amid this landscape, sport emerged as a proving ground for anxious men fearful of losing their manliness.[11] Sportsmen, specifically, represented the potential of American masculinity.[12]

This fascination with masculinity, the body, and spectacle forms the framework for this book. Americans easily identified wealthy individuals with their grand homes, cars, and elite educations. Men with names like Carnegie, DuPont, Fields, and the like were captains of industry, and those in their social circle were consumed with the future of the nation, be it militarily, economically, or morally. They attended Harvard or Yale and often studied abroad. At the opposite end, lower-class men were also easily identified by their coarse language, rough clothes, and tired countenance as they toiled to support their families working long hours for low wages. The rural and urban poor, recent immigrants, unskilled laborers, and recently freed slaves comprised much of this class. It is, instead, the more ambiguous, the newly established middle class of businessmen, managers, professional educators, and the like that serve as the core group under examination. The late nineteenth-century university was an institution of a few thousand primarily white, elite males from the Northeast that by the 1920s had to reconcile an influx of students and alumni, mainly from a rising, increasingly worldly middle class of the Midwest and even West. This was a generation of young men who had traveled the world as part of the Great War (1914–1918), who had seen the expansion of the railroad system that dramatically decreased the time it took to reach major urban centers, and who were more exposed to popular culture through the growth of vaudeville, circuses, newspapers, radio, and even early film. They were not the moneyed elites as most students had been at the turn of the century. Instead, they were part of a generation of students whose parents were newly minted professionals, lawyers, doctors, and businessmen as a result of the Industrial Revolution. And they were a generation versed in the appeal of sport, be it baseball, football, boxing, track, or basketball.[13]

Students were enrolling in a twentieth-century university that struggled with its identity. It had become, following the Civil War, a center of specialized modern intellectual culture that relied on individualized departments with professional, tenured faculties. It was also an institution that sought both regional and national recognition.[14] The challenge for university faculty and administrators was to make the seemingly esoteric disciplines of the social sciences, as well as professional business degrees, relatable to the citizen public so that they might understand the value of higher education and begin to consume new scientific disciplines. This was particularly important as these disciplines could be seen as dry and irrelevant to a public more obsessed with securing employment, feeding their families, and enjoying limited leisure time.

Football, simultaneously a game of rules and order, entertainment and violence, provided a common language for universities and colleges to articulate their values to the public.[15] "Football," writes the scholar Michael Oriard, "was locally rooted [between 1920 and 1950], serving as a powerful source of community identity and pride."[16] It defined an entire social and domestic world of American middle-class life. The rhetoric of college football espoused the fundamental aspects of early twentieth-century U.S. cosmopolitanism: the triumph of the collective over the individual, the active agency of athletes and spectators in supporting the community, personal responsibility and accountability, inclusiveness, and Christian morality. This particular function of collegiate athletics was important, especially as middle-class white male anxieties became written across the athletic landscape through the birth of large-scale stadiums, the staging of memorial campaigns to honor previous generations and fallen war heroes, and the creation of halftime performances. Sport, particularly college football, provided a space to release these anxieties because the story of American survival was bound in its rules and regulations and transmitted to a broad audience on pages of major newspapers, through projection on the silver screen, and across the waves of broadcast radio. Games were won by persistence and strength. Games were lost through a lack of physical ability or moral character.

The rhetoric of communal development and physical triumph was in part a response to the challenges college football had faced in previous years. As explored in the first chapter, gambling, vice, violence, coaches and athletes for hire, and the commodification of football all disrupted the rhetoric that universities relied upon in communicating with the public. It was the downside of American modernity, a moment when the public was just as fascinated with crime and criminals as they were with their heroes and when the evils of urbanization and modern commercialism were being excoriated daily.[17] Seeking to stamp out these negative forces, by 1926 universities had used not just the regulation of the game of football and its role as a formal discipline within the university but also halftime performance and athletic identities as a means of controlling and mediating the meaning of white male identity.

This book reveals that, while football was certainly a source of community identity and pride, the individuals and institutions engaged in producing college football were part of a transnational circuit of exchange that was decidedly not inclusive. The power of the sport to transcend its parochial roots relied on an explicitly racialized brand of American spectacle that extended the use of colonial tropes through faux Indian bodies, images, and music to maintain and grow its audience. Using the University of Illinois, Stanford University, the University of North Dakota, Miami University, and Florida State University between 1926 and 1952 as the landscape of this exploration, this book argues that halftime performance and racialized athletic identity were enmeshed in the project of higher education. Refocusing the lens of spectacle to consider college football and its environs as cultural production reveals that racialized performances of collegiate identity were continually being made and remade in the mid-twentieth century as white men worked to define the values of masculinity as white, educated, and heterosexual. That project relied on white men's desire to train and promote their bodies as aggressive, physical, and heterosexual. Returning to the opening vignette of this introduction reminds us of this broadly construed field of analysis and the variety of people engaged: athletes and coaches, band members and their leaders, spectators, newspaper writers, university presidents, alumni, faculty, fraternity members, artists, writers, and community members. College football was the vehicle that allowed white middle-class men to affirm their value to their families, friends, and even the public. Fans could publicly perform their allegiance to the cult of masculinity by celebrating their teams' success. Athletes could embody physical perfection as well as strength, gentility, and respect for order. Coaches were able to mentor and guide young men away from potential evils like gambling, hypersexuality, and other base ills. Newspapermen, musicians, artists, and even university faculty not only aided these efforts but also contributed substantially to the public understanding of the value of creating a white, masculine, middle-class citizenry.

The need to continually make and regularly enforce the boundaries of college athletics and its spectatorship resulted from the conflict between the original mission of land grant institutions—to educate the citizenry—and the reality that higher education was limited to those with means and opportunity.[18] Students accounted for a small percentage of the eighteen-to-twenty-one-year-old male demographic. Only 8 percent attended college in 1920, 12 percent in 1930, 16 percent in 1940, and just under 30 percent in 1950. In the eyes of administrators, audience members who previously had not attended college might provide an avenue for generating revenue for the expanding institution of higher education. For every single student who attended the university, there were potentially thousands more who could be reached through college football. Moreover, football and its associated spectacle provided a vehicle for disseminating a message about the boundaries of white middle-class masculinity for Americans in this period. It provided an outlet for men in their late twenties and early thirties to relive their youth through participation in football and its spectacle as audience members. Universities were able to generate large audiences for their events; however, they struggled to appeal to an increasingly diverse urban constituency that embraced popular culture and was either uninterested in or unable to afford to attend expensive institutions of higher education. Football, "partially democratized in the 1920s and 1930s by a tremendous mix of Italian, Polish, Jewish, and other eastern and southern European immigrants" for whom football was a vehicle for achieving American success, offered the opportunity to speak to men who could potentially donate to (for elites) or even (for the newly wealthy) enroll in the university. Urban, ethnic communities provided expanding markets for football. Many of their young sons took to the field to play college football in the 1920s.[19] They read newspaper coverage, purchased tickets to games, and invested in the future of universities as they sought access to education to remake themselves from immigrants to Americans. Under the guise of athletic teams and university monikers, elite and upper-class white men constituted, transformed, and transmitted ideas of Indian mascotry and physical triumph within the spectacle of college football using lower- and middle-class ethnic bodies.

MODERN ANXIETIES AND THE
MAKING OF NATIVE MASCOTS

In creating the opportunity for physically aggressive gentlemen to prove masculinity through athletic success, universities created opportunities for the public to affirm their belief that the future of America was a white middle-class future. Native American mascots became a key element of that articulation by providing a counterpoint to stories of progress and athletic success. Faux Indian bodies were used as proof that white men would ultimately be successful in their endeavors, be they athletic, social, or economic, just as white men were successful in colonizing America. Colonial tropes of Indian life and American expansion were embedded within halftime performances in music and imagery as well as within athletic identities. Indian-themed halftime shows and identities were far from being historical anomalies. In fact, Native Americans and sport shared a long history. John Steeprock (Seneca) competed in a footrace against thirty-seven white men before a crowd of 30,000 people in 1844.[20] In 1861, Louis "Deerfoot" Bennett (also Seneca) received international acclaim in England for his foot speed.[21] Between 1887 and 1945, forty-seven tribally recognized American Indians wore uniforms for major league baseball teams. Another eighty-five players had American Indian ancestry.[22] Baseball players Charles A. "Chief" Bender (White Earth Band of Chippewa), Louis Francis Sockalexis (Penobscot), John "Chief" Meyers (Cahuilla), and Moses Yellow Horse (Pawnee) were regularly covered in the sports pages.[23]

No Native athlete received more coverage or attention than Sac and Fox athlete Jim Thorpe.[24] A gold-medal-winning decathlete and pentathlete in the 1912 Stockholm Olympics, Thorpe's list of athletic accomplishments places him as the most storied athlete of the twentieth century. He was a two-time All-American college football player, major league baseball player (1913–1919), minor league baseball player (1919–1922), and professional football player (1915–1917, 1919–1920, 1921 Cleveland Indians, 1922–1923 Oorang Indians, 1924 Rock Island Independents, 1925 New York Giants, 1926 Canton Bulldogs, 1928 Chicago Cardinals). He even served as the first president of the American Professional Football Association, the forerunner of the modern National Football League. Thorpe and others were products of the world-famous Carlisle Industrial Indian School and Haskell Institute, Indian boarding schools that received extensive attention in non-Indian newspapers from 1890 onward, which will be explored later.[25]

Americans' fascination with Thorpe and other Native athletes is situated within what Native historian Philip J. Deloria has termed "nostalgic antimodernism."[26] Indians were simultaneously objects of racial repulsion who represented the base instincts of humans and the devolution of humanity. They were also racially desirable through nostalgia for community, spirituality, and nature. Indian athletes offered coaches, fans, and the public the opportunity to embrace primitivism by reading Indian bodies as inherently masculine.[27] Importantly, though, unlike white middle-class masculinity, which sought aggressiveness and physical strength tempered by gentility and moral uprightness, Indian masculinity provided a cautionary tale. Indian athletes were exhibits of barely restrained violence, brutes who might at any moment violate the rules of football and threaten the lives of those around them. White men juxtaposed the "natural" physicality of Indian men to the ills of industrialization and urbanization. Viewing Indian bodies during athletic performance in the first half of the twentieth century allowed fans, coaches, and the media to imagine that Indians were not grappling with the same anxieties of modern life that the rest of the country was. This, as Deloria notes, affirmed assimilationist policies, theories of social evolution where Indians would eventually decline (or die out altogether), and political and cultural policies that forced Indians to recognize federal authority. Indian athletes, particularly those who played on all-Native teams, were exoticized by white audiences. Exhibition football games and barnstorming baseball games were opportunities to see members of the "disappearing" race demonstrating their natural physical abilities. These games served as small-scale spectacles that primed audiences for what would develop around halftime performance: Indian dances, knife-throwing performances, and even theatrical exchanges where blanketed Indian athletes would wander around town looking at all the "big-city" extravagances. Native men became both an example for the desired physicality of white men and served as a warning that modernity could corrupt by enslaving men to the toils of industrial and office work. Despite the fact that Americans could not reconcile these tensions, they never abandoned the exoticism of Native mascots, because to do so meant completely accepting the perils of modernization.[28] As such, the white creators of halftime performance were primed for appropriating Indian spectacle for their own.

From large, urban universities to small-town schools, Indian mascots became a common feature of early and mid-twentieth-century educational identity. Dartmouth College (New Hampshire); St. John's University, Siena College, Syracuse University, and Colgate University (New York); Montclair State College (New Jersey); Juanita College (Pennsylvania); Miami University (Ohio); the University of Illinois at Urbana-Champaign and Bradley University (Illinois); Saint Mary's College and Mankato State College (Minnesota); Marquette University (Wisconsin); Eastern Michigan University (Michigan); Dickinson State University (North Dakota); Simpson College (Iowa); Oklahoma City University, the University of Oklahoma, and Southern Nazarene University (Oklahoma), Arkansas State University (Arkansas); Alcorn State University (Mississippi); University of Tennessee-Chattanooga (Tennessee); Seattle University, Eastern Washington University, and Yakima Valley Community College (Washington); Southern Oregon State University (Oregon); as well as Stanford University and Southwestern College (California) all featured Indian mascots. While each of these institutions deserves its own story, this book explores five sites that signal the dimension and depth of American engagement with the creation of halftime spectacles. From the fourth-largest university (the public University of Illinois), through the well-financed private research institution (Stanford University), to the rural liberal arts college (Miami University), the frontier agricultural school (the University of North Dakota), and the upstart southern institution that offered coeducation (Florida State University), these universities were part of a national network of performance and spectacle that surrounded college football and its attendant events. Selected to illustrate regional variations on the same theme of halftime and Indian performance, each school offers the opportunity to explore the appropriation of Native imagery, music, and performance through athletic identities.

Carefully monitored and policed by white men, the "Indian spectacle" of the University of Illinois at Urbana-Champaign's Chief Illiniwek, Stanford University's "Indians," the University of North Dakota's "Fighting Sioux," Miami

University's "Redskins," and Florida State University's "Seminoles" illustrate that this book is not just a narrative of college football, but is instead a history of culture and the ways in which Indian bodies were interwoven with white middle-class identity in the early twentieth century. Importantly, though, this book does not attempt to capture how Indian athletes performed their own cultural and racial identity for white audiences. Instead, it explores how faux Indians performed a set of behaviors that white audiences perceived as representations of Indian culture and race. This set of behaviors, termed "Indianness," coupled with the concentration on athletic bodies, is important as it highlights how white middle-class men imagined themselves and constructed their own form of Indian identity by sampling from historical tropes, perceptions, and misconceptions. By capturing brief moments and episodes with the narrative of college life around the country, I consider how these moments and episodes are always being contested, affirmed, negotiated, and constituted. Where possible, I highlight the contributions of Natives to these moments. Yet, ultimately, this book recognizes the racial and cultural boundaries that white middle-class men enacted around college football and their communities.

The challenges of modernity in the form of urbanization, immigration, industrialization, and the like threatened American masculinity. Produced through written, visual, and aural means, college football and its associated spectacles espoused and exposed racialized and gendered narratives that ultimately reaffirmed white male hypermasculine identity as the apex of American society. Individual sporting identities represented local manifestations of national consciousness about sport, race, and manhood. Football teams, bands, and literary and fraternal societies were individual but dependent expressions of the movement that worked to shape collegiate identity in the face of modern anxieties, including the closing of the American West, competition between institutions of higher education, the meaning of higher education and the intent of sport, as well as major events like the Great War (1914–1918), the Great Depression (1929–1941), and World War II (1939–1945).

THE MAKING OF AN "INDIAN SPECTACLE"

This book's title, *Indian Spectacle: Collegiate Mascots and the Anxiety of Modern America*, has an intentional double meaning. On the one hand, it directly recognizes the role college plays in the United States and in the American cultural imagination. College served, in the early twentieth century, as a site where boys became young men; where students could achieve academic, athletic, and personal accolades; and where America could invest its efforts to create hard-working, financially responsible citizens. The very people who held Native mascots and sports as arbiters for race and masculinity would rarely allow Jim Thorpe or other Indian athletes to cross those boundaries. They existed as a perfect specimen of athleticism, a controlled spectacle, but they rarely would be allowed to attend a white college to do so.[29] To attend, those who were Native would have to cast off their Indianness and embrace assimilationist (read: white) dress, religion, and cultural attitudes. Attending college was, in the American mind, an opportunity to better oneself for the common good, but that access was limited to those perceived as being potential contributing members of society. On the other hand, the title of this book alludes to the ways in which college relied on spectacle to fulfill its commitment to serve the general public. A site of performances of race, identity, and class that was uniquely American, halftime performance and athletic identity became an avenue for universities to engage with their public in carefully monitored and controlled ways. They expressed a multitude of complicated ways of envisioning community that relied on historical tropes of raced, classed, and gendered bodies and narratives of conquest familiar to the general public. Yet for all these complicated community dynamics, the underlying meanings remained extraordinarily consistent with their limited worldview: white men must carry on the legacies of their forefathers and become useful members of society in order to ensure the future of human and humane life. And, in doing so, they must carefully regulate their behaviors, their experiences, and even their physical bodies so as to preserve the social order.[30]

Studying college football with an attention to Indian mascots is situated as a firmly postmodern exercise that enriches our understanding of cultural history and the ways in which race, class, gender, and youth were enshrined within the expressions of American life, whether in the form of halftime spectacles, sporting identities, stadium campaigns, band performances, or newspapers. By attaching these instances to the larger milieu of minstrelsy, movies, literature, music, art, fraternal organizations, social clubs, and anthropological events like the world's fairs, a historically specific form of popular culture where middle-class men were engaged in viewing and producing racialized spectacles through the lens of cosmopolitan worldviews is revealed.[31] Mascotry and athletic identity were an integral way of mapping the meaning-making for these upper-middle-class men in their roles as bandleaders, coaches, alumni, athletes, fans, faculty, and newsmen. This type of mapping challenges bifurcated elucidation of culture into highbrow versus lowbrow endeavors by demonstrating how elites and upper-class men engaged in college athletics drew from lower-class practices of representation to speak to, and portray themselves as, middle class.

Shaped by industrialism, commercialism, capital acquisition and expression, mass democracy, and the nation-state, the modern American university of the early and mid-twentieth century was an innately political space that, while recognizing multiple identities, privileged young, male, white, middle-class, hypermasculine, and athletic as powerful. This was an oppositional identity read against a general public, who were perceived as masses of immigrants that needed education and protection from themselves.[32] Spectators could live vicariously through athletes on the field, be educated in appropriate social behaviors, and ultimately serve as a revenue stream that could support the next generation of America's leaders. Daniel Boorstin has extended the notion of pleasure and economy of performance by positing that complicit performances are "pseudo-events," fetishized moments of spectacle creation and dissemination where truths, realities, and meanings are complicated with ambiguity to arouse and capture the public interest.[33] As the game provided the opportunity for its performers and audiences (athletes and spectators), it muted their individual values, identities, and experiences in favor of the communal good. Thus, individuals who were not racially, economically, or even physically acceptable often became embroiled in supporting the desires of the community. The performance of mascots at halftime was just one expression of the needed ambiguity where the realities of life (especially Indian lives) were not needed. More specifically, it suggests that the very bodies of Natives were "reality, image, echo, appearance" rather than legitimate presences within the community.[34] This was the essence of modern communal identity that affirmed belonging through circuits of knowledge about sport, education, and race, and clearly positioned these men as disingenuous in their efforts to embrace the public.

Organizations including universities, the Boy Scouts of America, the American Bandmasters Association, and newspapers were invested in the creation of these images for the purposes of both entertainment and education.[35] One of the goals of these institutions was to create an able-bodied educated citizenry that could operate as an agent of the nation. For universities, this citizenry would be the next generation of white-collar professionals; the Boy Scouts sought moral training and skill-based aptitudes; the American Bandmasters Association imagined the creation of appreciative communities invested in their future; newspapers sought to sell their stories and enrich their potential share of the competitive newspaper audience. While each used varying definitions of what constituted "educated," they all used passing on, and the accumulation of, knowledge as its key social relationship. Each created hierarchical rules of success and belonging that continually affirmed the value of elite "white" (read: Euro-American) knowledge and of able-bodied constituents. An extension of Jacques Derrida's argument that the signified concept "is never present in and of itself," these rules suggest that it is the relationship of difference (past versus present, white versus nonwhite, athletic versus nonathletic, male versus female) that formed the very core of understanding white middle-class male investment in masculinity and modernity.[36]

This book explores these variations while underscoring the fundamental articulation of sport as a place for appropriating, producing, and disseminating racial identities. As such, it suggests new ways to consider the demarcations of on-field and off, local and national, individual and communal within the historical context of the early twentieth century. Sport was the fulfillment of the promise of universities and colleges to educate the next generation. Only those of a certain type could attend classes, but all could support the modern, industrial university by attending a game, listening to a broadcast, or purchasing a newspaper. In promising to make boys into men that could take on the world, inherit the land from their fathers, continue the narrative of American civilization, and simultaneously teach the general public appropriate behavior and collegiality, early twentieth-century universities constructed their "modern" identity: seemingly accessible to all, yet in practice firmly planted behind the intellectual and social hierarchies that they reified. This spectacle and its associated brand firmly established the roots of today's modern university, where the continual conflict between academics and athletics often overshadows the very process of education and obliterates almost entirely the continuing problematic nature of economic class and access to higher education.

If we step backward then and refocus our discussion of college football and university dynamics to the history of the performance of racialized bodies, there is a much more revealing historical thread with which this book is engaged. Philip J. Deloria's seminal texts *Playing Indian* and *Indians in Unexpected Places* deserve particular consideration for their exploration of tropes and identities that were the hallmark of Indian portrayals. In *Playing Indian*, drawing examples from the American Revolution to the late 1990s, Deloria suggests that Indian identity offered the opportunity for whites to imbue it with political, social, and cultural meanings drawing on tropes of Indian bodies as naturally athletic well beyond the colonial period. Playing Indian was simultaneously an affirmation of essentialist colonial stereotypes and a means of creating new interpretations. It allowed for calling "fixed meanings—and sometimes meanings itself—into question."[37] *Indians in Expected Places* has broadened these explorations by focusing on how Indians disrupted the stereotypes upon which white society relied. News coverage of Wounded Knee, Wild West performances, working and performing in Hollywood westerns, and Native use of "modern" machines like sewing machines and cars, as well as Native athletes and tom-tom-beat-driven music, offer the argument that Native peoples grappled with modernity just as white society did. Their engagement with these modern conveniences and mainstream cultural representations often startled white Americans who believed that Indians were either relegated to reservations or had disappeared altogether. While this book focuses on faux Indian bodies in the realm of sporting identity, it owes much to Deloria's revelations of how Indians grappled with the larger cultural milieu in the same period.

Since Deloria's *Playing Indian* and *Indians in Unexpected Places*, a variety of scholars, including Carol Spindel, C. Richard King, and Charles Fruehling Springwood, have analyzed dialogues about Indian mascotry and performance.[38] Sociologists, anthropologists, and cultural studies scholars have also embraced Indians mascotry as a site of investigation.[39] These scholars have focused on individual institutions, the relationship between sport and higher education, identity politics within individual communities, and the relationship between specific Native groups and the contemporary institution. They have overwhelmingly focused on individually localized debates over power and authority, cultural borrowing and exploitation, the meaning of democratic higher education, and the psychological rationale behind community identification in late twentieth- and early twenty-first-century contexts with only surface attention to the historical moments of appropriation, dissemination, and collaboration. This book differs by addressing the historical networks in which these individuals participated and the ways in which these productions were part of a larger national circuit of performing Indianness through athletic identities at colleges and universities in the first half of the twentieth century. These circuits led to the creation of a particularly modern brand of college football spectacle that embraced commercialism and the production of raced, class, and gendered bodies.

The following chapters are presented chronologically, with each having a particular emphasis on a mode of production. Progressive organizations, university bands and musical innovations, literary and newspaper representations, anthropological and artistic displays, collegiate football and Indian athletics, Florida regional identity, and humorous caricatures, when taken together, create a framework that illustrates local manifestations of national consciousness about Indian bodies. In structuring the chapters, I illustrate the dominance of a particular institution (the University of Illinois) in the creation of a racialized halftime spectacle that influenced the adoption of Indian-themed athletic identities at other institutions while simultaneously capturing the ways in which schools seeking large-scale football enterprises utilized and produced Indian identity for their own use. By capturing institutions leveraging Indianness throughout the university, I fundamentally affirm the notion that halftime spectacle and Indian-themed athletic identity were intrinsic aspects of the modern university from the late 1920s onward. Collegiate competition, coupled with the need to make education relevant to the masses, constructed the need for these commercialized community identities. Significantly, the vehicle of faux Indian bodies, imagery, and music not only appealed to the public but also was used to communicate continuing messages about what it meant to be a white man in a modern world. Where possible, I highlight the exploration of counternarratives and moments of contestation with the production of narratives about Indian bodies and acknowledge when Indians themselves were part of the production of spectacle. Yet unlike previous scholarship, which has focused on the history of mascots to underscore the contemporary issues around Indian mascotry and sovereignty, this book isolates itself as a purely historical analysis. It makes no attempt to grapple with contemporary debates, ethics, or voices, nor does it look at the psychological effects of these representations on current Native peoples. Instead, it focuses on the messages being transmitted by the actors engaged in the historical production and reminds us, in the conclusion, of the importance of historical contexts to our current understandings. The reception of those messages is, as Michael Oriard and others have pointed out, probably lost to the historical record. What is possible, though, within this historical approach is to demonstrate the continued persistence and relative similarity of these representations over the course of the pivotal fifty years where Americans grappled with the effects of industrialization, urbanization, and modernization. This suggests that these images were working well for universities and colleges and thus must have at least been perceived as functional in translating their messages to the public.

Chapter 1, "King Football and Game-Day Spectacle," sets the stage for the rise of Indian mascots by outlining the rise of college football, the debate over its meanings, and the ways in which college football represented white middle-class men's attempts to grapple with modern anxieties. It argues that college football, with all its rules and order, became the most visible expression of white middle-class male identity in the 1920s. Chapter 2, "An Indian versus a Colonial Legend," explores the performance of the first Chief Illiniwek and provides a revisionist history of the origins of the University of Illinois mascot tradition. This chapter offers a detailed exposition of the colonial encounters of the Illini Indians and explores colonial exchanges on the American frontier. "And the Band Played Narratives of American Expansion," chapter 3, examines the establishment of the University of Illinois band as a locus of a communications circuit that disseminated ideas about the theatrics of halftime performances and fan participation throughout the United States. Giving particular consideration to the role of "spectacle," this chapter relates the transition of university bands from secondary elements of athletics to the emotive voice of the action. It highlights the convergence of written, aural, and visual mediums on the athletic field.

Chapter 4, "The Limitations of Halftime Spectacle," discusses how two schools, Miami University and the University of North Dakota, grappled with establishing athletic identity when they could not marshal the resources or audience of larger midwestern and eastern schools. In the case of Miami University, we see how its efforts to compete with the University of Cincinnati led students and fraternity members to craft a "Redskins" identity. For the University of North Dakota, the physical presence of Indians on the sports field as well as in proximity to the university itself would lead students and administrators to construct a carefully articulated commercial identity that would combat eastern fears of the frontier university. "Fighting Sioux" identity would reassure the general public of the safety and security of the university only 300 miles and thirty years distant from Custer's Last Stand and the Indian wars of the late nineteenth and early twentieth centuries.

Chapter 5, "Student Investment in University Identities," analyzes the far-flung locales of Stanford University and Florida State University. My exploration of Stanford University seeks to understand the conflict between university administrators and their students. Additionally, the chapter explores the involvement of A. Phimister Proctor, an American artist, in producing Indian-themed athletic identity and the role of world's fairs in creating an appetite for Indian bodies. I then move to Florida State University to show how particularly southern anxieties about the influence of women at the newly established university would force students to campaign to adopt a borrowed "Seminole" identity from their local competitor, the University of Florida. Along the way, I highlight the multiple meanings of the other identities that were under consideration to demonstrate the influence of commercial institutions on Florida State University students and administrators.

Chapter 6, "Indian Bodies Performing Athletic Identities," explores how a female performer during World War II at the University of Illinois and a postwar Indian performer at Stanford University demonstrated both the tenuous nature of halftime spectacle and the success of its existence. For Illinois, we will see how Idelle Stith Brooks, an "honorary Osage," was first celebrated for her Indian identity and her femininity yet would ultimately be largely written out of the history of halftime spectacle. I also explore the genre of comedic representation in order to uncover how humorous depictions were used to communicate tropes of colonial encounters and Indian bodies in the 1940s and early 1950s. I then close the chapter by exploring the rise of "Prince Lightfoot" and how Williams's performance not as Yurok Indian (his own Indian heritage) but as a mish-mash of Indian identities demonstrates the success of the message that football audiences sought to alleviate white, young, male anxieties. In Williams's adoption of "Prince Lightfoot," an Indian appropriates colonial tropes for his own purpose.

Collectively, these chapters serve to provide a framework for considerations of identity politics, collegiate sport, and community identity as a mechanism of the white male middle-class heterosexual worldview in the early twentieth century. They illustrate that the production of Indian mascots was part of a long-held tradition of producing colonial encounters to affirm the project of American modernity. Along the way, they reveal why nearly 100,000 people might fill a stadium to not just watch football but to celebrate their "Indian" identities.

1 · KING FOOTBALL AND GAME-DAY SPECTACLE

Between 1876, when the Intercollegiate Football Association established the first common rules of football, and the mid-1920s, the game of football went from an unregulated leisure activity to an event that weekly transformed small towns into public bazaars. The sport moved from open grassy fields to massive concrete stadiums. In the process, it also became an American obsession. Embroiled in controversies over violence, amateurism, and profiteering, collegiate football began to communicate ideas of proper manhood to its audience. Reflecting broader American anxieties about the perils of modernity, early twentieth-century universities and communities invested in football as a social, cultural, and racial educational space that needed to be ordered, policed, and preserved for white men.[1]

Football originally formed as a playground game. With few rules and even fewer formal regulations, college football initially developed among elite eastern universities, where faculty members and students took to grass lots in order to challenge peer institutions.[2] The game closely resembled English soccer as it was played at colleges such as Columbia, Wesleyan, Yale, Tufts, Trinity, Stevens, the University of Pennsylvania, and Princeton University.[3] Only Harvard University, with its rugby origins, permitted players to run the ball forward or tackle opponents.[4] Opponents debated extensively each time they came together to play an intercollegiate match what the rules of the game would be.[5] In part, the debate over which system of rules would be adopted suggests the indeterminate nature of football in the late nineteenth century. College football could just as easily have been an Americanized version of rugby or soccer rather than the game that came to dominate the American public in the twentieth century.

Walter Camp, Yale student and director of operations of Yale athletics, transformed football into the modern game familiar to twenty-first-century Americans.[6] Serving as representative of Yale at the annual Intercollegiate Football Association meeting in 1878 and again in 1880, Camp proposed a number of changes to the game that were ultimately adopted. First, he suggested that the number of players be reduced from fifteen to eleven. Second, he argued that players should be permitted to retain possession of the ball by placing it on the ground.[7] While seemingly innocuous, these two innovations paved the way for the game that millions of fanatics watch today. Over the following years and decades, football would embrace additional rules: one-sided possession of the ball, the formulation of yard increments and downs to move the ball, set plays, the creation of assigned positions including the quarterback, tackling, the line of scrimmage, and many more.[8] By 1888, college football games resembled the modern contest, whereby a single player snapped a ball to the quarterback and then joined his fellow linemen in blocking opposing players in front of the ball carrier.[9]

New rules bred contact between players, who now rushed headlong into one another with knees, elbows, and heads smashing into their opposing counterparts. Wealthy alumni worked with football recruiters to identify, train, and even fund promising young athletes to attend their alma maters.[10] Many of these recruits were brought from urban cities in the Northeast or small towns of the Midwest, locations that recruiters thought matched the increased violence and physical strength common to the game. Fistfights, broken bones, blood, and even life-threatening injuries became common occurrences at college football games. Fans celebrated the potential violence of the game by yelling "kill him" or "break his neck."[11]

University faculty members and administrators raised concerns about the seemingly unsportsmanlike and ungentlemanly conduct of players and fans by focusing on the physical and moral consequences of the spectacle that had grown around the game of football. In 1906, Stanford University, as well as a number of other schools, discontinued football programs in favor of rugby squads, which it believed were much less violent.[12] Frank Angell, faculty athletic committee chairman, clearly delineated his concern in a report to university president David Starr Jordan:

1. The closed formations favored by the present rules make possible unfair and brutal playing which cannot be detected.
2. The game . . . has become a business rather than a sport.
3. The methods of play almost wholly exclude men of medium weight. This means that a large majority of students are shut out of the game altogether.
4. The game is in no sense a college sport; students do not form volunteer teams and play football for sport as they play baseball.[13]

Angell's critique exposed the early impetus to transform football from the pastime of faculty members and students on campus quads into a sport dominated by physically exceptional men who received monetary support for their athletic endeavors. In complaining about the business of football, where few could participate, Angell also demonstrated a larger frustration with the limitations of sport in addressing the universal needs of male students, rather than merely catering to the athletically gifted. More directly, though, Angell also commented on the role of athletes as laborers for the university. By no longer serving as volunteers, athletes had the opportunity to profit from their participation. By profiting, they no longer could claim that football was an activity for the betterment of the student population; it benefited both the athlete and the university, which collected fees from ticket sales. The attempt to replace football with rugby was met with staunch resistance. At Stanford, the football team initially threatened to go on strike, alumni protested, and even local newspapers took up the call, noting that the "only period of right living during their college career" was during the season when students were obligated to follow football training rules.[14] By 1908, Jordan (formerly president of Indiana University) lamented the low numbers of students actively participating in athletics or recreation because of the movement away from football: "Considerably less than a quarter of the men take part, and of this fraction, hardly half are active throughout the year."[15] In these arguments, football was positioned squarely as a moralizing force in the lives of young men. Some believed that football drew athletes away from the evils of drinking and carousing and placed them squarely under the oversight of coaches, who could monitor their behavior and morality.

For professional football associations, the movement away from football held tremendous financial consequences. Football associations received dues from member universities, so each university that eliminated football also threatened the profits of its fellow academies. These financial consequences raised concerns sufficient enough to incite the American Professional Football Association, at its meeting in San Francisco in 1909, to recruit a coach from the East Coast to train California high school students so that they would demand the sport at prospective universities.[16] The association feared both evaporating profits from waning membership and declining ticket sales from lax attendance. Rugby, the association believed, might weaken the commercial appeal of football by shifting attention away from the game it controlled and toward other sports. Rugby was perceived as less interesting, profitable, and competitive than football. Moreover, it offered fewer opportunities for competition with elite institutions that could bring large crowds, thereby increasing revenue. It also lacked appeal to the white middle-class males who were beginning to transform colleges and universities into sites where they could explore their anxiety with the modern world.

While rugby became the centerpiece of reform in the West, midwesterner David Jordan, a graduate of the University of Wisconsin, scathingly critiqued the University of Illinois, Northwestern, and the University of Chicago for their "unsavory recruiting" led by alumni who exhibited a "win-at-any-cost" mental-ity.[17] The complete series of articles, "Buying Football Victories," appeared in *Collier's* magazine in 1905 and lambasted the universities for providing financial support to athletes, arranging for football players to attend specially designated courses that would provide passing grades, and supporting irresponsible fiscal practices including going into debt just to secure football victories.[18] Jordan's critique was so vociferous that Wisconsin faculty member Frederick Jackson Turner, the architect of the "closing of the American frontier" thesis, joined the growing numbers of faculty protesting the lack of oversight being exercised over collegiate football.[19] With Turner as one of the most outspoken members of the Wisconsin committee on reform, representatives from the Big Nine Conference (the precursor to the Big Ten Conference) met in February and March of the following year to discuss supposed abuses at its member institutions.[20] Reports from the various institutions charged that Big Nine football was not just threatened by physical brutality and possible injury to athletes but also by the "moral evils attendant upon the gradual raising of the game into a thing of absorbing and sometimes hysterical public and collegiate interest."[21] In characterizing football spectacle as a "moral evil," Turner and his colleagues underscored the accepted interpretation of football's role as a site of inculcation for creating young men of worth who could participate fully as members of their local communities. The recently established Intercollegiate Athletic Association challenged the undemocratic practice that created seven geographical regions that would annually send a single representative to debate rules and procedures. Unsurprisingly, the association's first targets for reform were amateurism, recruiting, and intentional injuries by violent players.[22]

The increased vociferousness of critics who claimed that college sport was a site of "hysterical" interest illustrated an important transition taking place in the early 1900s: the convergence of football with commercialism. This change allowed for the creation of a nationwide circuit of communications that emphasized the desire for young, white, male, middle-class, football-playing citizens. Football offered the opportunity for coaches to support themselves and their families where previously they had to cobble multiple jobs together to make a living. Players had the opportunity to receive an education, garner a wage, and even rise from their social position by becoming a famous athlete. They could buy and sell themselves to multiple teams, and even send money home to their families. Football offered universities large-scale events that could be marketed to thousands of fans, generating massive annual revenue. And, significantly, it offered narratives of battles to be fought and wars to be won that were intriguing to the general public. Competition between teams, particularly those in close geographical proximity, was encouraged as it could foment community allegiances and demonstrate the superiority of one college's students over another's. Football spectacles fulfilled a need to communicate with the general public by using athletic bodies and sporting events as opportunities for white middle-class men to prove their masculinity and their worth.

GROWING PAINS

Despite increased violence on the field and complaints from faculty members at institutions of higher education throughout the first two decades of the twentieth century, the potential profit of college football appeared to offset the concerns in the minds of athletic directors and university administrators. The growing attendance of paying fans at college football games held the awesome potential to transform university communities. Athletic competition between schools might aid the university in recruiting wealthy students and donors. An important aspect of this transformation included the marketing of the university to the public through physical space and advertising.

The "preparedness crisis" of the Great War had placed an emphasis on the need for physically fit young men to participate in the country's defense, and Americans turned overwhelmingly to football as their training ground.[23] The male athlete came to represent the potential of American masculinity and its dominance internationally. He was physically strong, morally upright, educated, heterosexual, and gentlemanly. He did not carouse, challenge authority, or financially benefit from his skills. This young man respected his elders, supported his community, and looked forward to being a contributing member of society. The innovations developed by Walter Camp coupled with the adoption of football as one physical outlet during military service allowed for the rapid growth of football among young men. By the beginning of the Great War, football was reaching its second maturity, as the allure of revenue and the potential to transform young boys into modern men were cemented in the minds of university administrators.[24] One 1919 *New York Times* editorial exclaimed, "football owes more to the war in the way of the spread of the spirit of the game than it does to the ten or twenty years of development in the period before the war."[25] Football rapidly dominated campus life of colleges and universities, as the number of schools participating was growing.

Post–Great War prosperity allowed larger numbers of students to enroll in college, and the rise in veteran enrollment produced a strong uptick in the athleticism of teams across America.[26] The National Federation of State High School Athletic Associations, the National Football League (NFL), and the American Football League all formed between 1922 and 1926 to manage the growing number of teams. At a moment when college attendance for men eighteen to twenty years old was growing from 8 percent (1920) to 12 percent (1930), attendance at college football games increased 119 percent. By 1930, over ten million Americans attended college football games.[27] Over 60 percent of attendees were at one of forty institutions, including the University of Illinois and Stanford University.[28] More bodies to play the game led to more games being played, which generated additional revenue, fans, and audiences. Additional audiences and fans demanded more games, which then relied on additional bodies being brought into the institution to take part in the game. This circuit of dependency provided more bodies to engage with the university and more dollars into university coffers. Athletic departments and especially football programs relied on the continual reintroduction of new bodies, athletes, fans, audiences, and schools to remain financially viable and athletically superior.

A May 1927 editorial in the *Daily Illini*, the University of Illinois student newspaper, illustrated students' interest in the university: "it must be admitted at the outset that most of the personnel of the institution is here because 'going to college' is admittedly the modish, fashionable, accepted thing to do."[29] The author continues on to claim that those truly interested in the "academic life" are few, "although increasing year to year, wouldn't fill one section of the stadium. . . . The attraction of successful athletic teams cannot be overestimated in this consideration. . . . They have probably heard of that 'Illinois spirit,' which has been so generally advertised largely as a result of athletics here." Tellingly, that "Illinois spirit" that the author speaks of as being a selling point for new students is decidedly masculine. Women "go to mark time until they can 'get' married with the prospects meanwhile of making a 'good' sorority and 'rating' five dates a week." In gendering women's attendance at Illinois as part of a scheme to achieve social norms (getting married), the author illustrates the growing tension within higher education. As more families were able to afford to send their young men and women to college, the demographics of the student body shifted. Children of middle-class parents were able to take advantage of postwar prosperity and used college as an opportunity to increase their social standing and economic prospects in both the short and long terms. As Fred H. Turner, a University of Illinois dean, remarked in his 1926 missive, "Like Father, Unlike Son," most male students did not major in their father's occupation. They used the opportunity to explore new vocations, including commerce and engineering.[30] This unease, the distance between young men and their fathers, showed the slippage of the modern world that middle-class white men inhabited. Young men were out to "make their own way" while fathers were worried about having sons who could follow in their footsteps and support their families. For students who were thrust into a rapidly growing student body, extracurricular activities became an avenue to create community and to achieve social recognition that their fathers could be proud of.

For Reed Harris, former editor of the Columbia University student newspaper, college football consisted of a kaleidoscope of "commercialism, anti-intellectualism, distorted priorities, fraud," and "hypocrisy" that undercut the educational efforts of the university and mocked efforts to create the next generation of highbrow thinkers.[31] Harris lamented the "big business" of higher education and its "sordid business behind the gigantic spectacles that are college football games."[32] Believing that football "staged as a super-extra sideshow by academic moguls is as depressing as it is ridiculous,"[33] Harris decried the opening of universities to the masses postwar, the ways in which athletes were permitted to avoid the academic responsibilities of the regular student, the use of a separate financial model to fund athletics that relied on ticket sales and promotions, and leveraged complicity by students, faculty, administrators, sportswriters, fraternities, and the public in promoting the game.[34] In questioning football, Harris and others illustrated the uneasy allegiances between sport and education. Sport had to be continually affirmed as valuable to the university. Without that mediation and negotiation, dissonance within the community would come to the fore.

Football expansion, which was at the core of the debate, became viewed as a cause of the disconnect between the educational mission of the university and the spectacle of college football. The role of professionals, both coaches and athletes, in football was at the center of the debates of the 1920s just as it was in the newly created social science disciplines. Professional coaches were no longer part-time employees who supplemented jobs with low-paying athletic appointments. By the early 1920s, coaches like Knute Rockne of the University of Notre Dame and Robert Zuppke of Illinois were full-time employees who received salaries commensurate to faculty members.[35] In fact, Rockne's success as Notre Dame's coach propelled his salary beyond other Notre Dame faculty. Moreover, he acquired additional monies by endorsing a line of football equipment for Wilson Sporting Goods, serving as a motivational speaker for Studebaker Motors (at a salary larger than the company's president), and publishing books and articles on coaching football.[36] While Rockne is an extreme example of the ways in which college coaches could profit from America's fascination with football, coaches across America were embracing the financial benefits of professionalization while maintaining the rhetoric of football as an amateur game. They often led local training camps for youth, appeared at openings of businesses, and worked with their universities to market the game to the public.

The need for marketing resulted from threats offered by other organizations, be they the nascent professional football leagues, other universities, or town-based football. College players, who received little to no financial assistance from universities, often played as substitute players in professional leagues and town games. Usually appearing under fictitious names, these athletes drew large crowds and were integral to the local gambling circuit. More broadly, though, town-based teams often used football to demonstrate their town's superiority over other nearby towns. Illustrating how the evils of gambling were not just urban, two rural towns in Illinois received national attention for the lengths they would go to in order to defeat their rivals. In November 1921, bankers and businessmen in Carlinville (along with the Carlinville football team) rigged a game against local rival Taylorville by recruiting eight football players from Knute Rockne's Notre Dame team.[37] Each player received $200, and bets placed in favor of a Carlinville victory topped $50,000; local businessmen viewed it as an opportunity to aid the town's flagging economy. Taylorville, not to be outdone, recruited nine players from the nearby University of Illinois. Consequently, professional bettors raised the stakes of a seemingly friendly rivalry between two rural towns to a spectacle that drew nearly $100,000 in bets.[38] Taking place today, the small-town game in Illinois would have placed over $1.2 million in bets. With 10,000 people in attendance, the original Taylorville team showed admirably in the first half, securing a 6-0 lead before turning the field over to their University of Illinois ringers, who increased the lead by another ten points before the end of the game.[39] The event and subsequent scandal, which ended in suspensions for the collegiate players, demonstrated that even local football was big business.[40]

The Carlinville-Taylorville episode represented the worst of organized athletics—gambling and professionalism run amok—and highlighted the need for mentorship and order among the game. A highly trained coach could not only coax the best out of young men on the field, he could also provide a check against the stain of professionalism and gambling. The athletes from Notre Dame and Illinois who were caught in the Carlinville-Taylorsville scandal emerged simultaneously as the physical representation of J. C. Leyendecker's football-themed cover art—"the broad-shouldered, supremely confident male with shining skin, chiseled features, and steely eyes" who could secure the town's reputation—and the antithesis—the corrupt youth profiteering from their physical skills.[41] Leyendecker's images became wildly popular; by the 1920s he was receiving as many as 17,000 letters in a single month.[42] That football, and hypermasculine, rugged male bodies, was a place of amateur athleticism acting to aid young men was an obvious yet powerful illusion.

On December 27, 1921, forty-one coaches gathered at the Hotel Astor in New York City to discuss the formation of a national coaches association. Formally titled the American Football Coaches Association (AFCA) just a few weeks later, the AFCA included representatives Major Charles Daly, the first president of the organization and representative from the U.S. Military Academy, John Heisman of Pennsylvania (later of Washington & Jefferson and Rice University), Amos Alonzo Stagg of Chicago, J. W. Wilce of Ohio State University, Robert Fisher of Harvard University, and Fielding Yost of the University of Michigan. Early trustees of the organization included Robert Zuppke of Illinois, William Cowell of New Hampshire, Gil Dobie of Cornell University, E. C. Henderson of the University of Southern California, Knute Rockne, William Roper of Princeton, and Glenn "Pop" Warner of Stanford.[43] Importantly, the AFCA believed that the game of football should be preserved as an amateur sport and that off-the-record payments to players and coaches were ruining the game.[44] While not directly responding to the Carlinville-Taylorville game, which remained obscure and local until national news coverage appeared in January of the following year, AFCA coaches sought to preserve the sanctity of college football by prohibiting players from moving between schools or from

THE CRISSCROSS, a Football Story by GUY W. NORTON
THE MEANING OF VERDUN by WINSTON SPENCER CHURCHILL

FIGURE 1. J. C. Leyendecker, *Football Hero*, 1916. Oil on canvas, 30 × 21". Signed lower left. Reproduced in *Collier's*, November 18, 1916, cover. Courtesy of the Library of Virginia.

acting as substitutes for other teams, including the NFL. By wielding amateurism as a rationale, Zuppke, Warner, Yost, and others prohibited successful athletes from marketing themselves to the highest bidder. This permitted coaches (and, by extension, the colleges they worked for) to retain control over workers who were both highly profitable via their athletic success and highly important to the underlying ethos of community. In large part, the AFCA and other organizations like it allowed football to flourish by imposing greater rules and order that concentrated power for these decisions not in the hands of the athletes themselves (who could profit from the free-market system) but in the hands of coaches and college presidents. In their roles as leaders, they were reliant upon the success of the game for promoting themselves and their institutions.

Sportswriter John Tunis wrote in 1927 of what he called "The Great American Sports Myth." For Tunis, the myth was that competitive sports built character and facilitated a bond between nations and individuals.[45] A former Harvard athlete and author of over twenty articles for *Harper's* magazine, Tunis lambasted the ways the public revered football: "Football is more to the sports follower of this country than merely a game—sometimes it seem [sic] to be almost our national religion. With fervor and reverence the college man and the non-college man, the athlete and the observer approach its shrines; dutifully and faithfully they make their annual pilgrimage to the football Mecca, be it Atlanta or Urbana, Cambridge or Los Angeles, Princeton or Ann Arbor."[46] Quoting Willard Sperry, dean of the Harvard Theological School, Tunis continued, "the only true religious spirit to be discerned among large bodies of undergraduates to-day is in the football stadium."[47] At the core of this new religion of football is the "doctrine that only through 'college spirit' can a man be saved."[48] Tunis's sharply worded criticism of football as an American religion compared athletes, coaches, managers, athletic administrators, university presidents, and fans to a religious pantheon and noted the importance of ritualization to the successful deployment of any football event. "Certainly nowhere has the love of the average man for ritual been more completely and more fully satisfied than by the rich and intricate ceremony of modern intercollegiate football."[49] Speaking of high priests and acolytes, preaching and devotion, Tunis vividly recounted the streaming crowds of undergraduates who, worked up to a fever pitch by pep rallies, harassed those who dared to question football's importance before continuing onto game day and participating in the cheers and "demonstrations of ingeniously organized pageantry."[50] Tunis underscored the conscious way in which football was an integral part of the performance of white, middle-class, young, athletic identity in modern America. Football was essential to providing students, fans, and athletes with the opportunities to celebrate their masculinity.[51] Even former president Woodrow Wilson noted prior to the Great War, "the side shows are so numerous, so diverting, so important if you will—that they have swallowed up the circus, and those who perform in the main tent must often whistle for their audience, discouraged and humiliated."[52] For Tunis, the well-organized supportive football factions were not discouraged and humiliated. In fact, these communities of believers were all members of a "vast state educational factory" that relied on the publicity brought to their university by their football team to both build the size of the community and maintain its fiscal stability.[53] In comparing football fans to workers in the factory,

FIGURE 2. Harold "Red" Grange, December 8, 1925. Courtesy of the Library of Congress Prints and Photographs Division, Washington, D.C. LC-DIG-npcc-15254. http://hdl.loc .gov/loc.pnp/npcc.15254

Tunis was emulating popular Progressive Era concerns by reformers who feared that factory work was emasculating men. Fans were becoming mindless drones, no longer controlling their own futures, marionettes on a string mastered by capitalist elites who took advantage of the general public. By turning to the romantic past to lambaste the present in favor of a new and better future, Tunis was relying on the same methods that were being used to compare athletes to nonathletes, whites to nonwhites, young to old, citizen to noncitizen in the 1920s.[54]

The University of Illinois was prominently featured in Tunis's attack on the god football. Using publicity materials associated with Harold E. "Red" Grange, arguably the first celebrity college football player, Tunis wrote, "so long as the colleges persist in maintaining publicity bureaus and press directors to keep the nation informed of the doings and sayings of their heroes in sport, they can hardly accuse the public of having spoiled football."[55] "Each sport had a number of outstanding individuals, really stars. And they were publicized to death," Grange stated during a 1974 interview. "The First World War was just over; they had been trying times for everyone . . . everyone seemed to let their hair down after World War I."[56] Grange's highly publicized football achievements hardly mark his assessment as surprising. His 1924 twelve-minute-long four-touchdown effort against the University of Michigan at Illinois's Memorial Stadium dedication game became an American sensation, captured in print and on radio. A paid attendance of 67,205, with an additional 11,000 in temporary bleachers and over 600 others camped in the University Armory, were eclipsed by the estimated 100,000 football fans listening on the *Chicago Tribune*'s WGN radio station.[57]

Grange's success threatened the status of college football players as students. Although he generated massive profits for the Western Conference that Illinois played in, he also recognized his own personal control over his athletic success by announcing, just prior to his last game of the 1924 season, that he had signed a highly lucrative professional football contract with the Chicago Bears of the NFL and would be leaving Illinois prior to graduation.[58] Fielding Yost, the well-known coach of the University of Michigan, anticipated Grange's decision prior to his announcement by lamenting that he would rather Grange do anything other than play professional football. The NFL, and all professional sports for that matter, represented everything Yost and the college football associations had been working to prohibit: high-paid athletes who profited from the game, gambling and vice by fans, and the creation of an unruly public unconcerned with their moral and physical future. Professional football fans wanted a show, and team owners were willing to pay to ensure that they could provide one.[59]

CREATING THE SPECTACLE OF KING FOOTBALL

For colleges, though, the rise of celebrity athletes and standing-room-only games highlighted the need for modern stadiums that could accommodate more fans. The first modern stadium was built in 1903 at Harvard University. Modeled on the Olympic Panathenaic stadium that debuted in Athens, Greece, in 1896, Harvard Stadium represented the innovations of the industrial age through its use of steel-reinforced concrete.[60] Accommodating 21,000 fans on a regular basis, with an additional 13,000 potential temporary seats for special games, Harvard Stadium represented the first major investment by a college in competing with the urban athletic spaces that had been home to baseball games and intermittent football matches in the latter half of the nineteenth century. Yale, Princeton, and others followed throughout the first two decades of the twentieth century in creating massive edifices to host games. What was striking about these construction projects was not just the resulting transformation of educational campus space into a place where thousands of members of the public could enjoy a game but also the autonomy that football programs had in using stadiums to secure their own revenue streams. More bodies at the game meant more revenue for teams (and their associations), which allowed athletic departments financial autonomy from the concerns of faculty reformers who continued to lament the potential ill effects of the game on students and the general public.

The first major capital campaign on the part of the University of Illinois, founded in 1867, raised funds for its modern football stadium. Course instruction, maintenance, and even the general operation of the university were not selected as important enough to seek alumni donations. Instead, university officials privileged football as the target of their national campaign to raise funds. To raise these capital funds, the university reached back to its fictitious indigenous past.

The Story of the Stadium, a 1920/21 promotional pamphlet, featured a cover image of a campfire circle of Indian men with a lone Indian figure standing dressed in what appears to be a Sioux headdress, loincloth, and boots. The Indian male holds a peace pipe, with one hand raised before a full moon. Underneath, the caption reads, "We have a heritage from the Illini Indian—the Great Heart, the fighting spirit."[61] *The Story of the Stadium* continues by characterizing the Illini as "a hunter," a "fighter," an "individualist," "brave and self-denying." The publication continues: "No temples have these ancient Indians left us, and no books. But we have a heritage from them, direct through the pioneers who fought them and learned to know them. It is the Great Heart, the fighting spirit, the spirit of individualism, of teaching our children to be free but brave and to have a God—for these are the laws of our tribe."[62] The Stadium Drive Committee—composed of faculty, students, administrators, and members of the local community—reassured the public that the future of their world was one of progress and potential. The chronological progression asserted the "living vitally in [their] heritage of freedom, braveness, religion, and athletics." "Watch us play football," the organizers wrote, "see us on the cinder track, on the baseball diamond. We are different, somehow, we of the middle west—not particularly better but different. We are uniquely ourselves." The violence of the past, and even the modern urban world, frightened and discomforted midwesterners. In supporting the building of the stadium, the public could celebrate order, progress, and an understandable future where their roles were clearly defined.

Samson Raphaelson, a former University of Illinois student and then faculty member, orchestrated a mass meeting of students in April 1921 to generate support for the stadium project.[63] Appealing to current students, alumni, and wealthy members of the public, Raphaelson arranged seating in the overflowing gym annex in order to concentrate wealthy foreign students and their parents.[64] Following a call for $1,000 pledges by football coach Zuppke, foreign-born students rose one by one to make pledges. Not to be outdone by foreigners, local students quickly made matching donations to prove their allegiance to country and university. Even in something as banal as a stadium fund-raising campaign, hatred and fear of the foreign who were threatening the place of white middle-class men were used as tools to generate an opportunity for newly wealthy middle-class students to prove their value.

"We have a heritage from the Illini Indian—the Great Heart, the fighting spirit"

FIGURE 3. Cover illustration, *Story of the Stadium*, 1922. Image courtesy of the University of Illinois at Urbana-Champaign Archives.

The stadium was being constructed in memory of the young men who lost their lives during World War I. Clarence Welsh's 1921 brochure, *University of Illinois Memorial Stadium*, clearly explained the underlying motivation behind the capital campaign and its perceived role in the community.[65] Intended as a memorial to soldiers of the Great War, Welsh delineated three characteristics of the stadium and the unique Illinois man and woman who supported its build-ing: "culture, sportsmanship, and loyalty." The physical site of the stadium and the football game itself became an opportunity for community meaning: "the Stadium will become the symbol of a new, united, fighting, aspiring tribe of Illini, who know how to honor their living heroes and venerate their dead."[66] At least one member of the Stadium Drive Committee, Coach Zuppke, was interested in establishing the University of Illinois stadium as a replication of a larger trans-national athletic world: that of the Olympics. The stadium should be built on an "Olympic plan" that embodied the values of the new "tribe of Illini." "Illini is part of the word, Illiniwek, which means the complete man," Zuppke remarked, "and we want a stadium which will represent the complete man."[67] Fred Lowenthal, a 1901 alumnus, remarked, "What good member of the tribe can see in the stadium anything but a visible sign of, and a sacred shrine to, an invisible thing—the spirit of the Illini."[68] Memorial Stadium was alternately a "monument," a "shrine," and a "symbol" that gave white middle-class men the opportunity to participate in the ritual of the football game. Memorial Stadium, like other concrete stadiums of the 1920s, provided a physical space in a newly public place for white middle-class men to celebrate their identity in the modern world.

SPECTACLE AS THREAT

The decade of the 1920s read as a continuing struggle over who owned collegiate sport.[69] Was it the young men playing the game? Faculty educating the youth of America? Coaches who promoted athletic excellence? Universities that profited from big-time collegiate football? Or was it, as *Time* asserted in 1930, "the public, taking possession of a game which was once the private property of the colleges ... [who] changed it almost unrecognizably."[70] *Time* began its headline celebration of "Football's Public" by drawing an elegant yet ominous picture for readers:

> If a stadium were built big enough to hold all the U.S. football public at one time, it would be big enough to hold the entire population of Chicago, Paris, or of Rome, Hamburg and Glasgow put together. Its breath rising in a vast faint mist, its shout like the roar of an earthquake, its tiered ranks veiled with the smoke of innumerable cigarettes, its tremendous stare as heavy as sunlight, this crowd in its fabulous coliseum has no equal in the world.[71]

In depicting the stadium as a "veiled" giant replete with actual fire (from ciga-rette lighters), *Time* graphically illuminated the changing nature of the game.

> Once the crowd was one-quarter its present size. It was composed of undergradu-ates, parents, alumni, their wives, sweethearts, cousins. For years it has been growing until it has come to include every element in the country. Last year 450

college teams played games, 15,000 players participated, 1,400 games were played, 3,000,000 tickets were sold, the gate receipts were approximately $10,000.000. This year the figures may be even bigger.[72]

Importantly, it was not just the size of the stadium and scope of the games that alarmed *Time*. It was that football had become the purview of "every element" in the country. College boys and alumni, *Time* continued, might have to pay ticket sellers who charged exorbitant prices for the privilege of attending their alma mater while "sitting next to people who have never been to any college."[73] The preservation of both college and the game of football as a middle-class domain reads clearly within the language of the *Time* article, titled "Football: Mid-Season," which chronicled the game and its ardent supporters. College and the game of football was the domain of white middle-class men who had earned (or bought) their right to be there. It was fine for the general public to follow the game in newspapers and on the radio, but only the right members of the public should actually attend the game. It was okay for the odd second-generation male immigrant to attend the university because of his football prowess. Yet it was not okay for "every element" to potentially include the working class, the poor, non-athletic immigrants, African Americans, and even women, each of whom were threatening white middle-class men's social and economic place in the world. By failing to regulate the sale of tickets and allowing the attendance of these undesirables at football games, universities and colleges were endangering college football as an environment where white middle-class men could behave like men and prove their masculinity. If white middle-class men could not attend the games and participate in the ritualistic fervor of the game, then they were losing access to an avenue that could be used to affirm their manhood. Undesirables flooding football games illustrated the pressures of modern living for white middle-class men. They were consistently under threat from the encroaching classes and from women who were emasculating them through their increasingly public lives.

With upwardly mobile students entering the university and the public congregating weekly to join the university community in celebrating football victory, the very meaning of college football changed dramatically during the decade of the 1920s. Policing attendance at the game in order to preserve football as a space for white middle-class men suggested the need to preserve the game as a male, public ritual. College football teams like those at Stanford, Illinois, and others needed to create rituals and traditions that, while specific to each school, were familiar enough to everyone to be embraced unilaterally. It is that pivot away from small student bodies gathered around a football field to celebrate the game to large-scale stadiums that transformed rural communities like Palo Alto, California, and Champaign-Urbana, Illinois, every Saturday with tens of thousands of fans that underscores why it was not just the game of football that became a spectacle, but university identity itself.

2 · AN INDIAN VERSUS A COLONIAL LEGEND

On a crisp cerulean Saturday afternoon in October 1926, Lester Leutwiler introduced Chief Illiniwek to the University of Illinois. Leutwiler's buckskin-clad chief, who appeared during halftime of the University of Pennsylvania–University of Illinois football game, delighted fans as he ran from a hiding place north of the Illinois stands and led the band down the field with a frenzied war dance.[1] The band stopped in the center and played "Hail Pennsylvania" while the Indian chief saluted the UPenn fans.[2] Following performances by both bands, Chief Illiniwek and George Adams, another Illinois student dressed in a costume provided by UPenn, shared a catlinite pipe and left the field arm in arm.[3] While the game of football had itself become a spectacle of violence and danger, it was not until the late 1920s that elaborate halftime performances using mascots were introduced as elements of that spectacle.[4]

In the final decades of the nineteenth century, as football developed into an American obsession, university administrators and local communities began to construct larger public identities around their athletic teams. Social mixers, alumni picnics, game-day rallies, even parades through town all became commonplace events on game day. Community members were encouraged to participate in supporting local teams and often became enmeshed in the opportunities that were created around the game of football. At Harvard University football games, a local figure began appearing as "John Orangeman" at events prior to and during the game itself.[5] John Orangeman was, in fact, John Lovett, an Irishman who emigrated from County Kerry, Ireland, in 1855 and peddled fruit in Harvard Yard.[6] Bequeathed with a cart given to him by students, Lovett marketed his wares at Harvard football and baseball games where "the students decorated him with crimson streamers."[7] Harvard fans also sponsored John's travels to Harvard sporting events. At an 1888 game in New York, John, "arrayed in crimson scarfs and flags," joined Harvard students who "sat on the upper deck, singing songs and telling stories until nearly midnight; and naturally John was the central object of interest."[8] One year later in Springfield, Massachusetts, "his

FIGURE 4. Lester Leutwiler as Chief Illiniwek, 1928. Courtesy of the University of Illinois Division of Intercollegiate Athletics.

appearance on the field was announced by cheers, and cries of 'John! John!' all along the line. To these he responded by waving a couple of crimson flags, and shouting, 'Harvard! Harvard!' He was immediately seized and dragged to the grand stand, where a seat had been reserved for him."[9] Samuel Batchelder, a Harvard Law School student, wrote that John Orangeman and other local figures at Harvard made it "as full of characters as a novel by Dickens."[10] Lovett's proximity to the sporting field as well as the approximation of his racial identity to the whiteness of John Harvard, the Harvard founding father, embodied the efforts of those seeking to become white middle-class men.[11] This marked a dramatic representation of the possibility of America: an individual being remade through hard work, opportunity, and community.[12] Lovett's lower-class status, in the eyes of Harvard students and fans, could be mediated by his commercial acumen and work ethic, which would probably have appealed to the largely Protestant population who saw value in the myth of social ascendancy in America.[13]

The veneration of John Lovett's performances at football games rests in uneasy conversation with the more common appearances of African Americans at baseball games. As the baseball historian Adrian Burgos wrote, "diminutive, odd-looking, and often bearing some physical deformity, black mascots were the physical embodiment of black men as backward, brutes, or dandies." Contrasted with young white boys who served as batboys, a black mascot's physical appearance had to be "the reverse of beautiful."[14] This is what the 1888 Toledo club in the American Association accomplished with its "diminutive" mascot.[15] "His grin is broad, his legs limbre and his face as black as the ace of spades," wrote one Chicago newsman of the Chicago White Sox's Clarence Duval. "Whenever anything goes wrong, it is only necessary to rub Clarence's wooly head to save the situation, and one of his celebrated 'double shuffles' to dispel all traces of care, even on the gloomiest occasion."[16] Duval's role was clearly different than that of John Lovett, who did not "perform" in the comical sense. Lovett's decorations, while entertaining, were not embedded with the racialized overtones of subservience that were common in the vaudevillian, comical performances of Duval. Yet even these supposedly comical performances were explicitly derogatory. During an international tour stop in Cairo, Egypt, "several ballplayers forced [Duval] to wear a catcher's mask and glove and then paraded [him] about the Cairo railway station, tethered by a rope, 'as if he was some strange animal let loose from a menagerie.'"[17] This one example demonstrates how African American men were being derided. Native American athletes were also accompanied by stereotypes and cultural constructions of Indianness that furthered the purpose of affirming white male mastery.

MODERN MASCULINITY AND NATIVE MEN

Indians paraded daily through the pages of American newspapers, in dime novels, and as subjects of educational lectures and exhibits as the nineteenth century gave way to the twentieth. They also appeared at sporting events across the United States. Penobscot Indian Louis Francis Sockalexis, widely recognized as the first American Indian to integrate baseball, played for the Cleveland Naps.[18] "Sockalexis was the object of intense racial fascination," the historian Jeffrey Powers-Beck wrote, "which Cleveland management happily exploited in ticket sales, and also the object of intense racial bigotry."[19] Despite being athletically gifted, he was usually referred to as "Chief Sockalexis," "Sockalexis, the Big Medicine Man," "the Redskin," "the Indian," or the "genuine descendent of Sitting Bull." Cleveland fans between 1897 and 1899, when he formally left the club, remarked caustically on his supposed alcoholism, laziness, and irresponsible behavior.[20]

From reports of the conditions of Indians from Carlisle Industrial Indian School in 1890 through the death of Lucy Boston Johnson, the last of the Nipmucks, in 1900, men and women learned of Indians from the pages of the *New York Times*, *Chicago Tribune*, and *Washington Post*.[21] These written texts often conjoined with performances of "actual" Indians at Chicago's Columbian Exhibition, where the public visited touring shows like Buffalo Bill's Wild West show to relive the experience of American victory over plains Indians. Many adolescent men and women also learned of Indians through social organizations founded by Progressive reformers. Lester Leutwiler, the first Chief Illiniwek, learned about Indians from one such organization, the Boy Scouts of America (BSA): "I had learned the Sioux Indian war dance when I attended the 1924 Boy Scout Jamboree in Copenhagen, Denmark," he recalled. "My costume which was used at this first performance [of Chief Illiniwek in 1926] was made in 1925 when I attended Camp Ten-Sleep, operated by Ralph Hubbard, in Elbert, Colorado."[22]

The Boy Scouts "embodied the diffuse idealism of the Progressive Era. . . . They relied upon recreational programs to nurture and discipline capacities which they summed up as character."[23] By focusing on the "normal, morally wholesome, and socially respectable" young man, the BSA established itself, along with the Young Men's Christian Association (YMCA), as the premier organization to educate young men of their role in the growing nation.[24] The YMCA, with its Progressive tendencies, defined civilization as a spectrum of social identities with elite white male Protestants at the lead. In turn-of-the-century Philadelphia, the YMCA utilized evangelical Protestant rhetoric to "turn manhood into a tool for preserving class distinctions and cementing their own place among the country's educated elite."[25] YMCA secretaries attempted to quell working-class radicalism by inculcating the values of hard work, loyalty to employers, and Christian fellowship.[26] Young white middle-class men were supposed to lead America into the future.[27] BSA organizers occupied YMCA offices in New York City and sought out Progressive men interested in child welfare. Luther Gulick, the noted expert on physical education who spent the first fifteen years of his life in Hawaii as part of the American Board of Commissioners Foreign Missionaries, consulted for the nascent organization. So too did Jacob Riis, the master photographer of urban life in New York, as well as men affiliated with the Red Cross, Big Brothers, *Outlook* magazine, and public school systems.[28]

The involvement of these Progressive reformers, who were deeply invested in issues of race, citizenship, and nationhood, significantly shaped not just the BSA but its response to the pressures of modernity. James E. West, former YMCA man and government lawyer, suggested that the Boy Scout oath not only covered a boy's duty to God, country, and fellow man, but also a willingness to "keep myself physically strong, mentally awake, and morally straight."[29] Additionally, new BSA laws mandated a boy be brave, clean, and reverent. These concerns about morality, physical strength, cleanliness, and mental fortitude echoed Progressive reformers' concerns regarding the immigrant population in urban centers. BSA programs looked to social rituals, community development, and physical activities to provide young white men with training in how to cope with the ills of modern life. They looked to nature skills like camping, fishing, fire-building, and the like to remind young men that the roots of American life were not in modern cities with their industrial woes but instead in a more natural preindustrial world.

Incorporated into the new organization were Seton's Woodcraft Indians, founded by Ernest Thompson Seton in 1900. Its rules and suggestions for play were made widely available to the public in 1903's *How to Play Injun*, a collection of six articles. Drawing from his experiences running his camp at his Connecticut home for the local boys who had been caught trespassing and vandalizing his land, *How to Play Injun* offered a step-by-step guide in the skills, costuming, and rituals that could transform a young white boy into an Indian.[30] "The promotion of interest in out-of-door life and woodcraft, the preservation of wildlife and landscape and the promotion of good fellowship among its members," wrote Seton in 1906's *The Birch Bark Roll of Woodcraft Indians*. "The plan aims to give the young people something to do, something to think about, something to enjoy in the woods, with the view always to character building, for manhood not scholarship is the aim of education. . . . My foundation thought was to discover, preserve, develop and diffuse the culture of the Redman."[31] Seton's Woodcraft Indians was a response to increasing urbanization and a nostalgic longing for a rural romantic past, but it was motivated, at least initially, by the lack of moral character in local children.

Seton's Woodcraft Indians was "concerned not merely to preserve resources for man's use, the reigning form of conservation, but also to defend the ecological balances of nature in the wild."[32] The American writer John Burroughs visited one of the camps four years later and wrote President Theodore Roosevelt, "Seton has got hold of a big thing with his boys' Indian Camp. . . . All the boy's wild energy and love of devilry are turned into new channels, and he is taught woodcraft and natural history and Indian-lore in a most fascinating way. I really think it is worthy of your attention and encouragement."[33] The "new channels" Burroughs spoke of were a plan for camping education with Indian games, ceremonies, and awards. "Instead of pursuing vocational training [as the YMCA was encouraging] or the usual hobbies, boys could earn awards, called 'coups,' for single feats of campcraft, nature study, or track and field. Whoever won twenty-five became a 'sachem,' and fifty made one a 'sagamore.'" Boys assumed positions of social power based on their athletic and educational prowess. "In the evenings, Seton led in songs, Indian dances, and storytelling around the council fire and solemnly gave each boy an Indian name."[34]

The demonstrations of personal achievement culminated in a naming ritual that allowed boys to imagine themselves as an honorary member of a fictive Indian nation. In effect, each boy could become Indian through name and achievement. In reality, these ceremonies were social performances that allowed each boy to demonstrate his worth to his peers and leaders. Coupling the militaristic scouting program, with its regimented appearance, with Seton's

Indian lore created the standardized program of the BSA. Integrated into this was the technological emphasis promulgated by the Sons of Daniel Boone and its founder (and later adviser to the nascent Boy Scouts), Daniel Carter Beard. Like Seton, Beard was an illustrator and freelance writer who began the Sons of Daniel Boone as a "circulation-building device for *Recreation* magazine."[35] Using explicitly masculine language, Beard wrote, "we play American games and learn to emulate our great American forebears in lofty aims and iron characters. . . . We want no Molly Coddles."[36] Bridging the militarism of Robert Baden-Powell's British scouting movement, the YMCA's organizational structure and resources, Seton's Indian lore and games, and Beard's technologies, the BSA became by the early 1920s an organization devoted to masculinizing America's white youth through militaristic, racialized, and athletic performances. Targeting middle-class heterosexual Protestant adolescents between the ages of twelve and eighteen, the BSA became a vibrant part of young, male, middle-class American life. The BSA and other social organizations like it offered an initial opportunity for middle-class reformers to intervene in the influences of modern life on young men. Football would become not just its college-age corollary, but a destination for the first few generations of graduates of BSA programs.

In 1925, as Lester Leutwiler participated in Boy Scout events at home and abroad, a sociologist, E. S. Martin, wrote, "scouts are volunteers, every one of them, from the slim boy proudly conscious of his khaki uniform to the alert scoutmaster at the head of his troop. And that troop itself could never exist unless some institution, some community, some group of citizens want it and agree to cooperate with the Boy Scout Movement in making the program available to their boys."[37] Leutwiler had earned the title of Eagle Scout just prior to his departure for the Second International Jamboree in Denmark. Ann Leutwiler-Brandenberg, Lester Leutwiler's daughter, wrote of his international travel, "the experience overseas had a powerful impact on the young man who had recently been elected president of his senior high class."[38]

LEARNING TO DANCE

Ralph Hubbard taught Indian dance at his Colorado camp and participated in a U.S.-based circuit of educators who taught Indian dance to Boy Scouts. He was the son of Elbert Green Hubbard, a Bloomington, Illinois, native who worked as a farmhand in his adolescent years, and Bertha Hubbard, who held a bachelor's of arts degree and was fluent in French, German, and Latin. Elbert Hubbard enrolled in Harvard University in 1894 at the time that sporting events and campus functions featured its mascot, John Orangeman.[39] Following his tenure at Harvard, Elbert began to publish a series of books including *The Philistine* and embarked on establishing Roycroft, the family furniture and woodcraft business. *The Philistine, a Periodical of Protest* appeared in 1895 and featured the writings of prominent men, including Stephen Crane, Eugene Field, Bernard Shaw, and Rudyard Kipling.[40] With heavy ties to Thoreau, Emerson, and the American Romantics, *The Philistine* articulated longings for the distant past with implicit beliefs in American expansion. The Roycroft business became a de facto artists' colony that allowed Elbert and his children to engage in a transnational circuit of poets, artists, and writers, many of whom were exploring classism, racism, Progressivism, and Romantic naturalism. The list of luminaries who dined with the Hubbard family reads as a Who's Who of American intellectual life: suffragist Susan B. Anthony; writer Carrie Jacobs Bond; Mrs. William Jennings Bryan; *Uncle Tom's Cabin* author Harriet Beecher Stowe; Joel Chandler Harris, the author of *Uncle Remus* stories; American Red Cross founder Clara Barton; George Washington Carver; Booker T. Washington; Ida Tarbell; Mark Twain; Eugene Debs; Margaret Sanger; Clarence Darrow; and Gutzon Borglum, the American sculptor who carved Mount Rushmore.[41]

The close proximity of Hubbard's children to the Seneca Indian Reservation in upstate New York shaped Ralph's lifelong interest in Indians. Hubbard writes of his childhood experiences with the Seneca, "since we lived in close association with these people, and since Grandfather Hubbard, and Grandmother too, knew so much about them and their customs, even back to pioneer times, Sandy [his sister] and I absorbed all of this as we went along. We grew up with it, and it all seemed right and natural, a part of our lives."[42] Yet it was Ralph's grandfather, the Illinois farmer, who told him, "Ralph, if you really want to learn about Indians, go west until you can smell the sagebrush."[43] This encountering of Indians and experiencing their "lives" (albeit in mediated voyeuristic form) was an essential component of the ways in which the men involved in creating Indian mascots narrated their understandings of Indian bodies.[44] Attending high school in Colorado, Ralph spent the summer between his junior and senior years living among the Crow and visiting the site of Custer's Last Stand at Little Big Horn. Trained by his aunt Myrtilla, who held a doctorate and was the head of the museum at Cornell University in 1905, Hubbard was a botanist and taxidermist. He parlayed these skills during his education at Oberlin College in Ohio, Cornell University, and at the University of Colorado at Boulder.[45]

Boulder locals who knew that he was experienced in Indian dance and lore brought Hubbard into the Boy Scout movement. Old family friend Ernest Thompson Seton, Chief Scout of America, welcomed Hubbard's involvement. "I was only hip high to a dustpan when I learned the basic steps of Indian dancing," Hubbard wrote. "I loved to watch them dance, and then I'd go home and practice the steps until I had them memorized. Almost as far back as I can remember, I could watch a dance and then dance it. When I went West, I could watch any new kind of dance, performed by any of the different tribes I met out there, and then dance it myself. For all the basic steps are similar, but each dancer can use his own gestures, showing how he feels about it."[46]

Hubbard's role in the Boy Scouts was delayed by the sinking of the *Lusitania*, in which his father perished, and the entrance of the United States into World War I. By the time Hubbard returned from France, where he served on the front lines, the BSA had become a nationwide movement that was planning its first World Jamboree.[47] Hubbard was appointed to incorporate a display of Indian dancing and crafts. He gathered teepees and other materials from his Colorado ranch as well as costumes for ninety boys and set off for London. The first jamboree was highly successful. Performing before an audience of 10,000, including the British royal family, the American display featured a 325-foot-long scene of a pass in the Rocky Mountains. "To the roll of the drums the youth of the world marched over the pass and down its slope to take their places on the great stage. First came the American Scout Orchestra from Denver, followed by a group of American Indians in magnificent war bonnets, and then Scouts from all the rest of the world."[48] From England, Hubbard and his Scouts traveled to the 1920 Olympic Games, where they performed for sports fans. This moment of convergence between the Boy Scouts pageantry and the Olympic Games suggests an increasing level of spectacle associated with sport. Predating Leutwiler's performance by a scant six years, it provided a model of appropriation available to each of these Scouts. Hubbard wrote of the Scouts chosen to attend the international jamborees: "all of them had to be progressive, hardworking, ambitious lads."[49]

By early 1924, Hubbard traveled around the United States holding city jamborees to educate more young men. Hubbard stopped in every major northern and western city, including New York City, Chicago, St. Louis, Seattle, and Phoenix, and brought the Indian department to urban and rural Scouts alike. With courses lasting four weeks, Hubbard taught boys camp craft, canoeing, teepee construction, cooking, wilderness survival, and Indian lore and dancing.[50] The city jamborees, while controlled exclusively by Hubbard, featured invited guests. Artists, painters, musicians, members of the forestry service, and Indians themselves contributed to a program that would dominate many young white boys' understanding of what being an Indian meant. Relegated to the margins of Boy Scout history are men like Santa Clara Pueblo Indian Ben Naranjo and Navajo Richard Long.[51] Employed first on Hubbard's Colorado ranch as an assistant, Naranjo became instrumental to the touring productions offered at the city jamborees. A craftsman, singer, and drummer, Naranjo guided many young men in learning Indian dancing and drumming, while Long drove the Boy Scout truck and participated in the jamboree programs. Visits by famous Indian athletes including Jim Thorpe and Ben American Horse were used to educate attendees about "the ability and worth of Indians."[52]

Hubbard's jamboree also offered the opportunity for young male Indians to participate in the Boy Scout movement. Remembering their involvement, Hubbard writes, "Scouting was mostly for white boys in those days, but for Indians, too, whenever we had the opportunity to include them. The reason for the government's reluctance to let us have any Indians was that the Bureau of Indian Affairs and the Indian educational departments refused to recognize that Scouting had no military connections."[53] Importantly, in some cities, Boy Scouts could attend Buffalo Bill's Wild West show and receive behind-the-scenes tours to see the Indians and the spectacle of American expansion that was performed almost daily.[54] Appropriate lines of class, race, and ethnicity were carefully outlined through tales of the past where Indians fell to white progress, black men and women were slaves, and immigrants were the "other." The education of young white men by the BSA then became a prism through which they could begin to grapple with their anxieties about the social and cultural upheaval felt by immigration, industrialization, and new feminism.

HALFTIME AND THE SETTLER COLONIAL IMAGINATION

The performance of William Penn and Chief Illiniwek at halftime of the UPenn-Illinois game in 1926 signaled a direct form of cultural borrowing from Native American ritual: the catlinite pipe served as a signifier of the calumet ceremony that frequently occurred in political negotiations among differing Indian nations, and between Indians and Euro-Americans, during seventeenth- and eighteenth-century colonial encounters. The calumet ceremony allowed the owner of the pipe and the guest to both ratify peace and create a fictional kinship relation. The calumet ceremony was part of the negotiating process and ultimately became a symbol of both parties' investment in peace.[55] One seventeenth-century French priest, Louis Hennepin, remarked that the calumet was a "pass and safe conduct among the allies of the nation who has given it."[56] Leutwiler, as the Indian chief, and William Penn, who had been enemies in the first half of the football game, ceased their conflict, pretended to become friends, and negotiated bonds of responsibility that suggested equal sociopolitical standing and safe passage for white Americans. The chief and the UPenn mascot then left the stadium together, leaving behind an audience that effectively inherited and represented the success of the colonial encounter by enjoying the rest of the game.

The interplay between Leutwiler and the UPenn mascot can be read as a reenactment of American colonialism that elided actual consequences of violence, disorder, and disruption in favor of a more neutral narrative of equitable relations and white succession. Tropes of Indians as warring peoples, spectacles of entertainment, and vanishing into the colonial frontier were all present in Leutwiler's performance. His dance was not just a demonstration of his understanding of Indian dance, dress, and political ceremonies; instead, it can be seen as a manifestation of a broader circuit of knowledge about Indians within the context of twentieth-century conceptions of race that were shared between the band, its members, and these competing institutions. In this manifestation, there is no place for the "Indian" to remain in the stadium. He appears only to contextualize white inheritance of the field, the stadium, and the university, and, much more broadly, the persistence of America even in the face of modern ills like urbanization, immigration, social disorder, and political upheaval. By turning to rituals and images of bygone eras, white middle-class men could reassure themselves that they were key contributors to modern American society. Football and the spectacles associated with the game became a vital opportunity for white men looking to alleviate their anxiety through celebrations of masculinity and order, albeit tinged with violence and gambling.

The halftime performance began because UPenn bandleaders appealed to the Illinois band to help them stage a performance of "good sportsmanship." Ray Dvorak, the assistant band director at Illinois, turned to Lester Leutwiler, who was already performing as the chief at his local high school, to show the camaraderie between the schools. Leutwiler was a senior at Urbana High School, a few miles away from the Illinois campus, whom Dvorak had witnessed donning his handmade costume at the behest of classmates who thought he should demonstrate all he had learned from Scouting and the touring group of Boy Scouts and Indians.[57] Leutwiler would perform at Illinois with the UPenn mascot, Benjamin Franklin.[58] Interestingly, though, Illinois fans thought the performance was between William Penn, the founder of the state of Pennsylvania, and Leutwiler's Indian. In part, their misidentification suggested the strength of popular narratives about the founding of Pennsylvania.

The historian James Merrell has charted English and colonialists' historical amnesia: "Beginning shortly after the Founder's death in 1718, medals struck in England depicted Penn shaking hands with some Indian or, seated beneath a tree on a sunny day, passing the native a peace pipe across a cheerful fire."[59] Benjamin West's 1771 painting *William Penn's Treaty with the Indians* visually articulated similar historical amnesia associated with Indian-white relations. "On an autumn day in 1682, the legend goes, William Penn met leaders of the Lenape to settle a unique treaty of peace and amity. According to the story told and retold during the subsequent centuries, the Native people quickly lost their initial fear when they met Penn and his unarmed company in the diffuse morning light."[60] Benjamin West believed that the "savages [were] brought into harmony and peace by justice and benevolence" and "a conquest that was made over native peoples without sword or dagger."[61] His painting of the Lenape suggested strong classical European influences that elided the actual appearance and exchange between the Lenape and William Penn's treaty party. The historian James O'Neil Spady writes, "the story of Pennsylvania's benevolent origins is an allegory of colonialism propagated by Penn and later colonists that has obscured the significance of both the severe disruption of Lenape life that Pennsylvania created and the resistance of some Lenape to that disruption."[62]

In historical memory, the effects of colonialism virtually disappear under the weight of the myth of the founding of Pennsylvania as a site of religious freedom

FIGURE 5. Benjamin West, *William Penn's Treaty with the Indians*, 1771. 75½ × 107¾". Courtesy of the Pennsylvania Academy of the Fine Arts, Philadelphia. Gift of Mrs. Sarah Harrison (The Joseph Harrison, Jr. Collection).

with Penn as the icon of "the compassionate father." "These fundamental contradictions in American identity and history—the tension between the ideal of a free and democratic nation and the reality of racial hierarchies, the discrepancy between the myth of peaceful expansion and the history of bloody conquest—reemerge again and again in the cultural imagination. It is, perhaps, for this reason that Euro-Americans have always been obsessed with stories of the nation's origins, repeatedly retelling and reconfiguring their collective past in self-justifying ways."[63] These mythologized qualities of benevolence and goodwill for the purposes of self-justification ameliorated the effects of the modern world where violence was common. The newly enacted William Penn passively greets the Indian after watching his war dance, accepts the gesture of friendship, and facilitates the exit of the Indian from the stadium.[64] He does not suggest the complex and often violent process of colonial encounters between the Lenape and Pennsylvanians. Nor does the narrative of encounter between colonists and Indians in the state of Illinois come to the fore. Instead, the scripted exchange suggests a benign interplay between Indians and colonists without nuance or elaboration. This is, as suggested in the introduction, the height of the erasure of Indian bodies.[65] Indian bodies are only present on the field when in conversation with white performers and only accessible to the audience through their proximity to that which is different.

Returning to the exchange between William Penn and the chief then reveals that the origins of the chief performance, while having local roots in both Hubbard's and Leutwiler's lives, are, in fact, national stories constructed by social organizations like Seton's Woodcraft Indians and the Boy Scouts that have local manifestations. It was through the creation of football spectacles and the need for images and narratives that could reassure young, white, middle-class men of their place in society that educational institutions, including UPenn and Illinois, began to construct halftime spectacles. Individuals within these organizations and the organizations themselves were connected to international circuits of creation and dissemination of knowledge about Indians. This worldview recognized Indians but continued to affirm their absence and eventual demise, illustrating that the future of the modern world was a world where young, white, middle-class men would prosper.

3 · AND THE BAND PLAYED
NARRATIVES OF
AMERICAN EXPANSION

The University of Illinois band accompanied Lester Leutwiler as he danced his "frenzied war dance" of toe-heel movements, low ground kicks, and half moon and full moon dance steps down the Illinois football field. Leutwiler's dark beaded shirt with bone and porcupine breastplate was complemented by a spotted eagle feathered headdress, feathered bustle, and dark rope wig. It presented a dramatic counterpoint to the nattily attired men dressed in formal band uniforms of white pants and military-style jackets. While the previous chapter examined the origins of Leutwiler's performance and the centrality of the Boy Scouts of America and Ralph Hubbard to the formation of a national network of learning about Indians, this chapter interrogates the ways in which the university band produced a halftime spectacle on the football field. Bands were a central performer at games and during community events. Yet it was with their integration with mascotry that halftime offered the opportunity for white, male, middle-class spectators to grapple with their anxieties over modern life. By turning from militaristic drilling toward entertainment, university marching bands incorporated aural as well as visual representations of the past. Students and band administrators joined in the spectacle and helped reinforce concepts of Indianness that extended well beyond the playing field.

The University of Illinois band transformed modern marching music and, in doing so, established a national identity for the University of Illinois built around its performance and halftime spectacle. The band influenced Illinois youth through its music education programs, drew support for the university from across the state, and memorialized the notion of the University of Illinois as a community through its adoption of loyalty songs. As a result, college bands were yet another mechanism that white middle-class men used to reinforce racial and class-based ideas to younger white men grappling with the anxiety of a modernizing world.[1]

The initial performance of Leutwiler as Chief Illiniwek in 1926 was supposed to be a solitary experience. Fans though, indoctrinated in the spectacle that had grown up around the game, were thrilled with the appearance of an "Indian" to entertain them at halftime.[2] Leutwiler's performances at Urbana High School and with his Boy Scout troop were accompanied by troop members on the drum playing popular compositions. At Illinois, however, he danced that October day to the music of "Illinois Loyalty," "Oskee-Wow-Wow," and "Hail to the Orange," which had been recorded in 1925 by the Victor Talking Machine Company following a performance at the University of Pennsylvania. Moderate in tempo, these three compositions formed the original accompaniment to Leutwiler's performance.[3] Leutwiler had not, in all likelihood, ever formally performed to this particular combination publicly. Yet these selections tell us of the underlying motivation of the performance itself: all three were familiar to band members and fans alike and were designed as participatory songs. Spectators were encouraged to cheer on the university and its sporting teams with songs made familiar through the university band.

THE MAKING OF A MODERN MARCHING BAND

Albert Austin Harding led the University of Illinois band. Formerly a captain of his local town team, the Paris High School football team, Harding enrolled as a freshmen at the University of Illinois in 1902 and quickly rose to take over leadership of the university band a few years later.[4] Harding's involvement and rapid rise to bandleader was hardly a surprise. Between 1897 and 1905, Harding served as a musician in the Boy's Brigade, the Paris High School Cadets, the Paris Beacon Drum and Bugle Corps, the Paris Concert Band, and Goodman's Band, the official band of the Fourth Regiment of the Illinois National Guard.[5] In many of these, he served as the bandleader as well as a musician. Coupled with his hiring out as a substitute musician to bands across the United States from Denver east to New York City, Harding participated in a network of musical contacts from local young men to "the March King," John Philip Sousa, who provided an overwhelming number of military-based march compositions for the Illinois band.

Harding and his colleagues within the university and collegiate band network transformed the band from a secondary element of the game to the emotive voice of the action itself. "Basically parade bands with drills based on their strong military heritage," wrote the musicologist Jerry Thomas Haynie, football bands' formality lent an air of gravitas to the performances prior to 1907. These bands were generally all-male; garbed in military-style uniforms; led by vocal, whistle, or baton signals from a drill-master or primitive drum-major type; and trained in the rudiments of direction-change, open-order, and close-order marching.[6] Militaristic marches and revues were the standard program presented by the football band.[7] Yet military marches and music were no longer entertaining to an audience looking for popular music. University bands could, however, generate audience excitement through the innovative use of new approaches to on-field performances. Providing audio signposts for fans to mark the progress of the game and with the introduction of loyalty music, the university band presented a lively sound to accompany the action of the game. In 1907, Purdue University introduced the first on-field formation, the letter "P."[8] Tribute lettering, the process of forming a letter or series of letters as a tribute to the band's own school or its opponent's, allowed the band to move from its strictly regimented drill lines for the first time.[9] Just as the exchange between Leutwiler's Chief Illiniwek and UPenn's William Penn was created to encourage good sportsmanship, the use of tribute lettering was used to remind audiences that they were supposed to be gentlemanly competitors rather than violent ruffians. Purdue's innovation spread quickly. The University of Illinois band by November 1909 featured the block "I" during its halftime performance in honor of its own university. Band members segued from the "I" into a performance of the first bleacher song in America, "Illinois Loyalty."[10] By participating in "Illinois Loyalty," spectators could demonstrate their allegiance to the university and their community.

"Illinois Loyalty" premiered at the Spring Concert of 1906 and quickly became a staple performance for all university bands, including the orchestra and the Marching Band, the formal organization that grew out of the baseball and football bands. Composed by Rhode Island–born Thatcher Howland Guild, a newly appointed English professor, and Harding, "Illinois Loyalty" was an "all-occasion" college song.[11] Harding quickly published the song, copyrighted the band arrangements, and distributed it to bands across the United States.[12] Thousands heard:

> We're loyal to you, Illinois
> We're Orange and Blue, Illinois
> We'll back you to stand
> 'Gainst the best in the land,
> For we know you have sand,
> Illinois,
> Rah, Rah.
> So crack out that ball,
> Illinois.
> We're backing you all,
> Illinois.
> Our Team is our fame defender,
> On boys, for we expect a victory
> From you, Illinois,
> Che-he, Che-ha, Che-ha-ha-ha

Che-he, Che-he, Che-ha-ha-ha
Illinois, Illinois, Illinois
Fling out that dear old flag of Orange and Blue,
Lead on your sons and daughters, fighting for you.
Like men of old, on giants,
Placing reliance,
Shouting defiance,
Oskey wow-wow.
Amid the broad green fields that nourish our land
For honest Labor and for Learning we stand,
And unto thee we pledge our heart and hand,
Dear Alma Mater, Illinois.[13]

Celebrating the university, its role educating the next generation of young men, and its potential athletic victories, the bleacher song highlights the lessons that were being offered to its spectators. The Marching Band and its football performances featured only male musicians, and "Illinois Loyalty" suggests that the "boys" were supposed to secure athletic victory under the supervision of previous generations of successful men.[14] Women were seen as a distraction to male spectators, and they were encouraged to avoid attending games or, if they did, to sit in segregated sections.[15] "Illinois Loyalty" echoed the prevailing sentiments of hard work and "honest Labor" as well as the commitment to education that all students were supposed to have. Student enthusiasm was the cornerstone of the "Illinois Loyalty" performance with the phrase "Oskey wow-wow" being yelled by those on the field as well as those in the bleachers. "Oskey wow-wow" was entirely a creation of Thatcher Howland Guild that mimicked Indian sounds made present in popular songs.[16]

The immediate popularity of Guild and Harding's composition was not surprising given Harding's growing reputation as the premiere collegiate marching band composer. Yet his immediate licensing of the march composition suggests an understanding of the demands of the marching band market for new music as well as the profitability of these compositions in an increasingly commercial world of music. Harding was not just sharing his composition with his band colleagues across the United States in an informal manner. He created a profitable enterprise that was based on the market for band music. The "Illinois model" encouraged audience participation and created new possibilities for men who were unable to compete on the athletic field itself. The band provided an opportunity for musically trained men to participate in the ritual of belonging that was being created on the athletic field. It closed the division created by the masculinist rhetoric of the football field by suggesting an alternative method of male indoctrination and participation: as a band musician.[17]

The integration of ideas of Illinois students and faculty with the Marching Band program continued with a 1908 competition to write a musical comedy. While students Howard Green and Howard Hill never completed their musical comedy and thus could not compete with rival Purdue, they did enter a university-wide postexam jubilee contest. "Oskee-wow-wow," "Hail to the Orange," "Cheer Illini," and the Sigma Alpha Epsilon classic "Violets" were all composed for the Green-Hill entry. "Oskee-wow-wow" reflected the growing rivalry between the Illinois athletic teams and their opponents:

> Old Princeton yells her Tiger,
> Wisconsin, her Varsity
> And they give the same old Rah, Rah, Rah,
> At each University,
> But the yell that always thrills me
> And fills my heart with joy,
> Is the good old Oskee-Wow-Wow,
> That they yell at Illinois.
> Os-kee-Wow-Wow,
> Illinois
> Our eyes are all on you.
> Oskee-Wow-Wow,
> Illinois,
> Wave your Orange and your Blue,
> Rah, Rah,
> When the team trots out before you,
> Every man stand up and yell,
> Back the team to victory,
> Os-kee-Wow-Wow.
> Illinois.[18]

Green and Hill copied the imagery of "Rah, Rah," "Oskey-wow-wow," and "Orange and Blue" from "Illinois Loyalty." They transferred the sentiments of men's loyalty for their team that was included in "Illinois Loyalty" to their own compositions. While "Illinois Loyalty" suggested the importance of young men's character and their role as protectors of the land, "Oskee-wow-wow" concentrated entirely on athletic rivalries with Princeton and Wisconsin. "Oskee-wow-wow" suggests how Green and Hill, two students, imagined Illinois athletics: not as a site for the inculcation of sociocultural norms but instead as a site of athletic competition between rivals. This was the furor of football spectacle that was beginning to transform colleges and universities. Honor of one's opponents must be carefully balanced against the entertainment value of a successful football match. While local businessman Charlie Graham purchased the rights to "Oskee-wow-wow," he passed on "Hail to the Orange," the composition of Green and Hill's that would become the school anthem. Fraternity brothers and glee club members sang:

> Hail to the Orange,
> Hail to the Blue.
> Hail Alma Mater,
> Ever So True.
> We love no other,
> So let our motto be.
> Victory, Illinois
> Varsity.[19]

By the time Green and Hill returned to campus in the fall of 1910 for the first ever collegiate homecoming, "Hail to the Orange" was being sold in local stores and sung by university students on a regular basis, with the university band accompanying them.[20] All three compositions—"Illinois Loyalty," "Oskee-wow-wow," and "Hail to the Orange—were part and parcel of the musical repertoire of Harding's band by 1910 and were familiar to athletes and fans alike.[21] The sounds of the Illinois band were becoming part of the spectacle beginning to develop around college athletics and football in particular. In joining these compositions to the halftime performance of Leutwiler, the university band established a broader, more explicit meaning of "Illinois Loyalty," "Oskee-wow-wow," and "Hail to the Orange" to include a visual rendering of the University of Illinois's supposed relationship to Indians. Importantly, though, this conceptualization of the conjoined music and performance was fluid and was altered in the early years of Leutwiler's performance to include music commissioned explicitly for the performance.

FORMALIZING THE HALFTIME SHOW

Lester Leutwiler again took to the field in 1928, now under the formal guise of Chief Illiniwek.[22] Karl L. King, the director of the Fort Dodge Municipal Band in Iowa and owner of the K. L. King Music Publishing House, and Harry Alford, the ragtime composer and vaudevillian musician, were commissioned by the University of Illinois to produce music for the Chief Illiniwek halftime performance.[23] "They were asked to keep in mind the driving beat of the drums which were used at Native American pow wows," Leutwiler remembered. "They were also told that the music would have to live up to the power of the performance."[24] While Leutwiler suggests that it was the "power of the performance" of the band that was vital to preserve, instead it would be more accurate to say that Harding and others were concerned that it was the importance of football games as entertainment that needed to be preserved. As the decade of the 1920s was ending, more universities and colleges were embracing the growth of big-time football with its massive concrete stadiums and game-day events. Rituals like the annual homecoming weekend where alumni could return to campus to relive their glory days as young men became opportunities for universities to secure donors who could support the growth of the university. Halftime performance became yet another moment where the university could entertain its potential donors as well as the public.

King sent Harding his newest march, the "Pride of the Illini," as a tribute to Harding and the University of Illinois band.[25] An Ohio native, King was noted for his career with professional circus bands throughout the Midwest and was, surprisingly, a charter member of the American Bandmasters Association (ABA). Beginning with his involvement in Robinson's Famous Circus in 1910 and culminating with his appointment in 1917 as the director of Barnum and Bailey's Circus Band, King toured the United States and produced circus marches for entertainment purposes.[26] Musicologist Thomas Hatton elaborated on the important role of music in circus performances: "It set the mood for various acts, covered transitions between acts, caught the audience's attention for entrances, encouraged applause for exits, and built and resolved suspense. . . . A march begins with a great fanfare of blaring trumpets and trombones loud enough to stop the audience from talking and martial enough to warn them that something exciting was about to happen. Then the march itself would follow in a tempo slow enough to walk to but fast enough to continue the excitement."[27] King easily grasped the dynamic nature of the circus march and applied it to the spectacle that was a college football halftime show.

Composing what Philip Deloria has called "sounds of ethnicity,"[28] King's tenure with the newly merged Sells-Floto–Buffalo Bill Wild West show demonstrated the use of music laden with racial sentiment and stimulated the formation of a mobile community of attendees engaged in performative racialized rituals of belonging.[29] "On the Warpath," "Passing of the Redman," and "Wyoming Days" were composed to reflect the story of the American West and the cowboys and Indians who remained a vital part of the circus in 1914.[30] "During 'The Attack on Deadwood Stage' an audience member saw gunsmoke, smelled gunpowder, heard gunfire, was aware of the spectators nearest to him, as well as those across the arena from him, and a few audience members even experienced the tactile sensation of even riding the stage."[31] General manager John Burke described the progression of events that would accompany the bandleader's music: "Life as it is witnessed on the plains: the Indian encampment; the cowboys and vaqueros; the herds of buffalo and elk; the lassoing of animals; the manner of robbing mail coaches; feats of agility, horsemanship, archery, and the kindred scenes and events that are characteristic of the border."[32] Chicago's Columbian Exposition, the Louisiana Purchase Exposition in St. Louis in 1904, as well as the growing coverage of far-flung nations in the daily newspaper created a demand for music compositions that supposedly represented those peoples. Even "the March

King," John Philip Sousa, composed sounds of ethnicity for public audiences that demanded exotic spectacles for their entertainment.[33]

Participation in the Wild West show, even as audience members, allowed for a collective expression of the success of American progress. Each show led to the physical, psychological, and emotional defeat of the American West and its Indian inhabitants. King repeatedly led the soundtrack to American expansion and "contributed to (maybe began) the rhythmic cliché, often heard later in music, signaling the approach of 'wild' Indians into a 'civilized' scene or reenactment: one & two &, one & two &."[34] Attendees heard King direct repetitive tom-tom drums portending potential disaster: "*dum* dum dum dum *dum* dum dum dum" as scenes of American expansion were reenacted before them.

The dramatic success of the nascent days of the original Buffalo Bill's Wild West show was due in part to its ability to create a visual performance of historical and literary accounts of encounters between and among Indians and Euro-Americans. Borrowing from fiction with its popular dime novel format, newspaper accounts, photography, art, ethnographic and museum exhibitions, as well as theater and musical performances, the show, led by William Cody, constructed a dazzling array that delighted the senses and affirmed familiar narratives of American success even to international audiences. The enormous public appetite for the foreign, unfamiliar, and exotic was fulfilled by early motion pictures, historical reenactments and pageants, as well as widely circulated literary narratives.[35] Just as Indians of the silent film era did not speak from the screen, neither did Leutwiler's Indian from the field. Instead, the music itself was supposed to signal and portend the action on the screen/field.

FIGURE 6. Buffalo Bill's Wild West show Indians with William "Bill" Cody in Italy, 1890. Courtesy Royale Photographie, Vuillemenot Montabone 188 Via Nazionale—Roma (Italia).

King's "Indian" music, with its now familiar rhythm, was notably absent from his "Pride of the Illini" composition. It did not reproduce the stereotypical sound of the tom-tom drum, nor did it utilize melodies made popular in Cody's Wild West show and in the scores from early motion pictures. Instead, the rat-a-tat-tat of the drum drew attention to the martial nature of the composition and King's conceptualization that the legacy of Harding and the University of Illinois band was its formal marching compositions. Ray Dvorak's lyric followed neatly behind "Illinois Loyalty" and "Hail to the Orange":

We are marching for dear old Illini,
We are marching for dear old Illini,
For the men who are fighting for you,
Here's a cheer for our dear old Alma Mater,
May our love for ever be true,
When we're marching along life's pathway,
May the spirit of Old Illinois, Keep us
Marching and Singing with true Illini Spirit
For our dear old Illinois.[36]

Importantly, the commissioning of the march from King suggests that Harding and Dvorak conceptualized the halftime performance as a spectacle, an entertainment, and an opportunity to affirm the standards of the marching band. King, though, produced a standard military-style march composition that was not part of his "Indian" music tradition. The music itself was a traditional march, and Dvorak's lyrics could be seen as neutral when divorced from Leutwiler's performance.

Harry L. Alford sent Harding the "March of the Illini."[37] He, as well as King, demonstrated the mobility of composers, bandleaders, musicians, and arrangers between popular music and the more conventional orchestral pieces. Alford worked as a freelance musical arranger for companies, including Rossiters of Chicago and Hearst Music of New York.[38] With arranging credits for prolific writer-publishers Charles L. Johnson, Paul Biese, and F. Henri Klickman, as well as Bessie Smith, Alford was involved in the ethnic music craze of 1900 to 1915.[39] Originally composed years earlier under the title "Battle of Tippecanoe," the "March of the Illini" seamlessly merged Indian-sounding music with Alford's other interest, band arranging. The rapid tom-tom beat of the drum that King and early film had made popular was extended by Alford to include brass, wind, and percussion instruments. An "Indian-flavored march melody," the "March of the Illini" explicitly linked Indianness to the university band identity without using vocals. This continued the pattern of the silent Indian produced in motion pictures and confirmed the firmly established stereotypes of Indians as separate from social exchanges in polite society. The music itself legitimated Leutwiler's performance for the audience by presenting familiar themes and tones. By 1928, the standard Leutwiler performance no longer enacted the greeting and peace pipe ritual that was present at the initial performance. It relied entirely on the score adopted by the band to communicate an extended meaning of Leutwiler's ritual. In effect, the band fulfilled the role that William Penn initially expressed: that of the civilizing mission. Highlighting the shift from Penn to the University of Illinois band suggests the uneasiness of the spectacle outlined here. These were not ritualized performances that did not respond to internal and external forces (like changing opponents); rather these performances could substitute elements for one another so long as they shared the same meaning within a framework that affirmed white middle-class concerns over their place in the world.

"Pride of the Illini" was the first overture in communicating the narrative of expansion. Band members in their martial uniforms took their place along the end-zone line to perform. The standardized march of the band called the spectators in the stands to attention: "We are marching . . . Our love . . ." and so forth. Giving way to the "March of the Illini," with its Indian-sounding beat and dramatic visual rendering, implicitly suggested that the "true Illini spirit" could be that of an Indian past. The music called forth the "Indian" and signaled a shift in the performance by creating an aural demarcation for Leutwiler's performance. "March of the Illini" was a duel between "civilization" in the guise of the band and the "primitive" in the form of Leutwiler's Indian. As Leutwiler's dance accelerated, so too would the tempo of the music. The tempo was controlled by Harding, the bandleader. He signaled the rise and fall of Chief Illiniwek by beginning the song and drawing the song to a close. Leutwiler, in his Indian guise, could only enter the field to the signal offered by the modern audience and had to accede to progress by ceasing his performance when the music stopped. This mimicked popular conceptions of the process of Indian assimilation, where the value of Indians was only recognized as a contrast to white American society.[40] The finale and metaphorical demise of Chief Illiniwek was to cease movement completely at midfield and salute the crowd as "Hail to the Orange" was sung by band members and fans alike. Chief Illiniwek would then lead the Marching Band from the field, leaving behind the fans as the inheritors of the metaphorical land, the football stadium.

In leading the chief performance, Harding was affirming the continued existence of the university and its white, male, middle-class audience through persistence. Just as Memorial Stadium was constructed as a simultaneous remembrance of the past and a celebration of new, modern technologies, Harding's university band offered a dual veneration of the past and the future.[41] The university band quickly attracted highly skilled musicians and directors from across the United States who hoped to learn from Harding. During the High School Teachers Conference held annually on the university campus, high school teachers interested in band sought out Harding and his staff. Meeting individually and in groups with these men, by 1930 Harding had established a formal conference to train public school band instructors in the methods and technologies of the modern Illinois band.[42] Prominent individuals who directed commercial and town bands—including Dr. Edwin Franko Goldman, Herbert Clarke, Frank Simon, Henry Fillmore, W. H. Bicket, Victor J. Grabel, and Harold Bachman, then director of Bachman's Million Dollar Band of Chicago and later conductor of the University of Florida band—all attended Harding's conferences.[43] His formal educational program to train students as professional performers and as public school and college teachers capable of teaching instrumental music, band, and orchestral performances anticipated the tremendous need for leaders and musicians for regimental and Reserve Officers' Training Corps (ROTC) bands that would occur during the Great War.

Harding paralleled his effort to locally train collegiate band directors and musicians with an expanded touring program to promote the Illinois model of professionalism, innovation, and performance. The University of Illinois band had toured since the turn of the century within the state of Illinois, and by the late 1920s the university band was traveling across the country to exhibitions and performances that were arranged to highlight their musicianship and innovative techniques.[44] By including well-known conductors and bandleaders in his annual meetings, training up-and-coming music teachers, and publishing compositions for use by bands across the country, Harding cemented a network that postulated a standardized model of performance that joined the interest of elites in classical composition with the growing number of individuals interested in commercial music. This blending of the musical market as it was conjoined to collegiate athletics allowed Harding and his marching band to foment a theatrical style of performance that alleviated the tension generated by the hierarchy of musical interests. The halftime performance created the potential for a mass appeal both to elites, who were interested in training the next generation of young men to be good citizens, and to the rising middle class, who sought to alleviate their anxiety over their place in the modern world. Music became something that could unite the classes. College football bands were a community that, while they concentrated on standards and professionalism, understood the importance of entertainment and spectacle. The marching band provided an aural soundtrack to the community gathering and signaled the appropriate moments within the ritual to venerate the university and community.

INFLUENCING THE NATION THROUGH COLLEGE BANDS

In the six years after Leutwiler's original Indian performance with the band, Harding's assistant directors firmly established themselves at colleges across the United States and were embracing composers favored by Harding and the newly formed ABA.[45] Glenn Cliffe Bainum served as the band director at Southern

Illinois University and later Northwestern University, where Karl L. King composed "The Purple Pageant" for use by Bainum's Marching Band in 1933.[46] Bainum was the first full-time band director at Northwestern and enlivened the faltering band that originated in 1911 to "add a little pep and ginger during the football games." In just one year, Bainum increased the size of the band from seventeen members to eighty and began the 1927 season by spelling out "hello" to welcome fans to the football game.[47] King also composed "Wisconsin's Pride" in 1937 for Ray Dvorak, who left Illinois to lead the University of Wisconsin band. Under Dvorak's leadership, the University of Wisconsin band earned a national reputation for its excellence and attempted to claim its own series of firsts: "the singing band, mass singing, formations without signals, and animated formations."[48] These competing claims of ownership for band innovations suggested a culture of competition between these midwestern schools. The modern university should not just have a marching band but have an innovative band with its own spectacle. Between 1937 and 1939, King completed an additional series of collegiate marches that proved integral to the individual ritual of the football marching band: "Michigan on Parade" for William Revelli at the University of Michigan, "Hawkeye Glory" for Charles B. Righter at the University of Iowa, "Mighty Minnesota" for Gerald Prescot at the University of Minnesota, and, much later, "Black and Gold" for the Purdue University band.[49] The success of the "Big Ten" marches led to additional commissioning at the University of North Dakota, South Dakota State College, Wayne State University, Phillips University, Louisiana State University, the University of Chicago, the University of Idaho, and the University of Arizona. The spread of King's compositions and the theatrics of the marching band had far-reaching implications in facilitating the changing conception of halftime spectacle.

By the late 1930s, Harding and the ABA, including charter member Karl L. King, had embraced the growth of collegiate bands and the importance of standardized performance to the halftime performance. The regimental band and the informal pickup bands of the close of the nineteenth century had, by 1929, when A. Webber Borchers donned the Chief Illiniwek regalia for the first time, given way to the spectacle of the choreographed halftime show. Colleges across the nation, many led by individuals trained in the "Illinois model," were encouraging the transformation of halftime into popular spectacle to go along with football. At the University of Illinois, Leutwiler's Indian and the music of the halftime show had become the centerpiece of an explicitly racialized articulation of community belonging that took place within the confines of Memorial Stadium. That articulation would be replicated throughout the 1930s. Yet even as Illinois's halftime spectacle spread, the tension between the various groups that made up the university grew as well. It took agreement between administrators, coaches, students, alumni, and fans to allow halftime spectacle to grow and for athletic identity to dominate the university landscape.

4 · THE LIMITATIONS OF HALFTIME SPECTACLE

By the late 1920s, Americans were fascinated with the athleticism of football. Yet for many universities and colleges, the production of a grand football spectacle was beyond their financial reach. For these schools, basketball and baseball garnered as much attention as the game of football. This chapter examines how two institutions, Miami University and the University of North Dakota (UND), manifested their own spectacles that employed Indians as central elements to not just their athletic identity but that of their universities more generally. Both demonstrated that the convergence of university identity, college football, and commercial spectacle was more difficult for small schools that struggled to attract white middle-class men as spectators.

On an unusually warm Saturday evening in January 1928, five Cincinnati "Baehr-cats" stepped onto dimly lit hardwood floors in Herron Gymnasium in Oxford, Ohio, to take on the Miami University "Big Reds."[1] The basketball game signaled a decade-long struggle between the city of Cincinnati and Miami University.[2] Cincinnati residents had protested the establishment of Miami University at the remote muddy outpost of Oxford; Cincinnati, in its boomtown glory, did not have a major institution of higher education. With Cincinnati struggling to become incorporated, Cincinnatians believed the establishment of a college within city limits boosted their claim that the city was *the* destination in the new state of Ohio.[3] The athletic rivalry began in 1888 with an annual football game, but by the 1928 basketball season, the stakes of competition were clear: winning was to be secured by any means necessary. The Bearcats were strong, fast athletes who liked to push the tempo of the game early.[4] The Miami men were told that everything must be "done to keep them from doing that." Cincinnati fans, having driven over an hour from Cincinnati, gathered with county residents to line the upper deck that surrounded the court. Cheering on the game, these communities saw a match dominated by Cincinnati's high-scoring guards.

THE RACIALIZED LANGUAGE OF CONQUEST

"Bearcats Come to Oxford Saturday Seeking Hides of Big Red-Skinned Warriors" opined the January 1928 issue of the Miami University student newspaper, the *Miami Student*. "The Big Reds are out to add one more scalp to their collection, and it must be done."[5] The use of skin color and the practice of scalping within news of the basketball contest suggested the power of colonial tropes that lingered into the early twentieth century. "At the start of the eighteenth century, Indians and Europeans rarely mentioned the color of each other's skins. By midcentury, remarks about skin color and the categorization of peoples by simple color-coded labels (red, white, black) had become commonplace."[6] Linneas's 1740 *Systema Naturae* popularized red as the physical descriptor for Indians' bodies, and the use of the phrases "red men," "red people," and "red-skinned" appears prominently in discussions of Indian life from the mid-eighteenth century onward.[7] In many Indian societies, the color white represented peace, harmony, and friendship while red signaled blood, violence, and warfare.[8] The color coding produced a physical manifestation in the case of the Creeks of the Southwest: leaders of Creek warriors would paint their bodies red in preparation for warfare. The Meskwaki, or "people of the red earth," tell of their origins as people "made out of clay as red as the reddest blood."[9] As council speeches among the Iroquois (1687), at the Treaty of Augusta (1763), and at Shamokin, Pennsylvania (1769), illustrate, skin color was a critical divide between Europeans and Indians.[10] In leveraging skin color as the marker of identity, Indians and Europeans were able to demarcate biologies of belonging. In eighteenth-century parlance, one must be "red" to be Indian and "white" to be Euro-American.[11] The use of "Big Red-Skinned Warriors," explicitly faux Native bodies, drew on these cultural meanings in advertising the game. Miami University athletes, in the guise of Native bodies, were being stalked by Cincinnati's bearcat. While metaphorical, the analogy of young white men hunting each other to secure athletic success echoed anxieties of modern life where immigrants, African Americans, and even American Indians were placing pressure on white middle-class men by seeking economic, political, and cultural autonomy.

In "adding one more scalp" to its collection, the *Miami Student* was playing upon a second prominent historical trope: that of the warrior counting coup and scalping his opponent to celebrate a successful conquest. Scalping and the display of Indian heads were documented as early as 1535 by French explorer Jacques Cartier, who was shown "the skins of five men's heads, stretched on hoops, like parchment" during his second voyage up the St. Lawrence among the Stadaconans.[12] Hernando de Soto's men encountered scalp displays in west Florida among the Apalachees in 1540, and Creeks displayed scalps on a pole in the town center in 1560. Through the lens of contemporary life, it would be easy to perceive the collecting and display of scalps by victors as a particularly vicious form of warfare and taunting. Yet the collecting and display of scalps were highly ritualized among many tribes. Samuel de Champlain witnessed a victory ritual among the Montagnais of lower Quebec in 1603:

> Approaching the shore each took a stick, on the end of which they hung the scalps (*testes*) of their slain enemies with some beads, singing . . . all together. And when they were all ready, the women stripped themselves quite naked, and jumped into the water, swimming to the canoes to receive the scalps of their enemies which were at the end of long sticks in the bow of their canoes, in order to later hang them round their necks, as if they had been precious chains. And then they sang and danced. Some days afterwards they made me a present of one of these scalps as if it had been some very valuable thing, and of a pair of shields belonging to their enemies, for me to keep to show to the king. And to please them I promised to do so.[13]

Explorer Marc Lescarbot witnessed a similar ritual of collection, singing, and dancing among the Micmacs at Port Royal, Nova Scotia, while missionary Gabriel Sagard noted that the Hurons of Lake Ontario not only collected the scalps but also placed them on a long pole and displayed them publicly during times of war.[14] It is difficult to assess the motivation of these tribes in collecting scalps. Used as part of a cultural ritual, the scalps allowed tribal members to both remember the event itself and ritualistically celebrate the success of their endeavor. The case of the Hurons suggests that scalp collecting could also have been used to signal to enemies their physical prowess and hopefully to dissuade would-be attackers from waging war.[15]

European and Euro-American colonists encouraged the practice as it was in the interests of colonial governments to reduce the Indian population in the New World. The earliest bounties paid by Europeans to Indians required the presentation of the head, not just the scalp.[16] The English, French, and Dutch all presented Indians with monetary and material rewards for seeking out their enemies. In 1688, the governor of Canada offered ten beaver skins to the Indians of northern New England for every enemy scalp, Christian or Indian. Not to be outdone, the English regained the palm in 1696 when the New York Council "resolved for the future, that Six pounds shall be given to each Christian or Indian as a Reward who shall kill a French man or indian Enemy." By the close of the eighteenth century, a hierarchy of monetary value had been established where scalps of men capable of waging war were worth 100 pounds, ten times that of women and children older than ten.[17] In creating a structured valuation of Indian bodies that relied on perceived gender hierarchies based on potential violent behavior, colonists were previewing the nineteenth- and twentieth-century obsession with biological categorization made popular by ethnology and anthropology as well as the physical sciences. These were the disciplines that were being formalized at colleges and universities across the United States in the early twentieth century.

By 1928, when the *Miami Student* was celebrating its "red-skinned warriors," these disciplines had firmly established popular perceptions of Indianness that capitalized on colonial tropes and displays of the exotic.[18] Since 1824, varsity athletes were members of the "M" men, a campus club. The "M" was in reference to the university name, which, in itself, was drawn from the Native tribes who had lived on the land prior to colonization.[19] The only logo was a red "M" each man received.[20] In assigning a physical marker of achievement to athletes, athletic administrators were demarcating social boundaries of the haves and have-nots. In wearing an "M," young men were able to promote themselves as physically superior to their classmates, thereby enhancing their masculine worth.[21]

Fraternities played a similar role in creating both a community for young men away from their families and serving as an indicator of social status. Many athletes were fraternity members during their tenure on campus. Following the 1929 football win against Transylvania University, halfback Frank S. Games attended his fraternity mixer. A member of the Delta Kappa Epsilon fraternity, Games began a conversation with university president Alfred H. Upham, also a fraternity member:

PRESIDENT UPHAM: "The name Big Red is no longer appropriate for Miami teams. The papers refer to you as the Pony Backfield and surely there must be a better name than Big Red!"

GAMES: "Well, this is Indian country and they have been part of the folklore. The Indian tribe and the rivers are all named Miami. Why not use the words Redskins as the designation for Miami athletic teams?"

UPHAM: "I like your suggestion and at the right time I will place it before the Board of Trustees."[22]

The folklore Games pointed to was formalized in student publications just a few years later. The freshman handbook, or "M Book," featured an Indian head silhouette alongside the "Scalp Song." The "Scalp Song" reads in part, "The tribes go forth to war/their scalp-songs ring afar/bright the blood-red camp-fires gleaming/mad with thirst the war-hawks screaming."[23] An invocation of the game written about in the news, the "Scalp Song" demonstrated the way in which university publications began to produce Indian-themed identity as part of their university identity. The Miami University yearbook, the *Recensio*, acknowledged this status: "Miami University-Athletic teams are known as Redskins, honoring the fierce Tribe Miami Indians of early Ohio history."[24] Football players received tomahawk stickers to affix to their helmets to recognize superior athletic achievements.[25]

According to the 1930 *Alumni Newsletter*, "members of the athletic department went into a huddle not long ago and decided that Miami teams had a moniker [Big Red] and a symbol [M]. As the very name Miami is taken from

FIGURE 7. Illustration by J. O. Lewis of Mi-A-Qu-A, Miami chief, 1854. Courtesy Clarke Historical Library, Central Michigan University.

an Indian tribe and the term 'Big Reds' smacks of Redskins and the warpath, an Indian brave in war lock and feathers was thought a suitable insignia."[26] The original Miami depiction of the insignia was accurate in its depiction of the Miami Indians. Men of the Miami tribe were heavily tattooed across the face, chest, arms, and legs. They wore animal skin shirts, leggings, and moccasins during the winter and a breechcloth during the summer.[27] Miami men wore their hair short with sections loose in front of and behind their ears.[28] The first depiction used a silhouette image reminiscent of Mi-A-Qu-A, a Miami chief, with braided hair.

Miami University enrolled roughly 2,000 students in 1928. It lacked a marching band and a capital campaign to construct a massive concrete stadium, and there was limited public transportation into and out of the town of Oxford.[29] Miami University, while growing, was struggling to attract students to the rural community just an hour from Cincinnati. That effort to attract students to rural communities was a struggle shared with the University of North Dakota.

Founded in 1883, the University of North Dakota existed, by its twenty-fifth birthday, in an increasingly competitive world of higher education.[30] The North Dakota Agricultural College (now North Dakota State University) had recently been founded and provided vocational training including short courses on farming and mechanics that were popular with the populace who saw farming as one of its primary occupations.[31] "By 1909, it was a rare farmer—and hence a rare North Dakotan—who was not grateful for the Agricultural College's work in eradicating the Russian thistle, finding new seeds and improving old strains, solving the problem of 'flax sickness.'"[32] The University of North Dakota, on the other hand, presented a wide variety of curricula, including teacher education, arts and letters, as well as the more esoteric fields of Scandinavian studies and linguistics.[33]

From the outset, the two institutions competed for the scarce student-age population. On the eve of the Civil War, the U.S. Census recognized only 4,837 persons within the Dakota Territory, which included the current states of North and South Dakota, Wyoming, and Montana. Nearly half of those identified as Indian.[34] By 1880, 135,177 persons were listed as living in the Dakota Territory, the overwhelming number of whom (133,127) were male.[35] The Indian population increased just slightly to 1,391 persons. With a population of roughly 3,000, Grand Forks, where the university was located, served as a hub of commerce and trading for the northern Red River Valley. Grand Forks boasted a Hudson's Bay Company store, a station on the Red River steamboat line, a stop on the stage line, a courthouse, a Masonic lodge, two flour mills, four hotels, two daily newspapers as well as a Norwegian weekly, a brewery, brickyards, twenty saloons, and six churches.[36] Grand Forks might have been a big city on the edge of the American frontier, but in comparison with other university-driven cities, Grand Forks barely registered as anything more than a stop on the railroad.

Utilizing newspapers across North Dakota, UND faculty launched a publicity campaign to combat the influence of the university's rival by planting feature articles on the school and its efforts. Not content to just utilize the press, faculty leveraged UND students to participate by sending the first student annual, the *Dacotah*, to every high school in North Dakota in order to illustrate the virtues of attending the newly established university. This continued a pattern throughout the first twenty-five years of the university where university administrators, faculty, and alumni were deeply invested in constructing a student identity that could be used to generate publicity for the university and to simultaneously provide students with opportunities for self-advancement. Whether through football, the student newspaper, or cultural clubs like the literary society, students were encouraged to become active participants in securing the educational and athletic success of UND.

Early editions of the student yearbook included Indian-themed imagery that would have been familiar to settlers of the Dakota territories.[37] The 1912 *Dacotah* presented an elaborate history of the University of North Dakota that included Indian-themed elements. Filling almost the entire top half of the page was a black-and-white ink drawing of an Indian standing on a precipice next to a lake pointing off into the distance. Bracketed by a buffalo skull and his horse, the Indian featured two long tails of hair on either side of his face, three feathers atop his head, and a blanket wrapped around his mid chest and lower body. Below the composition, along the left side of the page, was a modified Indian headdress with a tomahawk; along the bottom, an Indian spear point; to the right, a pipe and arrow. Collectively, these elements were similar to those early images included as part of Leutwiler's Indian performance and university-themed identity more generally: the pipe a signal of friendship, the Indian posed on the precipice pointing into the distance a sign of guidance. While elements like the tomahawk and arrows signal the potential for violence, that violence was ultimately a thing of the past: the Indian standing alone with the buffalo skull at his feet with his horse at his back, pointing toward the future, yet riding into the past. By 1921, the Indian of the past had become highly masculinized. Chiseled pectoral muscles framed two braids leading upward into a thick neck, broad shoulders, and sharp facial features. Capping the Indian's head was a full Sioux headdress, the first use of this item in UND imagery. A trim waist leads the viewer's eye downward to the sharply edged lines of a breechcloth and the word "Dacotah." Interestingly, Art Deco–styled rendering features the Indian in color: an orange-red. Clearly an allusion to "redskin," which has been discussed previously in my exploration of Miami University, the use of color to highlight the hypermasculine body is quite telling. The UND Indian, by 1921, presented a masculine ideal of the physical body that students could strive toward: strong, sharp, stoic, and extremely physically fit.

University of North Dakota students continually reaffirmed that Indians were part of their state's past. The 1926 edition of the *Dacotah* notes that Indians were no longer of concern to North Dakotans:

FOREWARD [SIC]

Fighting Nodaks; lofty hours spent in halls of learning; evenings on the coulee; gayeties and complexities of campus life; men who have come, gone, and made good, make up the pages of this book.

We have gone for tradition and counsel to the Dacotah Indians whose trail, marked by the embers of smouldering campfires, is blazed across the pages of our history. We have attempted to depict, as applicable to college life, the many-sided colorful existence of the Indian. The calm of meditation, exhilaration of play, work, love and laughter—this was his life and is ours.

In honoring the Indian, we have tried to give you a Dacotah full of things remembrances are made of; a book that will live with you, and hold you fast to your Alma Mater- to the school "in the land of the Dacotahs."[38]

Love and play were the themes of the university-produced history of the Dakota Indians. There was no violence, conquest, starvation, or warfare that Dakota Indians of the period were experiencing. The Dakota Santees had exchanged most of the tribal lands in Minnesota for two reservations in North Dakota as part of the Treaty of Fort Laramie in 1851. The Upper Reservation (Upper Agency) followed the Yellow Medicine River south from the border of South Dakota and was occupied by the Wahpeton and Sisseton bands; the Lower Reservation (Lower Agency) reached through the Minnesota River valley and was settled by the Mdewakanton and Wahpekute bands. These reservations were located just a few hundred miles from the University of North Dakota and contributed to eastern perceptions that the state was a lawless frontier.

A HISTORY OF CONQUEST

The Santee Dakota Rebellion (Great Sioux Uprising) began August 17, 1862, when four Wahpeton warriors attacked and killed five settlers as part of an escalating series of dares that began with stealing the family's eggs.[39] Seeking refuge among their families, the following morning a war party of Lower Agency Santees, led by Little Crow, attacked and killed the traders, their clerks, government employees, and their families. Mobilized by survivors of the attack, twenty-four soldiers from Fort Ridgley were killed during an ambush at the ferry crossing on their way to put down the rebellion. In the following days, the trading post at the Upper Agency, New Ulm, and Fort Ridgley all faced bands of marauding Santee warriors. By mid-September, the violence had spread to include Forest City, Hutchinson, and Fort Abercrombie on the Dakota border. Colonel Henry Sibley finally put down the rebellion on September 23, 1862, resulting in the arrest of 2,000 Santees, 303 of whom were sentenced to death. On December 26, 1862, 39 of the convicted Santees were hung in the largest mass execution held in public in U.S. history.[40] The surviving members of the Upper and Lower Agencies were dispatched to new reservations in Nebraska or dispersed.

In June 1874, General George Armstrong Custer led a party of over 100 troops, geologists, and mining experts onto Lakota lands. Ostensibly a scientific expedition, Custer wanted to establish a post in the Black Hills (Paha Sapa) to serve as both a military post to control errant Lakotas as well as a central departure point for explorations for gold. The 1868 Treaty of Fort Laramie had recognized agency lands between the Missouri River and the Black Hills as well as unceded lands to the west of the Hills from the Yellowstone Valley to the Platte River and into northwestern Nebraska as the territory of the Lakotas. Custer's expedition opened the floodgates of gold miners who sought their fortune on Lakota lands. By December 1875, the relationship between federal officials and the Lakotas had deteriorated in the face of Lakota refusal to sell the Black Hills and federal refusal to enforce the boundaries of Lakota lands against illegal settlers. After the Lakotas were ordered to report at the federal agency by January 31, 1876, in violation of the 1868 treaty, the army launched an initial campaign to force the Lakotas, Cheyennes, and Arapahos into compliance from June 1876 to May 6, 1877. The death of Custer and his 215 men on June 25, 1876, in the Battle of Little Big Horn at the hands of Crazy Horse, an Oglala Sioux, and hundreds of Lakota and Cheyenne warriors enthralled and frightened the American public.[41] The July 6 edition of the *Bismarck Tribune Extra* headlined the "first account of the Custer massacre" with subheads including "squaws mutilate and rob the dead" and "victims captured alive tortured in most fiendish manner."[42] So great was the impact of the Custer's defeat and the Great Sioux Uprising that the first "great spectacle" staged by Buffalo Bill Cody's Wild West show ten years later was a reenactment of Custer's Last Stand.

In the aftermath of Custer's defeat and the eventual surrender of Crazy Horse, Congress moved to secure the Black Hills lands that the U.S. government had attempted to purchase multiple times. Forcing the cession of all lands west of the 103rd meridian as well as the dissolution of the Great Sioux Reserve, which had been created by the 1868 Fort Laramie Treaty, by 1889 the Sioux were faced with strident American calls for expansion. As North Dakota was being admitted for statehood, the U.S. government was able to garner signatures from select tribal leaders for the sale of nine million acres of land in exchange for $3 million.

In the early years of UND's existence, which saw the establishment of reservations and the beginning of the allotment era, there was a fragile coexistence between settlers and Indians. Sickness, death, starvation, and violence committed by white settlers threatened Indians' lives.[43] Faced with starvation during the winter of 1890, residents of the Pine Ridge, Rosebud, Cheyenne River, and Standing Rock agencies joined the Indian prophet Wovoka's Ghost Dance movement in hopes of alleviating the suffering they were experiencing. For reservation agents, including Standing Rock agent James McLaughlin, the gathering numbers of Indians participating in the Ghost Dance was eerily reminiscent of the gatherings that had preceded both the Santee Rebellion and the Great Sioux Uprising. With Sioux warrior Sitting Bull, a hero of Custer's defeat and vocal critic of reservation "chiefs" who supported allotment and compromise with U.S. officials, living at Standing Rock, McLaughlin used the opportunity to arrest Sitting Bull.[44] Agency police, along with a detachment of army troops, sought out Sitting Bull on December 15, 1890. Refusing to capitulate to the agency police, Sitting Bull was shot and killed. The death of the revered warrior sparked fear in Sioux leaders, who were afraid that they would be targeted by

agency police. Minneconjou leader Big Foot fled the Cheyenne River to seek
refuge in the Pine Ridge badlands with other Ghost Dancers. Captured by the
Seventh Calvary and led to Wounded Knee Creek, Big Foot and 350 other men,
women, and children were separated into two encampments, surrounded by 500
troops, and repeatedly searched for weapons. When warriors protested the sei-
zure of their rifles, the encounter quickly deteriorated following the firing of a
rifle. With Sioux warriors firing at the cavalry and the cavalry shooting Sioux, the
council fire area and the camp were instantly transformed into chaos. Targeting
both warriors and Sioux women and children, over 150 members of Big Foot's
band were killed, with an additional 50 wounded.[45] The Seventh Calvary sus-
tained losses of twenty-five dead and thirty-nine wounded.[46] "After Wounded
Knee, stories circulated that the battlefield was filled with cries of 'Remember
Custer.'"[47]

Laden with violence, these few events of the Dakota Territory and the states
formed out of it illustrate the ongoing conflict between the Sioux, the U.S. government, and white settlers. For many Dakotans, the Sioux were an imminent
threat, and confining them to reservations was not enough. The nearest reservation to Grand Forks was Standing Rock, over 300 miles away, yet concern over
Sioux behavior littered local and national papers. Newspaperman L. Frank Baum
(later author of *The Wizard of Oz*) responded to the death of Sitting Bull:

Sitting Bull, most renowned Sioux of modern history, is dead. . . . The proud spirit
of the original owners of these vast prairies inherited through centuries of fierce
and bloody wars for their possession, lingered last in the bosom of Sitting Bull.
With his fall the nobility of the Redskin is extinguished, and what few are left are
a pack of whining curs who lick the hand that smites them. The Whites, by law of
conquest, by justice of civilization, are masters of the American continent, and
the best safety of the frontier settlements will be secured by the total annihilation
of the few remaining Indians. Why not annihilation? Their glory has fled, their
spirit broken, their manhood effaced; better that they die than live the miserable
wretches that they are. History would forget these latter despicable beings, and
speak, in later ages of the glory of these grand Kings of the forest and plain that
Cooper loved to heroism [*sic*]. We cannot honestly regret their extermination,
but we at least do justice to the manly characteristics possessed, according to
their lights and education, by the early Redskins of America.[48]

Interestingly, Baum simultaneously ascribes to Sitting Bull a "proud spirit" that
embodied a "nobility of the Redskin" and describes the rest of the Sioux peoples
as "whining curs." This differentiation between "early Redskins" who put up a
valiant and manly effort but ultimately capitulated to the rightful expansion of
white civilization and those who were fighting for their survival in 1890 is quite
striking. The Indians of the past that universities were venerating were noble and

proud; Indians of the present were deceitful and problematic. On January 3, 1891, in his editorial on Wounded Knee, Baum underscored his belief that the only good Indian was a dead Indian: "Having wronged them for centuries we had better, in order to protect our civilization, follow it up by one more wrong and wipe these untamed and untamable creatures from the face of the earth. In this lies future safety for our settlers and the soldiers who are under incompetent commands. Otherwise we may expect future years to be as full of trouble with the redskins as those have been in the past."[49] Baum's editorial recognized the problems between Indians and the U.S. government but discarded them in favor of ensuring the safety of white settlers. Less than a generation later, UND students and administrators would be appropriating Indian identity to demonstrate how far the state had come in securing its future.

The imagery that accompanied the 1925 student yearbook visually depicted the distance that had been achieved between Natives and whites in just a few decades. A full-page depiction of an Indian in a breechcloth astride his horse with his head thrown back and silhouetted by the sun faces two other Indians perched upon a rocky outcropping. Carrying a quiver of arrows, they appear poised to disappear into the horizon. Significantly, though, the Sioux demonstrate the investment students made in Indian identity: one Indian holds aloft the University of North Dakota seal; another, with his hair in braids and wearing brief shorts and moccasins, is seen running across a landscape dotted with teepees, while the final Indian in full Sioux headdress and garbed in buckskin pants and moccasins, with a knife clutched in one hand and a tomahawk in the other, dances before the setting sun. In portraying themselves as having gone for "tradition and counsel" to the Dakota Indians and then presenting a Dakota Indian as guarding the seal of the university, student editors and the artist were communicating a version of university history where the Dakota Indians ceded their lands to inhabitants of the Dakotas and provided their support for the university. This was a visual representation of the rhetoric being used by white settlers and the federal government to justify their expansion into Indian lands. Given the presence of Indian imagery in the 1926 *Dacotah*, it is hardly surprising that UND students turned to an Indian-themed mascot in 1930: "But the name 'Sioux' is about ideal. It would lend itself to many colorful variations, is historically correct, and most important of all, immediately brings to mind the pioneer conqueror of the bison, bears, and the elements. . . . The change would be a drastic one, but the Student does not hesitate to endorse it and to recommend it to athletic and stadium officials."[50] The adoption of "Sioux" as the athletic name was, like the *Dacotah*, driven by the need for a clear message with a framework of competition. "A. Student" wrote:

With the emergence of the University from comparative athletic obscurity into some measure of fame, it seems to me that this year presents a great opportunity to change a name which served its purpose only during the years when nobody but the alumni and the students of the University knew that we had football teams here. With the agitation which has progressed for the past few years toward a change in colors, there has also been agitation for the changing of the name and symbol of the school. Nodak means nothing but what your imagination may derive from it, and Flickertail foists upon us the antics of an obscure and timid little animal. For years we have been pursued by a massive Bison, in all Aggie publicity, and now that the Flicker has grown up and will play the Army, it wouldn't be a bad idea to turn the tables and stage a buffalo hunt in the good old Indian manner. By the way, how's that for a name, the "Sioux"? Something Indian, or most anything that can come out on top in bisonic struggle, as we have been doing for the past forty years. Think of all the symbolism that one could gain from an Indian name and figure. Let's have a little action.

In capturing the struggle between the Bison of the Agricultural College and the "Flickertails" or "Nodaks" (the original athletic moniker of UND), the writer echoes the narrative within the first student yearbook.[51] Yet in mentioning Army, the writer underscores an important expansion being undertaken at UND. Prior to 1930, the UND football team was mainly a regional team that rarely traveled outside of North Dakota or played teams outside of its region. Minnesota was its traditional opponent. In 1930, though, the University of North Dakota began to open its athletic schedule to high-profile teams, including Army, in an effort to attract large audiences and increase revenue. Alumni Secretary Frank Webb was quoted one week after the first series of editorials as saying, "the name of 'Flickertails' hampers publicity, especially in a young school trying to establish itself with larger institutions of the country."[52] Telling student reporters that popular university dean V. P. Squires, while dying on his sickbed, had said that "the institution to which he had devoted his life should no longer be represented by a tiny animal on which a pest bounty had been placed," Webb illustrated his willingness to leverage local community figures for his own purposes.[53] Bandmaster John Howard offered his support by arguing that the success of the football team placed UND on par with larger institutions within the country and that competitiveness necessitated a name worthy of a massive publicity campaign. Even geology instructor Ewalt C. Pietsch, who preferred animal mascots, recognized the potential of "Sioux," calling it "something big and powerful."[54]

DISTANCING THEMSELVES FROM CONQUEST

Fred Traynor, president of the UND Alumni Association, wrote to Frank Webb, "it seems to me there is already too much of a notion abroad, especially in the East, that we are still Indian territory, and that there isn't much else in this state except Indian wigwams and we all go around with paint on our faces and feathers in our hair."[55] Traynor's concern over eastern perceptions of North Dakota speaks to the powerful legacy of the violence of the nineteenth century. Only a little over thirty years had passed from Custer's defeat, and, for many Americans, the image of Indian violence remained fresh. Traynor echoed concerns of second-generation immigrants who had flooded North Dakota at the turn of the century and were invested in being perceived as white. They were disquieted by the perception of North Dakota as an uncivilized or backward place and that North Dakotans were backward people. Railroads, public schools, and progressive zeal to civilize the land and its Native people were the images North Dakota wanted to promote to easterners who possibly looked to move west, not a North Dakota as a lawless place where citizens could, in any possible way, become Indian. Traynor's concerns, while significant, were not present in the minds of UND students: "There is another reason for changing the name of the school to 'Sioux.' Most of the students who aren't freshmen know what the Haskell Indians did to us last year, and with the Davis-Elkins team including some Indians, about the only way of combating them is to turn Indian and cook up a little 'bad medicine' for them. Imagine the embarrassment of a buck all turned up to wham a flickertail, and then finding himself suddenly opposed to an all-wool, yard-wide Indian."[56] In pointing to Indian opponents as yet another rationale for changing "Flickertail" to "Sioux," students were recognizing the history of athletic dominance of athletic teams from Indian boarding schools. In arguing for the adoption of the "Fighting Sioux" in 1930 and pointing toward previous defeat at the hands of the Haskell Indians, one student revealed the belief that "turning Indian" and giving "bad medicine" was the only way to secure athletic success. The trope of "turning Indian" echoed the anxieties of easterners who feared that the newly opened Dakota Territory could be tantamount to a flood of citizens who were not worthy of being members of the nation. It also recognized the physical superiority of the Haskell team but alleviated the possible upset of racial hierarchies by arguing that "bad medicine," an evil mystical force, was needed to defeat the Haskell team. If the university football team could not defeat Indian opponents fairly, then they too would have to adopt Indian ways to ultimately defeat their opponents.

In waging a campaign to move away from "Flickertail" and toward "Sioux," students, faculty, and administrators were turning toward an identity that had already proven commercially viable by the their university. The *Dacotah* had helped the university gain stability by generating interest in the young school. Carlisle and Haskell had proven the interest in Indian athletics. America's cultural fascination with Indians was written across the pages of newspapers. By choosing "Sioux," UND was able to converge these interests, providing community via an easily understood and possibly highly profitable symbol without having to build an extravagant football stadium. This was the critically needed convergence of "modern" America being sought by institutions of higher education: athletics, fandom, commercialism, and young, white, male bodies in service to the community. In turning to these meanings, UND administrators and the broader community were signaling their assent to the racial and class-based hierarchies being promoted as essential in "modern" America, but they also recognized their financial limitations. They could not build a 20,000-seat stadium for a populace less than half that size in the entire state. Embracing these identities signaled the University of North Dakota's interest in urbanizing and combating the stereotype of North Dakota as a rural, unsafe place.

In the next chapter, I turn to Stanford University and Florida State University to illustrate how university identity, Indian-themed mascotry, and football spectacle were bound up in anxiety over male students' perception that they were being controlled by administrators, women, and other undesirable influences.

5 · STUDENT INVESTMENT IN UNIVERSITY IDENTITIES

By 1930, college football had expanded to hundreds of colleges and universities throughout the United States. Football had shifted from a game of elites to a spectacle that appealed to working-class immigrants, who saw the game as an opportunity to alleviate their less-privileged status. The University of Illinois, along with rivals the University of Wisconsin, the University of Michigan, and the University of Chicago, had fully embraced the game as an opportunity to blend commercial revenue with the indoctrination of young men. "I've never found that race or nationality mattered on the grid-iron," Carnegie Tech coach Walter Steffen wrote in that year. He continued, "Football has ceased to be a game of the classes, and has become a game of the people. A few years ago a prominent coach—I think it was Bob Zuppke of Illinois—remarked that it was the poor boys who were playing college football, while the sons of well-to-do parents were sitting in the stands comfortable in coon-skin coach."[1] Despite what Steffen argued, though, race and nationality had been written all over the game since its inception. From the Carlisle and Haskell Indians, who paraded across the pages of mainstream newspapers, to university-created identities like "Illini," "Redskins," and "Indians," public fascination with Native bodies, as well as tropes of colonial violence, was central to the creation of modern football. Previous chapters have explored the debate over college football, the rise of halftime spectacle and the ways in which it relied on popular conceptions of Indians, and how semirural schools were unable to adopt the halftime spectacle because of a lack of financial and community support. Two schools in far-flung locales, Stanford University and Florida State University (FSU), demonstrate how that competitive ethos and anxiety about higher education's role in educating the public would manifest through explicit statements by students about how they imagined their university identities. Together, they illustrate the lengths students would go to in order to ensure that their universities represented their sense of who they were in the modern world.

THE RACIALIZATION OF RIVALRIES

Over 2,000 miles away from the dominant football schools of the East Coast and Midwest, Stanford University was attempting to compete against the football spectacles that Illinois and its well-known competitors had begun producing. Stanford had begun building its own concrete stadium in 1921 in an effort to compete against the more popular University of California, Berkeley (UC) and its recently completed California Memorial Stadium.[2] What made Stanford's $210,000 investment so remarkable was that the university had not played football between 1905, when it replaced the game with rugby, and the 1919 fall season. While a portion of that pause can be attributed to the Great War (when most universities concentrated on military training rather than athletics), Stanford also suspended its participation in the game due to debates over violence and the effect of the game on student behavior. Seating 65,000, the new stadium united a capital campaign with efforts to draw students to the semirural area. Stanford University administrators relied on alumni to support their efforts to recruit the next generation of young white men.[3] The irony of Stanford's attempt was that it was a private institution attempting to compete with UC, a public institution that had seen a massive infusion of wartime federal funding. In 1922, UC was the largest university in the nation, with 11,505 students; by 1927 that figure totaled over 16,000.[4] In part, the disparity between the two schools could be laid at the feet of their location. UC was an urban school that pulled students from the highly populated San Francisco area. Stanford University was semirural, located on converted farmlands outside Palo Alto. The motivation to keep up with UC and even elite northeastern universities would motivate attempts by Stanford University alumni and administrators to craft football spectacle in 1930.

The Board of Athletic Control noted on November 15, 1930, that "the General Manager reported that the Associated Students had adopted the Indian as the official Stanford symbol."[5] A 1931 *Stanford Illustrated Review* article, "Stanford Goes Indian," explained:

> There were unlimited possibilities for its development. For look you, all the other Western universities has [*sic*] their official symbols the names of various animals, such as Cougars, Bears, and the like (never mind the Trojans). The Indian was their original lord and conqueror. His superiority was unquestioned. Then, too, the colorful qualities of the Indian's costumes and customs would go well in rallies. Our Stanford Red might rightly be identified with the Indian red. And the war-dances that could be held around the bonfire! Truly, it was an inspiration.[6]

The article suggested that Indians, as "original lord and conqueror" of animals, were savage, superior, natural beings that Stanford students (previously identified by the color "Red") should emulate.[7] In positioning the Indian as "lord and conqueror" of the natural world, Stanford students articulated their own sense of worth. They could beat their opponents on the sports field and relish a sense of physical and social superiority. Given the rivalry among the four California schools that came to constitute the Pacific Conference and the particularly vociferous rivalry between UC and Stanford for the treasured "Golden Axe," the utilization of the Indian is hardly surprising. The fans' allegiance to the Indian symbol grew out of both the repetitive use of Indian warfare metaphors when discussing Stanford football by local sports writers and an earlier 1923 effort by Dr. Thomas M. Williams, an 1897 alumnus and founding member of the Board of Athletic Control, to utilize the Indian symbol.

Thomas Williams was born July 16, 1871, in Duo, West Virginia. Initially home-schooled on his parents' rural farm, Williams was a student at Greenbrier Male Academy (Lewisburg, West Virginia) and later the University of West Virginia.[8] Upon his arrival at Stanford, Williams met resistance from his classmates, who viewed his rural eastern upbringing and lack of previous involvement in football as problematic.[9] The reaction of his contemporaries, drawn from the Stanford chapter of the fraternity Williams had been a brother of in West Virginia, under-scored the role football played both at the university itself and within the male fraternal community. Those uninterested in football were not fully accepted. In joining the football team in 1896 and 1897 as a center, Williams was attempting to climb the social hierarchy. White male athletic bodies were to be celebrated and emulated. In the intervening years between his 1897 graduation and return to Palo Alto in 1904, Williams attended Columbia University, where he lettered in football as a graduate student, during his pursuit of his medical degree.[10] Williams was an active alumnus upon his return to Stanford, including serving as an honorary pallbearer at the funeral of Jane Stanford, as president of the Alumni

FIGURE 8. Indian-head symbol used by Stanford University football, 1930. Courtesy MissionInn.Jim.

Association in 1909–1910, and as first chair of the Board of Athletic Control beginning in 1917. During his tenure as chair, Williams worked with the university to modernize Stanford athletics. Stanford constructed a 3,000-seat basketball pavilion, a football stadium, a baseball stadium, a gymnasium, and new tennis courts.[11] Mirroring construction campaigns across America, including those at the University of Illinois, Williams's effort to create a commercial athletic program was highly successful. The Athletic Department leveraged more than $2 million to construct permanent university spaces.[12]

The university designed these newly built spaces to provide young men with large public platforms to demonstrate their athletic success and garner social rewards. As head of the athletic board at Stanford, Williams was tasked with matching the rising spectacles being generated out east. He needed to solidify the local community's interest in Stanford football in order to fill the newly constructed stadium. Football rivalries would be used to generate interest. Founded in 1915 in Portland, Oregon, the Pacific Conference consisted of four charter members: UC, the University of Washington, the University of Oregon, and Oregon State. Washington State and Stanford University joined in 1918, followed by the University of Southern California (1922), Idaho (1922), Montana (1924), and the University of California, Los Angeles (1928). With opponents from across the United States, the Pacific Conference was actively engaged in building a fan base while simultaneously challenging eastern notions of sporting dominance. Part of building the public audience was providing them with a comfortable, safe, modern experience when watching a football game. That experience, importantly, began outside the stadium with the construction of new transportation networks, parking, and even public artwork.

Williams commissioned Alexander Phimister Proctor, the sculptor who had dazzled many at Chicago's 1893 Columbian Exposition, to design a concrete Indian statue to be utilized as the university athletic symbol and placed at the open end of the university's stadium in 1923.[13] A contemporary of Frederic Remington and friend to Theodore Roosevelt, Woodrow Wilson, and other important national figures who encouraged the expansion of America geographically and culturally, the majority of Proctor's work was sculpted to reflect his lifelong interest in nature and Indian life.[14] "Few things in the entire exposition [of 1893]," wrote Lorado Taft, "were more interesting or impressive than those great motionless creatures, the native American animals as sculpted by Proctor."[15] So powerful were Proctor's contributions that Frank D. Millet, head of the decorations division of the grounds committee of the exposition, asked Proctor to complete two future statues, the cowboy and the Indian. Using a cowboy and two Indians from Cody's Wild West show camped just outside the gates as models, Proctor completed *Equestrian Indian and Cowboy* just in time for the fair's opening on May 1, 1893.[16] Proctor's Indian, drawn from an illustration in the Wild West show program, visually depicted the dominant theme projected by Cody's show: that of the vanishing Indian gazing off into the distance.[17] Surrounded by other artists of the fair, including Augustus Saint-Gaudens, Olin Warner, and J. Alden Weir, the thirty-two-year-old Proctor established himself as one of the most popular artists in America. The painter J. Harrison Mills, who served as Proctor's mentor, described his success in 1916: "A sculptor, now of national fame as among the foremost of his guild, graduated from the chrysalis bed of the mining regions, where the cocoon of romance was spun about the vanishing life of the last frontier and came to the full metamorphosis of the acclaimed Academician in a time so brief that comprehension is staggered. No more phenomenal success, based on real achievement, is to be found in the annals of American Art since the days of Benjamin West; perhaps I should say—none to compare with it."[18]

Following the success of his works at the exposition, Proctor became the first recipient of the Peabody Institute of Baltimore's Rinehart Scholarship and, with the support of his mentor and collaborator Saint-Gaudens, constructed his second Indian-themed statue.[19] *Indian Warrior* depicted a Blackfoot whom Proctor had met when hunting on the Blackfoot reservation in early 1896. Proctor had long engaged with Indians who were settled onto reservations. He traveled with George Pratt to gather specimens for the Smithsonian Institution, lived among the Nez Percé, and was adopted by the Cheyenne chief Little Wolf all prior to his move to Palo Alto, California.[20]

Williams provided Proctor a template to begin his statue: an Indian head symbol that Williams's wife had sewed onto the blankets given to each player annually.[21] The Stanford student body withheld their support of the proposed statue and associated Indian name. Their critiques echoed those of reformers in the period, yet with a student-driven focus. The athletic board was too commercially oriented and had diverted funds from athletic contests for other purposes—most notably, building the Stanford stadium and a dorm for football players.[22] Ill-timed, Williams's efforts were perceived as yet another way football was privileged at Stanford University. Although students were working to improve "the spirit of university life in this country" by leading rallies and school stunts, this episode between Williams, Proctor, and the student body demonstrates how a Stanford alumnus and the football coach failed to get students to agree to adopt "Indians" as the identity for the entire student body.[23] The power of the student body to determine its own name and symbolic representation contrary to the desires of an important university figure suggests the importance of students, who were needed to comply with the desire of those constructing football spectacle.[24] In formally turning away from the Indian mascot in 1923, students were expressing their lack of interest in football spectacle. Proctor received commissions for some of his most notable sculptures, namely *Pioneer, Broncho Buster, On the War Trail, Mohawk Indian, The Rough Rider,* and *Circuit Rider,* just prior to and during his tenure in Palo Alto. Between the lack of student support

FIGURE 9. Alexander Proctor, *Indian Warrior*, 1895–1897. Bronze, cast 1900–1902. Amon Carter Museum of American Art, Fort Worth, Texas. Purchased with funds provided by the Council of the Amon Carter Museum of American Art. 2002.5.

and his own workload, he failed to even attempt to turn the symbol into three-dimensional reality.[25] Despite receiving the commission, one of the foremost American sculptors left Palo Alto without ever having sketched a potential statue to be placed in the newly erected stadium.

Only 6,000 spectators had attended the December 20, 1922, football game.[26] It would take the recruitment of the legendary Glenn "Pop" Warner as well as the efforts of alumni to bring in more competitive players to change student feelings about football and its spectacles. Warner was the former coach of the Carlisle Indian School, a residential school that had become famous in the early twentieth century for its athletic prowess. Opponents from the Ivy League, Big Ten, and the Western Conference offered between $10,000 and $15,000 for the opportunity to play all-Indian teams from Carlisle as well as Haskell Institute. Coached by Warner, the Carlisle Indian squad in 1907 included future all-American Jim Thorpe, who regularly sat on the bench during games.[27] So great was the interest in watching Warner's team that the University of Pennsylvania game on October 26, 1907, boasted an audience of over 20,000 fans. Harvard's defeat on November 9, 1907, in front of 30,000 spectators was recorded by eastern newspapers as a "scalping" of the Harvard team at the hands of the Indian, similar to that recorded in the Miami University student newspaper. Examined from an economic standpoint, the success of the Carlisle team and its coach is undoubted: in 1907 alone, the Carlisle football team generated total earnings of over $50,000. Just like university departments of athletics, Warner maintained control of those funds directly via the Carlisle Industrial Indian School Athletic Association. It is hardly surprising, then, that Stanford University would recruit the aging Warner to revive its football team.

Warner's arrival marked a change in the way that Stanford students felt about football, Indian-themed spectacle, and the economics of building a well-known university. His experience with creating public interest in an easily recognized athletic identity refreshed alumni interest in creating a unified Stanford University identity in the 1929–1930 season. That public representation was badly needed as the Great Depression, which began in late 1929, affected student enrollments in 1930. Fewer families could afford to send their children to college. Competition between institutions only grew throughout the 1930 and 1931 seasons. In failing to legitimize Williams's vision of athletic belonging, Stanford students had initially controlled their own sense of community identity and belonging. Yet by 1930 the force of football spectacle and competition for football athletes would shift the tide from concerns about the place of football at Stanford to questions of how Stanford was going to survive the Depression without a more marketable identity.

While ultimately assenting to the formal adoption of the Indian in 1930, it is the brief moment of contestation between 1923 and 1930 that proves remarkable within this book. Students were not eagerly accepting of administrators' attempts to redefine their university identity. Instead, they demanded their own authority in determining what their university identity would be. Students could enable the efforts of university administrators and football coaches to create athletic identities as Illinois and Miami students had done. Yet they could also elect to contest the adoption of football spectacles as Stanford University students did. Despite their investments in football spectacle with the building of their stadium, at Stanford University, the hesitancy of the student body (outside of the football team) prohibited the creation of a university-wide identity. Football athletes at other schools, though, would take a direct role in ensuring that their university identity was representative of their worldview.

COMPETING TO BE A SEMINOLE

"The gridiron team you'll see rushing out on Centennial field daubed with war paint and clad in garnet and gold uniforms," declared the *Tallahassee Daily Democrat*, "when Florida State University has its next home football game, November 22, will be called the Seminoles." The writer continued: "In commemoration of the tribe of Indians whose descendants still live in the Florida Everglades, the name was chosen by the FSU student body in final elections Thursday and Friday. Only about 30 percent of the students voted on the six names selected to be run off in the election, and 381 of these cast the deciding vote for Seminoles. Statesmen was runner-up with 271 votes. Other names in the contest were Rebels, 107 votes; Tarpons, 107 votes; Fighting Warriors, 68 votes; and Crackers, 54 votes."[28] Published November 9, 1947, the local Tallahassee paper revealed the lack of interest most FSU students had in determining an athletic identity. Florida State University built its American spectacle as an articulation of sporting identity that was concerned not just with use of the past to build a young, white, male athletic citizenry as the other schools had but also with celebrating southern identity. Students at Florida State considered a variety of names before voting. Many of these selections were similar in construct. "Senators" was considered alongside "Statesmen," with "Indians" being considered along with "Seminoles" and "Fighting Warriors." The more salacious "Gold Diggers," "Tallywhackers," and "Pinheads" competed with "Golden Falcons," "Sandpipers," and "Fleas," before being cast aside in favor of "Tarpons."[29] Identities familiar to students balloted the strongest: "Seminoles" (used at the University of Florida) and its generic representation "Fighting Warriors," "Rebels" (from the University of Mississippi), "Crackers" (from both the Atlanta Crackers baseball team and the "cracker" culture), and "Tarpons" (from its antecedent Florida Female College–Florida State College for Women). From the explicitly racial "Seminole" and "Cracker" to the confederate "Rebel," Florida State students were actively engaged in imaging their football spectacle as one beholden to nineteenth-century expressions of southern agency: white, male, self-sufficient, athletic citizens. It was an identity tied to politics of race and representation that were particularly southern and affirmed the legacy of the nineteenth-century conquest of red and black bodies. Significantly, though, students at Florida State University drew from predecessor institutions and a myriad of other commercial identities in attempting to craft their athletic spectacle. The Florida State University students poached ideas from the University of Florida, the Florida State College for Women, and even the Atlanta Crackers baseball team.

Jim Crabtree, a student from Pensacola, remembered "Tarpons" as the chief challenger, and suggests it took a whole lot of vigorous campaigning to keep that name from winning: "The women's swim team was named 'Tarpons.' That name was submitted, and it just about overwhelmed some of us. Only other thing that seemed strong in the running was the name 'Seminoles.' A bunch of us got together and decided it would be a whole lot better to have an Indian name than a fish. We got a group of girls to go around knocking on doors. And that thing was turned around, just enough for 'Seminoles' to make it. To me the name could not have worked out better."[30] Other students remembered the choice as a little controversial at the time. "I think the name caught on primarily because of the things that go with it," one student said. "There were so many things— fancy dress, the war dances." In signaling the costuming and dance aspects associated with the "Seminoles" identity, this student was recognizing the need for a performance that could be used to create drama and entertain the community. Given the fetishization of Indians in westerns and as part of the Boy Scout movement, it is hardly surprising that "Seminoles" was seen as being an appropriate identity for community performances. As Crabtree alluded to, choosing an identity for FSU that had been so closely tied to the women's college that had merged with the predecessor to FSU would impugn its male students' masculinity. Florida State University men could not allow their athletic identity to be a herringlike fish that was synonymous with women's athletics. The lengths these men would go to in order to shape the balloting illustrate their intense need to have an explicitly masculine identity selected. Bill Bentz, a member of the first Florida State University football team, recounted at a 1986 reunion: "I watched every damn ballot that went through, and a whole lot of 'em that didn't have 'Seminole' on them, I threw away. I was a bigmouth in those days—still am. At the time, doctoring those ballots seemed the thing to do. When you played football there, you were actually bigger than you were, you know, and you could get by with a lot."[31] Did voting irregularities exist in the selection of "Seminole"? Bentz's claim remains unverified. However, given Crabtree's account of efforts to rally voters against "Tarpons," it is quite possible that male students intentionally attempted to skew the selection to avoid the perception that Florida State University was going to continue to be dominated by women and their athletic identity. The *Florida Flambeau* illustrated the community's decision to embrace the election results: "The selection certainly gives FSU a distinct title. There are no college teams that bear the name. . . . New nicknames . . . are apt to appear ill-fitting, but they take on polish with constant usage—and are mellowed, aged and honored with time. The name Seminoles will be just as good a name as Florida State University makes it in the years to come. . . . Okay, Seminoles, take over from here!"[32] The Seminole name was drawn from a variety of sources. In 1910, students at the University of Florida issued the first edition of their student yearbook, *The Seminole*, which recognized the local Native peoples of the Seminole tribe.[33] In the opening pages of the yearbook, students acknowledged Seminoles as contemporary peoples: "Among the hammocks and prairies of the Florida Everglades, in a land unknown to the white man, lives a remnant of the once large and powerful tribe of the Seminole Indians. Driven Southward, fighting desperately and contesting every foot of ground, they found at last in the mysterious fastnesses of the 'Glades at once a fortress and a home. Here they have remained unconquered, the only people living on American soil who do not claim allegiance to the Stars and Stripes."[34] In positioning the Seminoles as "the only people living on American soil who do not claim allegiance to the Stars and Stripes," university student Ralph D. Rader ignored the continuing history of Indian resistance to American rule.[35] By turning to an anthropological description of the Seminoles (their hunting and gardening practices, clothing and appearance, and religious rituals), Rader presented the Seminoles as an exotic remnant of the nineteenth century. He emphasized the unusual nature of the Seminoles by recounting the story of "Coacoochee," or "Wild Cat," during the Seminole War. Supposedly told to young Seminoles by their elders "so that the present generation is as suspicious of the white man as their ancestors were," Rader compared the attempts to catch Wild Cat and his men by American soldiers as possible as attempts to capture the "Spirit Torch" or "Will-o-Wisp," the "ghostly" light that hovers over swamps at night. Even as Rader recognized the role of white colonizers in the decline and defeat of the Seminoles—"the white man came to rob the Indian of his land, and turn his hunting grounds into farms and cities"—the parallel of the Seminoles as mysteriously powerful beings that could evade capture by soldiers evoked a familiar trope of Indians as supernatural beings marked by their ties to the land.[36] He celebrated the Everglades as "an Indian's paradise" with "oasis-like hammocks" and "profuse" flora where "birds of brilliant plumage abound and game is plentiful" and seemingly suggested that the Seminoles drew power from the wilderness of the Florida swamps. "His wants are few and the genial climate makes very little in the way of shelter and clothing necessary." In cautioning that the "the tribe is gradually dying out" and that efforts to cling to old traditions and customs as well as propositions to drain the Everglades will lead to their eventual demise, Rader emphasized the holistic, "natural" connection of Indian peoples to their lands. "Never a thought is given the Indian who [sic] domain it is by right of conquest and exploration. Cannot at least a part of it be set apart for him? Surely this much is due to the people who at one time owned all of Florida and Georgia—the only people who ever engaged in war with the Unites States and remained unconquered."[37]

The origins of the Seminoles lie in the colonial encounters of the Deep South. The decimation of the Florida tribes of Apalachees, Calusas, Timucuans, and

other smaller groups due to slave raiding, forced migration by Spanish colonizers, disease, and war had opened up Florida for Creek settlement by the late
seventeenth century.[38] Settlement occurred in three general phases: 1702–1740:
Creek raids against the Spanish and their Apalachee allies; 1740–1812: six initial
settlements in northern Florida that allowed roving parties of hunters to search
for deer, bear, and other big game; 1812–1820: widespread settlements due to fractures within Creek society.[39] Warfare and the need for deerskin created a genera-
tional split among the Creek peoples, Muskogee-speaking Indians who inhabited
Alabama and Georgia. Young warriors, resisting the "traditional" storytelling of
the older generation who used such historical recounting as a means of social
control, coupled with the weakening of ties between the generations due to
epidemic disease, facilitated the establishment of permanent Creek settlements
in the Alachua prairie of north-central Florida.[40] As early as 1680, these Creeks
were being characterized as "*cimarrones*" by Spanish colonizers. Alternately "free
people" or "runaways,"[41] the *cimarrones* whom the Spanish and English encountered were "not subject to the town governments" of the Creek peoples and were
considered allies to the English, who provided them with gifts.[42] Co-opted into
the word "Seminole," these settlements included Muskogee (Creek) speakers
as well as Mikasuki (Hitchiti) speakers. By 1763, the newly appointed governor
to Florida recognized that peace negotiated with the Lower Creeks would not
extend to the Seminole settlements at Santa Fe, La Chua, and Satile.[43] Over the
next forty years, as Florida moved from a Spanish colonial possession to a British
possession, then back to a Spanish possession, the Seminoles continued to exert
pressure on colonizers via raiding and resistance to land boundaries. Influenced
by the Yamasee War of 1715 and the Red Stick War of 1813–1814, as well as by
the growing population of English colonizers in Georgia and South Carolina,
roughly 3,000 Indians lived in Florida, independent of the Creek Confederacy,
by the early nineteenth century.[44] The Seminoles, recognized as separate from the
Upper and Lower Creeks, offered an alternative community to Indians fleeing the
encroaching Indian and Euro-American populations as well as escaped slaves.

Encounters between Americans and Seminoles were continually complicated
by the perception of southerners that Seminole lands were havens for escaped
slaves and ne'er-do-well Indians. Slave catchers and bounty hunters repeatedly
violated the territorial borders of Spanish Florida and the Seminole settlements.
The continuing encroachment of white Americans onto Seminole territory
forced some to move southward while leaders chose, in 1823, to sign the Treaty
of Moultrie Creek. Opening the Atlantic and Gulf Coasts to American settlement, the Treaty of Moultrie Creek assigned central Florida to the Seminoles.
In part, the treaty was driven by the belief of American governor William P.
DuVal that "the area between the Suwanee River and the Alachua, where most
of the Seminoles lived, was one of the richest and most valuable in the territory
and should belong to whites."[45] Almost twenty-four million acres of land were

provided to the United States (for resale to American settlers at \$1.25/acre) in exchange for moving expenses, a \$5,000-a-year annuity for a twenty-five-year-long period, food for a year, payments for improvements made to the north Florida lands, and provisions for farming, schooling, livestock, and government agents.[46] The Seminoles also agreed to move onto formal reservations either in the Apalachicola River valley or farther south between the Peace and Withlacoochee Rivers, just north of Ocala, Florida. By 1832, James Gadsden was appointed lead negotiator to convince the Seminoles to follow other Indians under President Andrew Jackson's Indian Removal Policy to territories out west. At Payne's Landing, leaders of the Seminole people agreed to move out west within three years provided a delegation of Seminoles could select and approve of the new reservation site in Oklahoma. Almost from its signing, the Payne's Landing agreement was fraught with problems. Seminole leaders thought their ability to approve of the reservation also gave them the right to refuse removal should the land out west not be to their liking. They also believed they had twenty years to complete the removal process rather than three. Further, during the selection visit to Oklahoma, the Seminole selection party was forced to sign the Treaty of Fort Gibson before they would be allowed to depart the territory. The treaty affirmed that the region selected for them by government agents was sufficient for the new reservation and that the Seminoles would move posthaste. Accusations of bribery of the interpreters in the initial agreement coupled with what, in effect, amounted to the Seminoles being taken hostage in Oklahoma led the Seminoles to refuse to honor the removal agreement. Antiremoval chiefs, led by the young warrior Osceola,[47] were imprisoned in June 1835 by General Wiley Thompson of the Georgia militia, who was charged with securing Seminole agreement to removal. Released only after agreeing to move to Oklahoma Territory by January 1836, Osceola and other Seminoles stockpiled arms, attacked supply trains and troop patrols, and even executed a pro-removal chief. For the next six years, the Seminoles fought American troops to avoid deportation to reservations. It was only in 1842, after significant military defeats, that the Seminoles were forced to choose between an Oklahoma reservation or an isolated reservation west of Lake Okeechobee. Of the roughly 1,300 Seminole and African American warriors, 600 chose to remain in Florida. The banishment of the Seminoles to the isolated reservation west of Lake Okeechobee that Ralph Rader would refer to over sixty years later as an "Indian paradise" was not without continued struggles with American troops. Fifteen years later, the Seminoles continued to clash violently with American troops as they resisted infringement on their rights by the U.S. government and Florida settlers.

In this moment of appropriation in 1910, the University of Florida mimicked a process that took place throughout the United States in the early twentieth century. Students at the University of Florida were, in the early decades of the twentieth century, positioning themselves as the inheritors of the land occupied by the

"Seminoles." Distancing themselves from a past fraught with violence between settlers and Native inhabitants, students at the University of Florida were positioning themselves as survivors of the educational turmoil being foisted upon them by the reorganization that had taken place in 1904. The Seminoles were, in Rader's depiction, survivors of colonial encounters who created their own communities of people who desired freedom from their communities, be they traditional Creek society, slave life, or European settlement.

The University of Florida *Seminole* documented the survival of students at the University of Florida. With Florida State's appropriation of the Seminole name, they too were aligning themselves as inheritors of a Native past. The opening greeting of the Florida yearbook affirmed this sense of progress:

> In presenting to the students, faculty, and friends of the University, this, our first volume of the *Seminole*, we trust you will keep in mind that as your our Institution is quite young (a four-year-old); that as yet we are living in the early morn of what promises to be a bright and prosperous day; that as yet we are few in numbers and consequently not free from financial embarrassment. Nevertheless, in this as in all undertakings, success is our goal and to this end we have worked. If we have failed, it is our misfortune and not our faculty and the satisfaction of the undertaking still remains. But if, when you look through these pages either now or in later years, you derive some pleasure or benefit there from, then we will feel that our efforts have not been spent in vain.[48]

Athletic identity was vital to the survival of the institution. By 1911, the University of Florida solidified its own athletic identity with the use of a "Gator" mascot, which was shown in university publications with its jaws clenched around a Citadel "Bulldog" and a Clemson "Tiger," among others. Gators were considered strong, fierce animals that were an integral part of Florida culture.[49] "Gator" was also the nickname of a young University of Florida athlete who was well known for both his athletic prowess and his aptitude with local women. "According to a football player of [Florida State College, which was dissolved in 1905 under the Buckman Act], Florida State called itself the Gators before it became the State College for Women in 1905. Florida State's last coach [prior to the reorganization] was Jack 'Pee Wee' Forsythe, who became Florida's first coach in 1906."[50]

Larger than the University of Florida in both student enrollment and campus buildings, the Florida Female College (which merged with other Florida schools to become Florida State University) and its female students actively engaged in promoting both intellectual and physical pursuits during the same period. Athletics was such a large part of campus life that college administrators were concerned about the spectacle associated with young women playing sports before nonfamily members. With the 1909 prohibition that only males who were faculty or family members were allowed to attend games, the Florida Female

College athletic teams lost the majority of their competitors and were forced to create two campus-based teams, the Stars and the Crescents.[51] In legislating the gaze of men on female bodies, the university reinforced gender-based norms that relied on beliefs of the female body in motion as sexually alluring. Physical educators were actively constructing a hierarchy of approved athletic activity where sports like golf, tennis, and gymnastics were considered more appropriate for young women. Young women were encouraged to be active, but only within carefully patrolled spaces that rewarded athleticism but not excessive exertion.[52] By 1928, the Florida State College for Women had over 1,642 students walking the halls, necessitating a dramatic growth in residential housing, sorority houses, and approved off-campus housing.[53] The university, recognizing the spatial limitations of the campus flooded by so many students, chose to improve property that the college already owned to create more space. Camp Flastacowo (Florida State College for Women), a university property located lakeside, allowed female students to participate in water games, lounge around the lakeside, and compete in water-based athletics, including rowing and swimming.[54] The use of the camp as a training ground for female athletes can be seen in the success of the synchronized swimming team, named the Tarpons in 1936.[55] Sponsored by the Life Saving Club, which oversaw water recreation at the school gymnasium and Camp Flastacowo, the Tarpons achieved nationwide fame for their elaborately choreographed water ballets. Fox Movietone attempted to capture a Tarpon performance for a national newsreel in 1937, and Grantland Rice Movie Sportlights filmed twenty-five swimmers for a movie short in 1939.[56] In selecting "Tarpons," student athletes were memorializing a large herringlike fish found in the Gulf of Mexico that could grow up to eight feet in length. Prized not for their taste but for their antics in fighting against anglers, the choice of "Tarpons" by student athletes undoubtedly was meant to signify their desired agility in the water.

Thirty-seven years after the University of Florida began its *Seminole* yearbook and adopted its Gator mascot, on May 15, 1947, Florida governor Millard Caldwell signed into a law a legislative act to return the Florida State College for Women to coeducational status. Dropping "College for Women," the newly designated Florida State University celebrated its founding on June 9 by granting 432 women and twelve men diplomas bearing the phrase "The Florida State College for Women issued by the Florida State University."[57]

Service to their country in World War II was precisely what these Florida State University students were attempting to memorialize with the selection of "Statesmen" as one of their athletic identities. Narratives of athletes as leaders were explicitly laden with notions of citizenship in the form of military service. Highlighted on the walls of Memorial Stadium at Illinois and in the campaigns of stadium-builders across America in the 1920s, young men were portrayed as physically fit bodies in the service of their country. The use of this trope increased as a result of World War II. Just as Nordsiek claimed that "these men" would return to normalcy by partaking in campus activities, the articulation by FSU men that their identity was as wise elders versed in worldly affairs (the training and killing of enemies of state) suggested a reification of their place within the social hierarchy. Gendered male, the inclusion of "Statesmen" in the competition for an FSU athletic symbol suggested the exclusion of young women (including those who served in auxiliary units) and unfit men.

SOUTHERN INFLECTIONS OF MASCOT IDENTITY

Two final selections illustrate the ways in which FSU students were articulating their community and identity through a southern lens. The choice of "Rebels" for inclusion in the 1947 contest was unsurprising given that the University of Mississippi had adopted "Rebels" as its nickname eleven years earlier. Selected by southern newswriters from over 200 suggestions, the choice was facilitated as part of a promotion by the student newspaper of "Ole Miss," the *Mississippian*.[58] Suggested by Judge Ben Guider of Vicksburg, Mississippi, eighteen of the twenty-one newswriters selected "Rebels" as their choice over "Ole Massas," referring to the white masters of black slaves.[59] Students celebrated the selection by stating it was "suggestive of a spirit native to the Old South and particularly to Mississippi."[60] Just two years later, the student yearbook promoted its first mascot, "Colonel Reb," who appeared throughout the publication. The "Rebels" and "Colonel Reb" were directly derivative of southern elite plantation imagery. Initially depicted with "flowing white hair, bushy mustache, wearing a long coat nipped at the waist, light pants, dark shoes, and a big broad-brimmed hat," Colonel Reb was a seemingly elitist version of "Johnny Reb."[61] "Johnny Reb" was a familiar fixture in literature of the war celebrating the everyman, yeoman soldier who was valiantly battling the oppressive Northern government. Outfitted in Confederate uniform, "Johnny Reb" as symbolic of the South's battle was tied not just to the antifederal, proslavery articulations that consumed nineteenth-century America during the war but also to the postwar Jim Crow "New South." Southerners continually imagined a uniquely southern narrative where artifacts of defeat (including soldiers themselves) were repeatedly celebrated.[62] The University of Mississippi's decision to promote an upper-class version of the "Rebel" in the form of the plantation master, most of whom could purchase their way out of Confederate service, was quickly subsumed by the common image of "Johnny Reb" and racially explicit imagery. Performances of "Dixie" by the university band were sung before a waving Confederate battle flag in the late 1940s. While the historical record is silent as to the motivations of the students who nominated "Rebels" as one of Florida State's athletic identities, it is quite likely that they were aware of the University of Mississippi "Rebels" and its neo-racial expressions in Oxford, Mississippi. In selecting its inclusion, students were likely attempting to continue their own cross-institutional traditions of white privilege: students at the University of Florida had long been involved in campus minstrel shows where blackface performances were commonplace.

Selection of racialized identities for Florida State by its students continued with the consideration of "Crackers." "Cracker," first documented in 1509 in *Palmer's Folk Etymology* as a "braggart or liar," functioned as a cultural signifier that demarcated specific class and race-based identities. Four main theories suggest a variety of signifiers for "cracker": it referred to poor migrants from Alabama, Georgia, North Carolina, and South Carolina who drove livestock to Florida in the nineteenth century using whips; it was an allusion to the use of dry corn as a dietary staple by poor southerners who had to "crack" the corn before using it; it was an abstraction of the Spanish word "*cuáquero*," meaning Quaker, in reference to a Quaker settlement in Spanish Florida; it was a slur for poor Scotch-Irish migrants to Florida who replicated class boundaries of yeomanry against aristocrats.[63] Referred to as "hooligans" who plagued civilized society throughout the eighteenth century, crackers were portrayed as lawless, hard-drinking, poor whites who flaunted colonial authority:

> As skilled as the Indians in hunting, willing to dare immense rivers with fragile rafts or to track man and animal through dense forests, these [crackers] erect Indian-style huts in the first unpopulated space fit to grow corn that they stumble upon in order to give shelter to their wives and children. Once done, they move again, always keeping themselves beyond the reach of all civilized law. . . . The desire . . . to escape all legal authority is so strong that they prefer to live in Indian or better still, Spanish territory rather than live under the gentle yoke of civilized society.[64]

Florida's transition to American hands in 1821 facilitated an even larger flood of poor whites, particularly the Irish, into these lands. They encroached upon Indian lands and frequently challenged colonial rule, which required deeds for land use. So influential were these men that Lieutenant Oliver Otis Howard observed during the Third Seminole War that cracker volunteers were a detriment to military order: "as a general thing they are a very corrupt set of men. They drink, gamble, and swear and do all manner of discreditable things, and are not withal very good soldiers."[65] Military aptitude aside, by the end of the nineteenth century crackers firmly were established as nonslaveholding whites on the lowest rung of the socioeconomic class who held isolation as a key cultural feature.[66] Alternately portrayed as strong, independent yeoman working to provide for their families (poor southerners) or as unkempt, shiftless vagabonds preying on civilization ("crackers"), these men and women were fixtures in travelogues, which provided colorful narratives of their lives for the entertainment of the reader, "the genuine, unadulterated 'cracker'—the clay-eating, gaunt, pale, tallow, leather-skinned sort—stupid, stolid, staring eyes, dead and lusterless. . . . Stupid

and shiftless, yet sly and vindictive, they are a block in the pathway of civilization, settlement, and enterprise wherever they exist."[67] Frederic Remington, who
shaped perceptions of the American West through his art, was just one visitor
who saw Florida's crackers as rogue independents who plagued society.[68]

Cracker identity was imbued not just with class-based politics but also with
racial constructions. Throughout the eighteenth century, poor whites were
positioned, and positioned themselves, against free and enslaved blacks. Of
particular concern for poor Irish, as the historian David Roediger has revealed,
the ability to sexualize, exoticize, and penalize African Americans allowed lower-
class and working-class Irish to prove their worth to elitist whites. They could
become white through racial and economic justifications. Within the southern
context, the transition of enslaved blacks to freedmen (albeit only technically)
created confusion for elite whites, like those who were engaged in building the
University of Florida and the Florida Female College, and who continued to
hold the equation of black to subservient. For poor southerners, the continued
subjugation of African Americans was needed to preserve their own economic
positioning. Crackers, a subsegment of poor whites, undoubtedly expressed
their own feelings regarding race, yet the historical record remains largely silent
as to the interplay between African Americans and crackers.

"Cracker" became a fondly used term that connoted a community of self-
sufficient men and women who took pride in their family heritage and
backwoods knowledge in the waning days of Jim Crow. So powerful was this
rehabilitation that in 1914, the local Deland, Florida, baseball team referred to
itself as the Deland Crackers. Further uses of "crackers" within the realm of
sport abound. The Class AA southern minor league team the Atlanta Crackers,
founded in 1901, drew an audience of 40,000 the following year, with well over
221,000 by 1920.[69] The selection of "Crackers" as the team name has alternately
been posited as a reference to poor white southerners as outlined above or as a
shortening of the nineteenth-century baseball team name "Firecrackers," a team
headquartered in 1892 in Atlanta.[70] In either manifestation, by 1946 "cracker"
firmly represented a social ideal of highly successful athletic young men who
articulated an identity of personal independence and subsistence. In considering
these conjoined representations, there is a convergence of identity politics for
Florida State students: young, male, athletic, independent, and self-sufficient.

By July 1948, Florida State University created its "Seminole" identity. A formal
university seal that featured an Indian in profile flanked by the words "Florida
State University Seminoles" was created.[71] The seal was quickly adopted for use
in university publications, including the yearbook and the student handbook.
The football players who may have had an instrumental role in the shaping of
balloting embraced "Seminoles" as their identity: en route to the Cumberland
game in the fall of 1948, player Don Grant, using lipstick, lettered the outside of
their bus "Florida State Seminoles."[72] In claiming the space of the bus and the

university itself through their ballot campaigning (and possible fraud), FSU football players were sending a very clear message about their desired identity. "Seminoles" were young athletic men who would shape their everyday worlds.

"Seminoles" was a familiar identity for the young men of Florida State University who were making Tallahassee their home in 1947. Drawn from the University of Florida, these students were balloting a complex rendering of southern identity where racial identities were used to reify their own positions as young, white, male southerners. In the end, it is this reification and appropriation across schools and institutions, including the University of Florida, the University of Mississippi, and the Atlanta Crackers, that marks Florida State University as an identity in dialogue with other institutions. In recognizing the interwoven nature of the use of the Seminole name, I reveal the unique brand of American spectacle being illustrated in the South. Just as the University of Illinois was concerned with innovating new band performances and football strategies, and the University of North Dakota was concerned with combating its rural image, and Miami University was interested in constructing small-scale spectacle, so too was Florida State University interested in leveraging spectacle for its own purpose. However, unlike the University of Illinois and Stanford University, both of which focused on generic "Indianness," Florida State University students were using Seminole identity in order to signal Florida State's privileging not just of male students but of rebellious male students who persevered in the face of opposition—be it a demonized North of the mid-nineteenth century, expansionist settlers of the eighteenth, or the women of the Florida State College for Women who were considered a challenge to the dominance of the newly arrived male students. In considering this particularly "southern" brand of spectacle, we see then a nuance of the national articulation of college football but not a significant divergence. Each of these institutions inculcated its spectacle with differing representations, yet at the core, all of these schools embraced the same narrative that privileged white male athletic bodies.

6 · INDIAN BODIES PERFORMING ATHLETIC IDENTITY

By early 1948, the University of Illinois, Stanford University, the University of North Dakota, and Florida State University had all created athletic identities that utilized racial identifiers. With a desire to produce young, athletic, middle-class male bodies in service to their nation, football and sports mascots acted as the vehicle by which communities convinced themselves of their need for commercial performances of race. Having earlier explored the spread of college football and ways in which it represented modern anxieties about white middle-class identity, this chapter highlights the ways in which female and Native bodies troubled the meaning of halftime performance in the 1940s and 1950s. In part, this chapter reveals the explicit role of nationalism as the culmination of the process of portraying, learning, and interacting with halftime spectacle. Yet it does so by showing how tenuous halftime spectacle and athletic identity were for the white middle-class interest groups that shaped college football. This chapter traces the responses of Miami University and Stanford University to these developments and illustrates that, while these institutions at the time embraced slight changes in the meaning of their spectacle, the core articulations and meanings that privileged white male athletic citizenry remained whole in the face of external tensions brought upon by war and masculine anxiety.

THE GENDERED LIMITATIONS OF INDIAN MASCOTRY AT ILLINOIS

As women entered the university in greater numbers and the university became central to the project of building an American fighting force during World War II and the Cold War, the production of explicitly female narratives of athletic bodies unsettled the relative homogeneity of college football and its environs.

December 7, 1941, changed the daily lives of men and women at colleges and universities across America. On the campus of the University of Illinois, where football had faltered due to the retirement of Robert Zuppke, three navy training schools quickly opened while women's residence halls were turned over to officers. Illinois Field, the former home of Illinois football and baseball, became the training ground for over 200 enlisted men.[1] World War II created the opportunity for women at the University of Illinois to assume prominent positions on campus. Both the student newspaper, the *Daily Illini*, and the yearbook, the *Illio*, had their first female editors, and more women were included in the concert band. So stark was the drain of men from Illinois athletics that the 1943 football team was known as the "Disappearing Illini" after over 100 eligible athletes were called into service.

As a result of the war, the University of Illinois fundamentally, but temporarily, shifted its portrayal of Chief Illiniwek. In 1943, Idell Stith (later Idell Stith Brooks) of Fairfax, Oklahoma, donned the Chief Illiniwek headdress to portray "Princess" Illiniwek.[2] The petite Stith was dwarfed by the fifty-pound headdress that had become part of the authorized costume purchased in 1930 by the second Chief Illiniwek, Webber Borchers. Having only performed at home games in his homemade costume similar to Leutwiler's prior to 1930, Borchers began to travel with the football team to away games in the newly made garments:

> In the summer of 1930 I went, at my own expense, to the Pine Ridge Reservation in South Dakota. I hitch-hiked out, called on an Indian agent and explained my mission. He and an Indian trader called in an older Sioux Indian woman. She and two younger women made the suit. I stayed there nearly a month. The suit was not ready when it became necessary for me to return home for the fall term. The regalia was not ready for the first few games, but was ready in time for me to wear in the Army-Illinois game in Yankee Stadium, New York, November 8, 1930.[3]

"Illiniwek was all decked out in his new eagle feather outfit," wrote the *Alumni News*, "and later obliged with a whooping war dance up and down the field." Borchers's sense of drama, whether in the form of his costume, which he said was created by a Sioux woman who supposedly was involved in mutilating the dead at the Battle of Little Bighorn, or in the presentation itself, tested the ritualized nature of the Illiniwek performance. Borchers, a member of the university's Reserve Officers' Training Corps (ROTC) program, once rode bareback on a pinto pony to begin his performance. Stopping on the beat of a drum, he would slide off the pony to begin his dance. His attempt to change the ritual lasted only two games when the pony damaged the rain-soaked football field.[4] Coach Zuppke forbade the pony entrance to any future games. Zuppke illustrated the limits of halftime spectacle: the performance still took place on a working football field, and damaging the field, and possibly injuring the team's ability to win, was non-negotiable. More broadly, Borchers's desire to add a new, even more dramatic element in the form of the animal suggests a consciousness that the Chief Illiniwek performance might have been becoming banal. By changing costumes and adding the thrill of an interaction between rider and horse (who could possibly misbehave in the face of 60,000 fans), Borchers seemingly recognized that the performance needed to remain fresh and stimulating for the community. Altering the opening sequence of the performance acted as a form of resistance where Borchers, in his role as the authorized performer, suggested an alternative relationship of Chief Illiniwek to the space itself vis-à-vis the pony. Through his introduction of the pony, Borchers was attempting to directly replicate the opening sequence of Cody's Wild West show and movie westerns in order to imbue the performance with dynamic action. Significantly, it was not the audience that challenged the change to the ritual; it was Zuppke. Zuppke's refusal to allow the pony entrance to the field can be read as a way of underscoring that racial performances like Chief Illiniwek were in service to the community's desire: young white male athletes stimulating community interest in the commercial education institution.

Like Leutwiler, Idell Stith's first Indian performance began before her selection as Princess Illiniwek. On November 2, 1942, Stith performed an "Indian dance reminiscent of Chief Illiniwek" for a university club, Club Commons.[5] Selected by her Pi Phi sorority sister Nancy Kollman, Stith donned the chief's headdress and top almost exactly a year later.[6] Student author Milcy Sloboda headlined an article "Idelle Stith Dons Chief's Moccasins [sic] to Keep Another Tradition Alive." Sloboda continued: "Not unacquainted with Indian customs and rituals, Miss Stith has lived on a reservation of Osage Indians all her life. Her neighbors in Fairfax, Okla. are Indians—Beartrack and Red Eagle. She was made an honorary Indian princess of the Osage tribe, and has witnessed many rites, powwows, and ceremonies which usually are verboten to the White Man. Miss Stith's abilities as a dancer are not unknown on the campus for she was a frequent performer at Club Commons floor shows. Often her partner was Glenn Holthaus, formerly Chief Illiniwek."[7] Stith's "honorary status" as an Osage was a key feature for the few articles produced during her one-year-long tenure. She is referred to as the "Indian maiden," a "witness" to the forbidden rituals of the Osage. This portrayal of Stith as a white witness to exotic, secretive Indian life is highly suggestive. In presenting Stith as not just an observer of Indian life or a frequent participant but an "honorary" member, student writers and Stith herself were creating a mantle of authenticity to her performance. Illinois students, including Sloboda, were presenting the community with an easily understood rationale for Chief Illiniwek's transformation into Princess Illiniwek that accounted for variations in appearance and performance. Stith, because of her femininity, could not be narrated as an integral part of the Illini nation. Her involvement in

FIGURE 10. Photo of Princess Illinwek, Idell Stith, October 26, 1943. Image courtesy of the University of Illinois at Urbana-Champaign Archives. RS: 39/2/20, Box ATH 1, Folder ATH 1–2, Stith, Idelle 1943. Negative Number: 9871, Record Series 39/2/22.

the halftime ritual was seen as a last resort, the only way to continue a tradition that was in danger of being lost. It is significant that the university turned to a female student to keep the ritual alive and not a new male student. In turning to Stith, the university underscored the importance of the chief performance as being simultaneously masculine and patriotic.

Male students who remained on campus and who could have donned the chief's headdress were likely to have been either designated with a 4-F classification, unfit for military service, or actively enrolled servicemen stationed at the university for training purposes. The 4-F designation, no matter the underlying cause, had significant ramifications, and to choose such a student to perform would damage the social hierarchy where popular, athletic male students were positioned at the top of the social ladder. By continually repeating Stith's honorary status among the Osage (however accurate or inaccurate that might have been), the university attempted to mediate the loss of its authorized performer and the significant change to its ritual. Coupled with the loss of significant numbers of band musicians who had been drafted meant that the halftime performance itself was dramatically reduced. Although the music continued to be performed and Stith replicated the chief's dance, the 1944 *Daily Illini* remarked that "football fans will be happy Saturday afternoon to see an Illini marching band, made up of V-12 trainees [men receiving medical and dental education so that they could provide medical care in the navy]. . . . Come onto the gridiron at the half to make the traditional Illinois formations so missed at last year's games."[8] Playing the navy march, "Hail Purdue," and "Anchors Aweigh!," the band completed its performance by welcoming back Chief Illiniwek. Kenneth O. Hanks, a navy trainee and former football player, donned the chief's headdress to perform.

Stith's tenure as Princess Illiniwek lasted just a single year, and her involvement in the "chief's" performance is perhaps best memorialized by the resistance of the Chief Illiniwek performers after her to include her in their private ritual. Beginning in 1930, each Chief Illiniwek performer would inscribe the "chief" headdress with his or her name. In the years following Stith's tenure as Princess Illiniwek, her name was removed from the headdress by "chief" performers, who viewed her inclusion as inauthentic. In part, Stith's Princess Illiniwek performance was not just about her gender but also about the fact that she was not educated in the same manner as other Chief Illiniwek performers. The Boys Scouts of America and its program of "Indian" education were a usual, but not mandatory, qualification of the first six Chief Illinwek performers: Leutwiler, Borchers, William A. Newton (1931–1934), Edward C. Kalb (1935–1938), John Grable (1939–1940), and Glenn Holthaus (1941–1942).[9] "A 100 percent, American style dancer—*real* American style—is wanted at the University," one 1941 *Daily Illini* article began. "The moccasins and war bonnet of Illiniwek are empty. He is the Indian chief who dances before the band at football games and other events and is a living symbol of the University's Indian tradition."[10] Continuing on, the article relayed that while not a requirement, the chance of Chief Illiniwek being a young man with Boy Scout training was almost certain. All six Chief Illiniwek performers before Stith credited their Boy Scout training with their success as Chief Illiniwek. Echoing Lester Leutwiler, it was not just Grable's Boy Scout experience but also his time training with Ralph Hubbard that qualified him to perform as Chief Illiniwek. "Grable met Hubbard at the 1933 Boy Scout circus in St. Louis. . . . As a result of the circus contact, which was Grable's first public attempt at Indian dancing, he spent three summers at Hubbard's Colorado ranch for boys learning and teaching Indian lore and working as a horse wrangler."[11] As a woman, Stith had no access to the Boy Scouts or to Hubbard.

In highlighting the contrast between Stith and the six previous Chief Illiniwek performers, Stith's honorary status as an Osage Indian is challenged. She was met with resistance by other Chief Illiniwek performers. John Grable was noted in almost every article on his performances as Chief Illiniwek for his ability to "trace [his] line to Choctaw Tribe." Supposedly one-sixteenth Choctaw, Grable's Indian heritage passes by with little discussion. The lack of elaboration, coupled with the elaborate narratives of Grable's training with Hubbard, suggests that, for community members, Grable's status as a Boy Scout was more important than his tribal affiliation. Placing emphasis on his participation in the Boy Scouts, which had similar meanings and emphasis on young, white, athletic bodies in service to a nation-building project, mediated any possible questions regarding Grable's racial status. He could "trace [his] line" to the Choctaws, but there was no discussion of his knowledge of Choctaw dance or ceremony. Instead, the more generic Sioux Boy Scout dance tradition was emphasized. The obscuring of Grable's heritage and the highlighting of Stith's "honorary" status as an Osage can be read as a continuing effort to mediate the boundaries of who could participate in the community. Community members could be knowledgeable about Indians, have Indian-themed experiences, and even have been affiliated with Indians in the long-distant past, but Indian bodies themselves were not welcome within the cosmopolitan world of collegiate sport except in specifically defined situations (that is, as members of an Indian team like Haskell or Carlisle).

MIAMI'S CHIEF AND DEFINING NATIONALISM

Illinois was not the only school grappling with the war, its aftereffects, and authenticity. At Miami University, President Upham declared: "College is not an escape from the responsibilities of patriotic citizens. . . . College is not an alternative to service; it is actually a preparation for better service." In 1946, as thousands of young men and women returned from war, the "Redskin" athletic identity was transformed into artistic expression. The *Miami Tomahawk*, the student magazine of "campus life," published its first edition in February with sections including "The Chief Says" and "Smoke Signals."[12] "The CHIEF says: HOW! This is the story of a shoestring. This is the story of faith. It is the story of success. . . . Wrapped up are the many hours of fun, hopes, realizations of ideas, and just plain hard work . . . UGH!" In using the guttural "ugh!" and the stereotypical "how!," students at the *Miami Tomahawk* were continuing a practice of misappropriation where tropes of Indians speaking were deployed in racialized terms and tones. Just as the "sounds of ethnicity" that were being produced by the University of Illinois band and others within this cosmopolitan network, the attribution of pseudo-Indian speak for the purposes of advertising a college humor magazine affirmed the use of racialized identities for creating communal identity. A cartoon depiction of a large-nosed, buck-toothed, big-eared young man wearing a headdress accompanied "The Chief Says" and "Smoke Signals" columns. In this artistic rendering, the exaggerated features of the nose, teeth, and ears suggested a slightly befuddled man. Although wearing a headdress, the cartoon depiction presented a dubious ethnic picture. Drawn in black ink, the features of the face contain no shading or crosshatching to suggest darker skin. When positioned against the second artistic rendering within this edition of the *Miami Tomahawk*, it becomes apparent that "The Chief Says" cartoon represented a young white student. In effect, this "Chief" was wearing signifiers of communal belonging through the wearing of the headdress but failed to completely become Indian as his skin remained white.

The *Tomahawk* extended the use of racial signifiers and created an alternative artistic rendering through a tribute to the men returning from war. Franklin McKensie Shanos, class of 1945, published a drawing of three men representing the U.S. Navy, Army, and Air Force. A sweater-clad male is situated prominently in the rendering with his "M" letter sweater. An imposing figure positioned slightly behind and above the men rides a horse. The figure, a three-dimensional version of the logo, wears only a loincloth. Underneath the image is a four-verse poem by Muriel Nordsiek that recognizes the emotional events of World War II and their effects on Miami men:

> They have returned, these men, and proudly wear
> The emblematic discharge pin, and stand,
> Who all too recent battle skies have scanned,
> Full in the moonlight of a peaceful year.
> Who knows what echoes of war they hear,
> These ribboned heroes who so late have manned
> A fleet, and stalked a red Pacific sand,
> Or with hot tracer flame have seared the air?
> Who knows what silent voice still may ring
> Within their memories, what screams of dead
> And dying rise now from the past to sing
> A melancholy dirge about their heads;
> What violent recollections may be stirred
> By some small happening, one spoken word?
> But they are back, and echoes of war
> Fade fast among the happy campus throngs.
> Back home at last, they know Here they belong;

Here the road led, though they had traveled far.
Leaders in other days, they lead once more
The campus life that lagged while they were gone;
They laugh the same, and sing the same old songs,
And know perhaps, this was worth fighting for.
These are our men, who stroll Slant Walk secure
That they have won the right of all free men;
Join what they want to join, sit in the Pure,
Talking of "good old days," remembering when—.
We waited long: through Tarawa, and Rome,
To greet our men, and tell them "Welcome home!"[13]

It is unsurprising that the images of both the mascot and the surrounding figures are highly masculine given the arc of the poem. Nordsiek opens with "these men" as distant beings involved in collective violence facing the screams of the dead and dying. She suggests, in their return to campus life, that the memories of the dirge will fade and through participating in campus life and rituals, including walking the Slant Walk between campus and Oxford, that these distant affected men will become part of the community again. "We waited long," she writes, "to greet *our men* [emphasis added]." In this transition from the words "these" to "our," the hypermasculinity that promoted the control and development of the nation as a growing force underwent a shift. Within the image, the square jaws and fierce countenances of the soldiers suggested competence that masked the violence of war. The hypersexualized image of the Indian brave further rendered the gendered nature of the image even more prominent. The chiseled chest and abdominals, coupled with the clenched muscles of the thigh of the warrior-brave, were intensely athletic and sculpted. While this could be read as a suggestion of superior masculinity, the image was softened by the warrior's flowing windblown hair. Indexed against the military and shorn locks of the Miami athlete and soldiers, the Indian was no longer acceptably masculine but uncomfortably defiant of the masculine ideal. More simply, he was no longer gendered male but instead gendered neutral. Shanos's image was less about the mascot and the racialization of Native Americans in that contemporary moment of 1946 than it was about the historical memory of nation-building. The mascot, although depicted centrally, was a memorial figure (similar in many ways to the images of God looking down from the heaven so popular in painting). The warrior-brave was the psychic overseer of the Miami effort to aid in the project of preserving the nation from tyranny. Importantly, this historical obfuscation of white Americans' role in oppressing Native American nations is rendered invisible. Instead, the canonized moment is of strong individuals preserving the nation from any aggressor, at home or abroad. Taken together, "The Chief Says" cartoon and the Shanos depiction illustrate a flexibility of representation where markers of Indianness could be scaled based on interest. More simply, the community could emulate either an Indianness that was depicted as racially other or one that was not.

By March, comedic representations of Indianness dominated communication within the *Miami Tomahawk*. While it would be tempting to pass off the humor magazine as subsidiary to the community's imagining of itself, the importance of the *Tomahawk* and other student literary publications cannot be understated. The *Tomahawk* shared offices, resources, and personnel with the staff of the *Recensio*, the Miami University yearbook, and stated openly in its first issue that its goal was to generate subscriptions and advertise for the university. The role of the comic Indian here deserves note. As digital artist and theorist Michael A. Sheyahshe has noted in *Native Americans in Comic Books*, visual depictions of Native peoples were tied to the genre of the western.[14] From line drawings in "penny" novels to full-fledged multiscene illustrations in newspapers, the use of Native Americans in cartoons was intimately tied to colonization and stereotypes of the American West, including that of the "noble savage." American fascination with Indian bodies extended to comic strips. In 1936, the first full-length Indian depiction for comics was created by Publisher's Syndicate. Initially based on film star W. C. Fields, the leading character, J. Mortimer Gusto, sold Ka-Zowie Kure-All to naive men and women looking for a quick medicinal cure. Accompanied by "Big Chief Wahoo," his Indian sidekick, Gusto toured America seeking quick money. Gusto's tenure as leading character was brief when publishers realized that "Big Chief Wahoo" was the more entertaining of the characters. The feature cartoon appropriately titled "Big Chief Wahoo" was the first full-length cartoon with an Indian as the main character. Supposedly free to roam America using wampum from the sale of oil discovered on his land, the character of "Big Chief Wahoo" in its entirety suggested the trope of the wise Indian who could outwit dubious people through his Indian sense but was out of touch with "modern" America. Portrayed as good-humored throughout, the character "Big Chief Wahoo" offered many of the same conventions later used in the *Miami Tomahawk*: he "spoke" Indian with many "ughs!" and had a large, hook-shaped nose.[15] Published throughout the 1940s, students at Miami University had likely viewed at least one comic strip featuring "Big Chief Wahoo."

Just as other schools had positioned their athletic identity within international contexts, so too did Miami University in March 1946. "Off the Reservation," a regular feature that sported a white man clad in a tuxedo and a Sioux bonnet, began its first column with a commentary on the case for Filipino independence.[16] Telling of an ex–air force lieutenant and his squadron stationed in the Philippines and their "lively interest in the native sport of cockfighting," "Wings without Victory" continued: "For months the white hope was fed and exercised. At last the great day arrived. The feathered gladiator and its trainer were bundled off to Manila. Most of the smart money of the squadron rode along, for by this time the American contender was in great shape, weighing in at a cool twenty pounds. After the bets had been judicially placed with the gullible Filipinos, the warrior was prepared for combat."[17] Continuing on, the authors recounted the loss of their money and the killing of their cock after the bird fled the fighting arena in the face of the national challenger, a scrawny bird with bloodshot eyes: "In the camp next day, there was little of the usual easy banter, and less of the smart money. Feeling ran high against the Filipino who had sold them the craven bird, and they all tended to suspect that the incident was typical of the native mind. To this day no member of that squadron feels that we could gain anything by continuing an association with such a race. A shifty lot, our friend assures us, and the sooner we wash our hands of them, the better."[18] With nationalistic language at the fore, the battle between the "white hope" and the "scrawny bird" functioned as a metaphor for the ongoing battle between Americans and their Filipino neighbors. Leveraging ideas of race within the column to affirm white identity, the authors also expressed anxiety regarding the growing "atomic age" in the same column. Taken together, "Off the Reservation" and its contents illustrated an intersection of colonial representations of Indianness with the rhetoric of foreign involvement and global politics. Another example of the anxiety about living in the rapidly changing modern world, the significance of the pairing of Indian mascots with narratives of midcentury war and Cold War anxiety cannot be understated. Anxieties about the nation and the need for young, male, athletic citizens were integral to the expressions of cultural meaning surrounding college athletics and mascots.

The magazine, in its December issue, initiated a quest for an artistic version of the school's athletic identity. The name "Hiawabop" was contributed by senior John McDowell, a member of Sigma Chi fraternity who "said the reason why he slapped this collection of letters on [Hiawabop] was because he once knew an Indian whose name was Hiawatha."[19] The cartoon featured a short man with a protruding belly and a loincloth with a block "M" on it. Hiawabop sported glasses as well as a large, hooked nose, continuing the image made familiar in earlier issues of the *Miami Tomahawk* and through comics like "Big Chief Wahoo." The comedic nature of Hiawabop intersected with athletics on the October 1948 cover celebrating football victory. Hiawabop carried a football and wore a round ribbon proclaiming, "Sun Bowl Champs."[20] He was surrounded by the mascots of the Midwestern Athletic Conference: the University of Dayton (an aviator in a plane), Western Michigan (a bronco), [Case] Western Reserve University (red cats),[21] Marshall University (bison),[22] Ohio University (bobcat), University of Cincinnati (bearcat), Xavier University (musketeers), and Virginia (cavalier). This graphic representation of athletic identity illustrated the competitive element of colleges and universities in "modern" America. A central expression of the ritual of college football being explored here, the cover demonstrated the continuing dehumanization of Indian mascots by placing them in context with animal representation.[23]

Formal university publications at other schools embraced the use of cartoon representations for their athletic identities. In 1947, the Stanford student handbook featured a section entitled "Worktime and Playtime." Students opening their handbook saw a bare-chested Indian seated at a desk writing a letter. In a thought bubble over his head was a striking young woman with her hair in braids and a braided headband across her forehead. This rendition was striking in that the Indian figure was drawn with dark skin (signified by cross-hatching) while the young woman was not. In delineating an artistic demarcation of skin color, the rendering suggests that the young woman was an object of desire by the "red" Indian. The fear of Indian men stealing white women was a common trope in colonial literatures and throughout both western films and comics. At the hands of an Indian, a white woman could be physically assaulted and, most horrifically, become the mother of a "half-breed" child. In effect, it was not just the lust but also the control over white women's bodies that was at the core of these anti-Indian depictions. That an Indian could possibly debauch (and by extension pervert) a white woman would destabilize white male control over female bodies and the perception of men as defenders of the household. Given that the Indian cartoon portrayed the youth at work, the suggestion that white women are part of "playtime" activities is troubling. In part, this positioning of white women as objects of desire was part of a much longer trend of the sexualization of female bodies to idealize and reinforce gender norms within the constraints of white, male, heterosexist conventions. As the historians John D'Emilio and Estelle Freedman revealed, to paraphrase, mid-twentieth-century America witnessed the collapse of social norms regarding sexuality as public portrayals became more commonplace with the collapse of legal prohibitions.[24] For a magazine such as the *Miami Tomahawk*, which featured "Teepee Tintypes" (photographs of young female coeds), and the Stanford University handbook, the portrayal of comely young coeds whether in photographs or through cartoons suggested a further repetition of the hypermasculinity that was an essential expression of higher education's desires to create young, male, athletic bodies in service to the community and the nation. By emphasizing female bodies, students at these universities were alternately expressing desire (for marriage, sex, and family through female bodies) and repressing possible criticism associated with the hypermasculinity being expressed as part of the university's identity. J. C. Leyendecker's football-themed cover art for *Century, Popular Magazine, Collier's,* and *the Post*—with the "the broad-shouldered, supremely confident male with shining skin, chiseled features, and steely eyes"—continued to be presented throughout the 1940s and 1950s in photographic form.[25] Athletes in their articulated representation of successful masculinity were used to advertise college and university programs throughout America. The production of these images offered the possibility of transgressive behavior regarding male athletic bodies. They could be objects of desire not just of the women of the community but of men as well. By portraying female bodies in conjunction with athletic identities like Hiawabop and the Stanford Indian, students were policing the boundaries of acceptable behavior by drawing a clear line between heterosexual and homosexual behaviors.

POLICING BOUNDARIES AT STANFORD UNIVERSITY AND THE UNIVERSITY OF NORTH DAKOTA

The 1951–1952 student handbook represents the policed boundaries at Stanford University. Featuring introductory pages to each section with cartoon representations of students with Indian markers, the handbook communicated the community mores regarding male-female student behavior. "What Every Freshmen Should Know" depicted a trio of students, two male and one female. Farthest right was a figure, startlingly similar to Miami University's Hiawabop rendition with the exception of the bulbous nose, portrayed as a freshmen (demarcated with a block "F" on his loincloth) staring at the female student. In a three-quarter-length dress with deep décolletage, the female student, with an excessively curvy body, sported a single feather in her parted hair. With hands outstretched, she faced the third student. Standing almost twice as tall as the freshmen student and wearing a letter sweater with an "S" to denote senior status, the male student holds a book in one hand, with his other drawn into an upward position showing off his bicep. The message: when students arrive at Stanford University they are transformed throughout the years into specimens of masculine perfection that are attractive to female students. By including the letter sweater on the senior student, the role of athletics as a training ground for manhood becomes apparent. Further, the inclusion of the female student suggests that conquest of the female body could transform the lowly freshman into a strapping young man.

The "Fighting Sioux" of the University of North Dakota were also being presented in both masculine and comedic ways. The 1942 *Dacotah* yearbook included the first comic representation of the "Sioux": "Here we introduce to you a senior escapist, Sammy Sioux."[26] Sammy, wearing a headband with two feathers and his hair in braids tied with a bow, stands suggestively with one finger touching his lower lip with his eyes closed. His left hand trails along the edge of cloth, holding it aside from his fringed pants. Photographs of campus events captured decorations that presented images and tropes strikingly similar to those in the 1930 yearbook. Welcoming visitors to campus in 1935 was a banner framing the campus gates that read, "Welcome to the land of the Civilized Sioux."[27] Three Indian women characters garbed in fringed dresses held up a display entitled "Sioux in Education," which featured two male Indians garbed in breechcloths and full headdresses supplicating before books.[28] A similar composite of Indian men framed by books featuring an Indian dancing atop a glowing world was noted as the winning house decoration in 1937.[29] Titled "Sioux Tops the World," the display was part of the 1936 homecoming competition. The images produced by Gamma Phi Beta fit within the carefully constructed images that were being produced at the University of North Dakota. Indianness was a means of expressing community identity and belonging. The University of North Dakota replicated many of the same images that the University of Illinois was using. While Illinois's image captured a full-frontal view of Chief Illiniwek, the University of North Dakota "Sioux" was framed in profile. The images themselves are strikingly similar: each includes a Sioux headdress and a starkly carved male face with a stoic expression.[30]

Interaction with Indians marked the University of North Dakota as uniquely different from the University of Illinois, Miami University, and Stanford University. The University of North Dakota did not create a halftime performance from its own community. It turned to neighboring Indians to provide the performance. Documenting homecoming festivities of 1937, the *Dacotah* yearbook reveals a single instance of Indians performing at halftime at the University of North Dakota. A group of six Fort Yates Indians appear in multiple photographs throughout the yearbook.[31] Entertaining the audience during halftime festivities, the inclusion of Indians on the field who were not carefully constituted by the university itself suggests two fundamental understandings: that "real" Sioux were needed to accurately demonstrate the history of the University of North Dakota, a fundamental narrative of all homecoming festivities; and that it was the space of halftime and the musical narrative provided by the band that created the opportunity for Indians to enter into the space of the university. The fact that the Sioux performers were brought to campus at all suggests recognition of the ways in which Indianness had been leveraged to create community for the university. Having these performers only appear at halftime with band accompaniment suggested a replication of the ritual that the University of Illinois had constructed in 1928. Finally, the choice of Fort Yates deserves particular notice. Fort Yates, founded by the U.S. Army to oversee Blackfeet, Hunkpapas, and Upper Yanktonais, was renamed in honor of Captain George Yates, who was killed at the Battle of Little Big Horn in 1876. Headquarters of the Standing Rock Agency and over 300 miles from Grand Forks, Fort Yates Indians, led by Sitting Bull, were instrumental in the Sioux uprisings that challenged Dakota settlers. In contrast, the Spirit Lake Indian Reservation of the Sisseton Wahpeton Sioux bands was less than 100 miles away. The historical record remains silent on the decision to include Fort Yates Indians and not Spirit Lake Indians. Perhaps Spirit Lake Indians were invited and declined.

The final choice to include the particular tribe that was involved in some of the most notorious uprisings leading into the founding of the state of North Dakota and the university suggested a desire on the part of the university to explicate the full extent of the civilizing mission. It was not just about Indians performing but also about Indians descended from warriors representing the temporality of their culture. More simply, they appeared as exotic at halftime, performed to the delight of the audience, and returned to the sidelines to watch the university continue to celebrate its successful colonization of the land. As demonstrated in the creation of the cartoon "Sammy Sioux," the University of North Dakota was continually negotiating performances that relied on fictive considerations of racialized bodies.[32] At the height of the negotiation were the patriotic young white men who rallied their communities and served their country. Collectively, between Miami University, Stanford University, and the University of North Dakota, we see the expansion of the circuit of knowledge about Indianness at a critical moment where national issues about gender increased the emphasis placed on the communal desire for white male bodies in service to their communities. Significantly, with greater emphasis on male bodies being performers and actors within the network, the muting of female and homosexual desires continued.

Returning to the opening vignette of this book illustrates the extent to which college football and its attendant events became a site of constituting raced, gendered, and classed bodies for the purposes of building a white middle-class community. Performing at halftime before the Pasadena audience, Chief Illiniwek was presented for the first time to a national audience simultaneously in the first commercial televising of the Rose Bowl game. No longer tied to radio, where athletic feats had to be described verbally, or to news films that were only shown in theaters, the ability of racial performances and athletic feats to increase their communities exploded. Yet Chief Illiniwek was not alone on the field. Another "Indian" performer would take to the field and, in doing so, evince the strength of the circuit of cultural production that has been explored here. Stanford's Prince Lightfoot appeared at halftime with the Stanford University "Dollies," four female cheerleaders in calf-length skirts, three-quarter-length-sleeved sweaters, and faux-pearl necklaces. Dancing to the sounds of the university band, Prince Lightfoot was garbed in the "familiar headdress of the Sioux" with a "feathered cape of the Southwest Indians' 'Eagle Dance.'"[33]

"Prince Lightfoot" was H. D. "Timm" Williams, a longtime supporter of college athletics in California. A resident of San Jose, Williams began attending Stanford University football games at the invitation of the Stanford Rally Committee.[34] In exchange for tickets to the annual "Big Game" between Stanford University and California in 1951, Williams donned his costume. The first Prince Lightfoot performance was initiated, not from the field, but instead from a student committee that was seeking halftime entertainment. In subsequent performances, Williams would stand and cheer along the sidelines of the field in addition to dancing during the halftime performances of the university band. In writing of these first dances, Williams's performances are alternately spoken of as "a barely recognizable version of a Plains eagle dance" that he would use to "cast a 'hex' or 'spell' on the opponent" or as "traditional Yurok dances in traditional Yurok regalia."[35]

FIGURE 11. H. D. "Timm" Williams as Prince Lightfoot dancing at the California football game, 1953. Courtesy of the Stanford University Archives, Stanford Quad, 1953, 205. LD3047.Q4 V.60 1953.

Why the association with the Yuroks? The Yuroks, Algonquian-speaking Indians who migrated to California between the tenth and thirteenth centuries, were inhabitants of a reservation in the Klamath River valley in Northern California. First encountered by the Spanish in 1775 when a ship anchored at the coastal village Curey, the Yuroks had sporadic contact with Spanish and English colonizers prior to the mid-nineteenth century. In part because of the concentration of English colonial authority along the eastern seaboard, the Yuroks were relatively untouched by colonial Euro-American encounters prior to the 1849 California gold rush. In 1855, they were forcibly relocated to the Klamath River Reservation. One historian wrote in 1881 of the colonial encounter with the Yuroks: "A few years to come will see the last of these Indians, who once roamed the forests and mountains of Del Norte [County] in large numbers, and who could truly boast that they were 'monarchs of all they surveyed.' Flying before the march of civilization like chaff before the wind, they have rapidly been reduced in numbers, until at the present time [1881], a mere remnant of the earlier tribes are left to go down with the setting sun of their declining strength."[36] The common trope of the disappearing Indian was echoed by anthropologist A. L. Kroeber, who wrote of the Yuroks as having disappeared in the face of colonial encounters. In reality, the Yuroks, while dramatically affected by disease and the decline associated with colonialism, continued to fish, harvest, and work as loggers into the twentieth century. A subject of Edward Curtis, who also documented the Sioux, the Yuroks were presented in a variety of regalia. Performers of the White Deerskin Dance wore deer hide coverings, dentalia necklaces, and wolf-fur headbands, while Jump Dance performers were costumed in headdresses of woodpecker scalps, feathers, and deerskin robes. More commonly attired for the Curtis photos, Yuroks were usually dressed in loose-fitting pants and shirts with a beaded skullcap or headband.

Significantly, Williams was of Yurok ancestry. He initially performed along the sidelines, but rarely on the field. Williams's first authorized performance as Prince Lightfoot was at the Stanford University–Illinois Rose Bowl game. Dancing at halftime, Williams appeared in a plains war bonnet, a half-star painted along his cheeks and chin, a fringed shirt with a loincloth, and fringed boots. In this moment of Yurok appropriation of Sioux identity, we see the culmination of the efforts by white middle-class men to create an American spectacle of college football that has been explored throughout this book. In Williams's choosing to portray himself as Sioux, the hierarchy of race that had positioned Indians as "echoes" of American racial attitudes and colonial fears was inverted. The Illinois community had mentioned John Grable's supposed Choctaw heritage but quickly obscured it in favor of recounting his Boy Scout training. At Stanford University, Williams, an active member of the nonfederally recognized Yurok tribe, consciously created an Indian performance that was not Yurok in appearance but rather Sioux. In adopting the persona of Prince Lightfoot, Williams consciously subverted his own Indian identity in favor of the more commonly recognized Sioux trope that white Americans comprising the audience would recognize.

In concluding with this last instance of mascotry, where an Indian played Indian, the simultaneity of counternarrative of Indian performance and the success of halftime spectacle and Indian-themed identity unfolds. Just as Princess Illiniwek offered opportunities for counternarrative articulations, so too did Prince Lightfoot. Williams's performance could be read as a redemptive act where one Indian's body was "reality," not just an echo of colonial encounters and a romantic past. Williams was an active and vocal member of the Yurok community who spoke frequently through his role as Prince Lightfoot about Indian culture, history, and issues. "To me, however," Williams wrote in his 1959 autobiography, "there is a satisfaction that stands out even above [the good times and friends made at Stanford]. I realize now that I have achieved recognition and self-respect, not through passing for something I am not, but for being what I am—an Indian."[37] Believing he had his worth through his performance of Prince Lightfoot, a hodgepodge of Indian representations in the form of a Yurok body, Sioux headdress, beading, and dancing, and a southwestern Indian cape, Williams illustrates the extreme tensions felt by men throughout the first half of

FIGURE 12. Edward Curtis, The smelt fisher—Trinidad Yurok. Reproduced from Edward Curtis, *The North American Indian, 1907–30*, vol. 13, pl. 469. Courtesy of the Library of Congress Prints and Photographs Division, Washington, D.C.

the twentieth century. That a Yurok would consciously embrace Sioux and other identities to construct his performance of Indianness suggests the extent of the diffusion of ideas about racialized bodies that were communicated through college football. By not dancing traditional Yurok dances and instead favoring the familiar quasi-Sioux performance that was long a part of cultural productions of Indianness made famous through halftime spectacle and Indian-themed performances, Williams demonstrated his perception of his own limitations as an Indian.[38] In creating a "Sioux" version of himself, Williams was affirming the dominant trope that tied Sioux identity via the University of Illinois to the circuit of consumption and competition on the part of colleges and universities. In effect, Williams was the apotheosis of the "modern" Indian man; he was so "Indian" that he himself cast aside his Yurok identity in favor of a Sioux performance during halftime festivities. Significantly, Williams and others have overlooked that, at Stanford University, without Prince Lightfoot, Williams would never have had access to the Stanford University football field or the Stanford community.

In drawing parallels between the gendered performance of Princess Illiniwek, those of cartooned Indians, and that of Yurok Timm Williams, the boundaries of community identity negotiated as part of an ongoing expression of the anxiety of World War II and the Cold War are revealed. Expressing unease with gender and nationalism, this chapter underscores that at the close of any performance of athletic identity, the collegiate community always reaffirmed its desire for white male athletic bodies in service to the nation.

CONCLUSION

The spectacle of two Indians (one a "white" man and one "red") on the field in Pasadena in 1952 closes the exploration of modern anxiety and the rise of halftime spectacle and football identities that began here with an analysis of William "Bill" Hug's Indian performance and the performance by Yurok Indian H. D. "Timm" Williams. Enriching our understanding of cultural history and the ways in which race, class, gender, and youth were enshrined within the expressions of American middle-class life, whether in the form of halftime spectacles, sporting identities, stadium campaigns, band performances, or newspapers, this book has demonstrated the historical underpinnings of a consciousness that would come under fire in the second half of the twentieth century. Colleges and universities patrolled the uneasy boundaries of their identities so long as the majority of the community ascribed to the underlying meaning: that white, young, heterosexual athletic male bodies were needed for the future of the country.

In his book *American Historical Pageantry*, David Glassberg relates public rituals such as this pageant to belief in future progress. "Its [historical pageantry's] combination of elite, popular, and ethnic cultural forms depicting images of a 'common' past would break down social and cultural barriers between local residents, triggering the release of their underlying emotions and the revitalization of their overarching civic commitments."[1] The spectacle of college football was more than a game; it included bands and musical performances, newspaper writers and narratives of athletics, artistic productions and commercial athletic identities, and carefully constructed portrayals of historical narratives that capitalized on raced, classed, and gendered bodies. Yet by the close of the 1950s, the narrowly defined communities at most institutions of higher education were under direct siege. African Americans, Native Americans, and other minorities began to enroll in these institutions in larger and larger numbers. In doing so, they brought with them new considerations of race, gender, and community identity. Black Power, the American Indian Movement, and the Second Wave feminist movement all began to converge and threaten higher education, and the football field in particular, as a space for white middle-class men to act out their rituals of belonging to assuage anxiety about their role in modern America.

Throughout the 1960s, the fractures that began with the performances of Idelle Stith Brooks and Timm Williams continued to expand. In 1972, an ad hoc committee of the Dartmouth Alumni Council, working in conjunction with administrators at Dartmouth College, suggested that the "Indian" moniker be used less prominently in favor of the "Big Green" moniker. Across the country at Stanford University, administrators were also considering the effects of their "Indian" mascot on Native students. "I used to say that when I died and they opened me up they would find Stanford Indian written across my heart, the way Queen Mary Tudor said they would find Calais, the last English holding on the continent of Europe that she lost, written across her heart," remarked former Stanford University president Richard Lyman in a 2005 video interview for *The Stanford Presidency*:

> Nothing afflicted me more than the decision to abolish the Indian mascot. It happened by stages. We began to take in Indian students. We began to have a program to recruit Native American students in about 1972. They were unanimous that the Indian mascot was a no-no and should go. Prince Lightfoot, the Yurok Indian who danced at football games, offended them because his dances included religious motifs from various tribes and mixed them all up together. And they thought it was sacrilegious to have that going on at halftime at a football game. The whole idea of the Indian savage noble on horseback was bad because it gave people a romanticized and misleading view of what American Indians were all about.[2]

In February 1972, Stanford University ended its use of the Indian and its halftime spectacle around Prince Lightfoot. Miami University ended its use of "Redskin" in 1997; Illinois followed in 2007 after a decision by the National Collegiate Athletic Association (NCAA) to prohibit schools with Indian mascots to serve as postseason tournament hosts. The National Congress of American Indians, an intertribal political consortium founded to protect American Indian and Alaska Native sovereignty, estimates that roughly two-thirds of over 2,000 derogatory Indian mascots have been eliminated within the last fifty years in the face of protests by Native peoples. At North Dakota, the university finally retired its "Fighting Sioux" nickname and logo in 2012. So vociferous was the response by students and the public that a three-year "cooling-off" period was needed before the selection of a new mascot.

At Florida State, the Seminole mascot continues. Florida State was "authorized" by the Seminole tribe of Florida to continue its use. Scholarships now support a number of Seminole students to attend the university. If you read polls about the use of Native mascots, on one side of the issue are "Americans" who believe that the use of Native American names and imagery by college and professional sports teams is not offensive. And on the other side are Native Americans who are vociferously defending their right to determine the appropriate use of their own culture and heritage, even when it is pejorative. *Sports*

Illustrated and the Peter Harris Research have weighed in with a poll that says most Indians are supportive of the use of Indian identities.³ *Indian Country Today*, a leading Native American–run news media network, has put forth its poll, which found that 81 percent of respondents found Native American mascots offensive.⁴ More recently, the Associated Press, in response to a symposium held by the Smithsonian Institution's National Museum of the American Indian, revealed that four out of every five respondents did not think that the professional football team the Washington Redskins should change the team's name.⁵

Defenses of Native American mascotry often rely on personal anecdotes and polling data, the four out of every five respondents that do not find such mascotry offensive. Significantly, though, these polls are not statistically sound. The AP poll surveyed just 1,004 respondents out of a total U.S. population (as of July 2011) of 311,591,917 people. For those doing the math, that is 0.000322 percent of the population. There has not been a large-scale statistically significant poll done of mascotry. Setting aside the mathematics of opinion, alternative defenses often chide that the attempt to do away with mascots is about "political correctness," often code words for "politically liberal." The political correctness defense uses language of "honoring Indians" with the evidentiary basis often being personal testimony from one of the 5.2 million Natives pointing out that he or she does not find the use of "redskins" offensive. Quotations usually comprise some version of "I, as a Native, do not have a problem with this so you should not either."

Even when Native peoples argue that they have a problem with mascot performance and Native imagery, their concerns are often dismissed. Antimascot opponents though would argue that these problematic behaviors continue. The "tomahawk" chop where fans mimic the scalping of their opponents relies on cultural memory of the violence of colonization where whites and Natives alike lost their lives. The use of sacred iconography in the form of clothing and headdresses that are divorced from their communities of practice distorts and corrupts their meanings. And, more explicitly, the use of "redskins" is a racial epithet that continues on college campuses, in mainstream media, and at sporting events throughout the country.

For all the public discussion and debate over contemporary peoples, though, it is easy to forget that at the core of the discussions over the use of Native American representation are the historical conditions that influenced the creation and use of "Redskins" and other Indian monikers as sports mascots. Native athletes playing in professional sport in the late nineteenth and early twentieth centuries experienced their own forms of racial degradation even as white and African American mascots performed along the sidelines. Louis Sockalexis, Charles A. Bender, John Tortes Meyers, Jim Thorpe, and others faced taunts from fans that decried their Indianness in virulently racist language. Some were physically assaulted. All were treated as less than their white counterparts in everything from playing time to contract negotiations to housing. Often in the discussion over contemporary mascotry, these historical roots are glossed over. Those behaviors and experiences are past; the corollary then is that contemporary Americans have outgrown these explicitly racialized exchanges.

Sport is the focus of the contemporary debate just as it is within our historical exploration because sport serves as a microcosm of life. Sport is the 800-pound gorilla in American culture. It focuses issues of capitalism, market economies, cultural belonging, and play around consumptive behavior. Sport is play, except at the collegiate and professional levels (and increasingly the select youth level), when it was a million-dollar-a-year and is now a billion-dollar-a-year business that relies on quantities of young healthy bodies who perform for the benefit of the institution or organization. It generates massive streams of revenue wrapped in the rhetoric of enjoyment. Sport is an industry with thousands of contributors: owners, employees, athletes, fans, news media, even the U.S. government. As a nation, we have built (and continue to build) shrines to it that set it apart as privileged space.

In 2010, the collective revenue of the fifteen largest-grossing teams in the Collegiate Division 1A topped $1 billion, as reported to the U.S. Department of Education. What marks this figure as even more impressive is that it does not take into account university-derived income from the sale of athletic and university-related apparel.[6] When groups of University of Illinois students and alumni join together annually to petition for the return of Chief Illiniwek, it is not just about honoring our forefathers. It is, on the one hand, about a legacy of violence, oppression, and cultural heritage and, on the other, the right of corporations,

FIGURE 13. Chief Illiniwek, 2009. Image courtesy of the University of Illinois Division of Intercollegiate Athletics.

even public institutions, to use that heritage to profit in the contemporary global economy and the competitive world of higher education. Thus, it is unsurprising that at the University of Illinois, the University of North Dakota, and Florida State University, students, alumni, donors, and even administrators continue to support the use of these athletic identities and Indian spectacles.

The in-person audience of nearly 100,000 that would watch Chief Illiniwek and Prince Lightfoot perform in 1952 was minuscule compared to the audiences of today. The introduction of television as a mechanism for expanding and exploiting the marketing of university identity would transform halftime spectacle. With the advent of the Internet, mascotry has become a global phenomenon. Universities no longer compete locally or even nationally for students. They compete against institutions across the world. Football spectacle, with its halftime performance, remains one way they communicate their message of university identity. And for students, facing the fast-paced world where 24/7 communication and consumption are common, their allegiances to university and athletic teams have proliferated. Thus, it is vital that we return to the historical roots of mascotry to understand its colonial contexts. By understanding mascotry as one element in a larger milieu of representation of Native peoples, we more clearly understand the pervasiveness and uniformity that comprise contemporary representations in sports, film, music, television, and American material culture.

NOTES

INTRODUCTION

1. Originally published in a slightly different form in Jennifer Guiliano, "An American Spectacle: Collegiate Mascots and the Performance of Tradition" (Ph.D. diss., University of Illinois at Urbana-Champaign, 2010).

2. For ease of reading, when mentioning Chief Illiniwek and Prince Lightfoot, I am referring to the created portrayal rather than to the person performing the role.

3. Williams would later become director of the California Indian Assistance program.

4. "Illinois Football Team Gets Rousing Welcome at Pasadena," *New York Times*, December 19, 1951, 46; Bob Myers, "Bands, Cheering Crowds Greet Illini on 2d Visit to Coast," *Washington Post*, December 19, 1951, B5; Wilfrid Smith, "It's Bowl Day! Illinois Meets Stanford," *Chicago Daily Tribune*, January 1, 1952, C1; Wilfrid Smith, "Illinois Routs Stanford, 40–7, in Rose Bowl," *Chicago Daily Tribune*, January 2, 1952, 1; Paul Zimmerman, "Illinois Defeats Stanford, 40–7," *Los Angeles Times*, January 2, 1952, 1; Wilfrid Smith, "Late Deluge," *Los Angeles Times*, January 2, 1952, A2; *Oskee Wow Wow Illinois Football*, directed by Lawrence Miller (Champaign: University of Illinois, 1990), VHS.

5. Michael Oriard, *King Football: Sport and Spectacle in the Golden Age of Radio and Newsreels, Movies and Magazines, the Weekly and the Daily Press* (Chapel Hill: University of North Carolina Press, 2001), 11. On culture generally, see Clifford Geertz, *The Interpretation of Cultures* (New York: Basic Books, 1984), which remains a seminal and relevant text; on the invention of popular culture, see John Storey, *Inventing Popular Culture: From Folklore to Globalization* (Malden, Mass.: Blackwell, 2003); on popular culture in the 1930s, see Gary D. Best, *The Nickel and Dime Decade: American Popular Culture during the 1930s* (Westport, Mass.: Praeger, 1993); on Native Americans and popular culture, see S. Elizabeth Bird, *Dressing in Feathers: The Construction of the Indian in American Popular Culture* (Boulder, Colo.: Westview Press, 1996); on the working class and popular culture, see Michael Demming, *Mechanic Accents: Dime Novels and Working-Class Culture in America* (New York: Verso, 1987); on tradition and popular culture, see David Glassberg, *American Historical Pageantry: The Uses of Tradition in the Early Twentieth Century* (Chapel Hill: University of North Carolina Press, 1990); on memory and popular culture, see George Lipsitz, *Time Passages: Collective Memory and American Popular Culture* (Minneapolis: University of Minnesota Press, 1990).

6. On post–Civil War industrialization and capital accumulation, see Eric Foner, *Reconstruction: America's Unfinished Revolution, 1863–1877* (New York: Harper & Row, 1988), 460–511; Edward L. Ayers, *The Promise of the New South: Life after Reconstruction* (New York: Oxford University Press, 1992).

7. Bernard Bailyn et al., *The Great Republic: A History of the American People* (Lexington, Mass.: D. C. Heath, 1985), 569. On the theme of American expansion, capitalism, and the cultural changes they wrought, see Alan Trachtenberg, *The Incorporation of America: Culture and Society in the Gilded Age* (New York: Hill and Wang, 1982); Robert H. Wiebe, *The Search for Order, 1877–1920* (New York: Hill and Wang, 1967); Michael McGerr, *A Fierce Discontent: The Rise and Fall of the Progressive Movement in America* (New York: Oxford University Press, 2003); T. J. Jackson Lears, *Rebirth of a Nation: The Making of Modern America, 1877–1920* (New York: HarperCollins, 2009); Dan Walker Howe, *What Hath God Wrought: The Transformation*

of America, 1815–1848 (New York: Oxford University Press, 2007); Charles Sellers, *The Market Revolution: Jacksonian America 1815–1846* (New York: Oxford University Press, 1991).

8. Michael Kimmel, *Manhood in America: A Cultural History* (New York: Free Press, 1996), 84. See also E. Anthony Rotundo, *American Manhood: Transformations in Masculinity from the Revolution to the Modern Era* (New York: Basic Books, 1993), 222–247. For a useful history of manhood and nationality in particular, see Dana D. Nelson, *National Manhood: Capitalist Citizenship and the Imagined Fraternity of White Men* (Durham, N.C.: Duke University Press, 1998); Mark C. Carnes, *Secret Ritual and Manhood in Victorian America* (New Haven, Conn.: Yale University Press, 1989). On cultural hierarchy, see Lawrence Levine, *Highbrow/Lowbrow: The Emergence of Cultural Hierarchy in America* (Cambridge, Mass.: Harvard University Press, 1988); Joan Shelley Rubin, *The Making of Middlebrow Culture* (Chapel Hill: University of North Carolina Press, 1992). On religion and cultural boundaries, see Kathryn J. Oberdeck, *The Evangelist and the Impresario: Religion, Entertainment, and Cultural Politics in America, 1884–1914* (Baltimore: Johns Hopkins University Press, 1999).

9. Gail Bederman, *Manliness and Civilization: A Cultural History of Gender and Race in the United States, 1880–1917* (Chicago: University of Chicago Press, 1995), 11.

10. Ibid., 12.

11. Baseball player Babe Ruth, boxer William Harrison "Jack" Dempsey, golfer Bobby Jones, and tennis player Bill Tilden achieved national recognition not just for their athletic success but also for their representation of middle-class values. Ruth was famous for his many sexual relationships, which reinforced white male masculinity; Dempsey for his physical force; Jones and Tilden for their gentility and strength. Celebrated in film, photos, and newspapers, the physical bodies and behaviors of these athletes consumed the American public, be they elites who profited from owning teams, middle-class men who sought to regain lost opportunities to prove themselves, or lower-class men looking for leisurely outlets to alleviate the tension of being responsible for supporting their families. See Allen Guttman, *From Ritual to Record: The Nature of Modern Sports* (New York: Columbia University Press, 1978); Robert F. Burk, *Much More Than a Game: Players, Owners, and American Baseball since 1921* (Chapel Hill: University of North Carolina Press, 2001); Robert W. Creamer, *Babe: The Legend Comes to Life* (New York: Simon and Schuster, 1974); Steven A. Riess, *Touching Base: Professional Baseball and American Culture in the Progressive Era* (New York: Greenwood Press, 1980); Frank Deford, *Big Bill Tilden: The Triumph and the Tragedy* (New York: Simon and Schuster, 1976); Roger Kahn, *A Flame of Pure Fire: Jack Dempsey and the Roaring 20s* (New York: Houghton Mifflin Harcourt, 1999); Randy Roberts, *Jack Dempsey: The Manassa Mauler* (Baton Rouge: Louisiana State University Press, 1980); Jeffrey T. Sammons, *Beyond the Ring: The Role of Boxing in American Society* (Champaign: University of Illinois Press, 1989); Michael Oriard, *Dreaming of Heroes: American Sports Fiction, 1868–1980* (Chicago: Nelson Hall Press, 1980); Ron Rapoport, *The Immortal Bobby: Bobby Jones and the Golden Age of Golf* (Hoboken, N.J.: John Wiley & Sons, 2005).

12. Bederman, *Manliness and Civilization*, 41–42.

13. Melvin L. Adelman, *A Sporting Time: New York City and the Rise of Modern Athletics, 1820–1870* (1986; repr., Urbana: University of Illinois Press, 1990), 110–116. See also Steven A. Riess, *City Games: Evolution of American Urban Society and the Rise of Sports* (Urbana: University of Illinois Press, 1989).

14. Brian Ingrassia, *The Rise of the Gridiron University: Higher Education's Uneasy Alliance with Big-Time Football* (Lawrence: University Press of Kansas, 2012).

15. On the history of football and popular culture, see Oriard, *King Football*; John Sayle Watterson, *College Football* (Baltimore: Johns Hopkins University Press, 2000); Reed Harris, *King Football: The Vulgarization of the American College* (New York: Vanguard Press, 1932);

Michael Oriard, *Reading Football: How the Popular Press Created an American Spectacle* (Chapel Hill: University of North Carolina Press, 1993).

16. In *King Football*, Oriard argues that the power of mass media between 1920 and 1950 resided in their ability to determine which stories were told, what meanings were expressed, and what overarching ideologies circulated about collegiate sport. Limited in its consideration of racialized bodies, particularly African American and Native American bodies, Oriard's work primarily tells stories of the white middle class and its efforts to embrace football.

17. Anthony Giddens offers a useful definition of modernity as a starting point for understanding American modernity. "Modernity" is "a shorthand term for modern society, or industrial civilization. Portrayed in more detail, it is associated with (1) a certain set of attitudes towards the world, the idea of the world as open to transformation, by human intervention; (2) a complex of economic institutions, especially industrial production and a market economy; (3) a certain range of political institutions, including the nation-state and mass democracy." See Anthony Giddens, *The Third Way: The Renewal of Social Democracy* (Cambridge: Polity Press, 1998), 94. On the evils of modernity, see Charles Shindo, *1927 and the Rise of Modern America* (Lawrence: University Press of Kansas, 2010), 93–134. On modernity and its manifestations within the American context that inform this work, see Houston A. Baker Jr., *Modernism and the Harlem Renaissance* (Chicago: University of Chicago Press, 1987); Ray Batchelor, *Henry Ford: Mass Production, Modernism and Design* (Manchester: Manchester University Press, 1994); Nancy F. Cott, *The Grounding of Modern Feminism* (New Haven, Conn.: Yale University Press, 1987); Ellis W. Hawley, *The Great War and the Search for the Modern Order: A History of the American People and Their Institutions, 1917–1933* (Prospect Heights, Ill.: Waveland Press, 1992); T. J. Jackson Lears, *No Place of Grace: Antimodernism and the Transformation of American Culture, 1880–1920* (Chicago: University of Chicago Press, 1994); Roland Marchand, *Advertising the American Dream: Making Way for Modernity, 1920–1940* (Berkeley: University of California Press, 1985); Nathan Miller, *New World Coming: The 1920s and the Making of Modern America* (New York: Scribner, 2003).

18. On the history of American higher education, see John R. Thelin, *A History of American Higher Education* (Baltimore: Johns Hopkins University Press, 2004); Laurence R. Vesey, *The Emergence of the Modern University* (Chicago: University of Chicago Press, 1965); Christopher J. Lucas, *American Higher Education* (New York: St. Martin's Griffin, 1994); Frederick Rudolph, *The American College and University: A History* (1962; repr., Athens: University of Georgia Press, 1990). On the history of higher education, state formation, and the Morrill Land Grant Act, see Allan Nevins, *The Origins of the Land-Grant Colleges and State Universities* (Washington, D.C.: Civil War Centennial Commission, 1962); Coy F. Cross, *Justin Smith Morrill: Father of the Land-Grant Colleges* (East Lansing: Michigan State University Press, 1999); Edward D. Eddy Jr., *Colleges for Our Land and Time: The Land-Grant Idea in American Education* (New York: Harper, 1957); Alan I. Marcus, "'If All the World Were Mechanics and Farmers': American Democracy and the Formative Years of Land-Grant Colleges," *Ohio Valley History* 5, no. 1 (Spring 2005): 23–37.

19. Oriard, *King Football*, 9.

20. Philip J. Deloria, *Indians in Unexpected Places* (Lawrence: University Press of Kansas, 2004), 115.

21. Joseph B. Oxendine, *American Indian Sports Heritage*, 2nd ed. (Lincoln: University of Nebraska Press, 1995), 163.

22. Jeffrey Powers-Beck, *The American Indian Integration of Baseball* (Lincoln: University of Nebraska Press, 2004), 177.

23. On the history of American Indian athletes and athletics, see Oxendine, *American Indian Sports Heritage*; Powers-Beck, *American Indian Integration of Baseball*; John Bloom, *To Show*

What an Indian Can Do: Sports at Native American Boarding Schools (Minneapolis: University of Minnesota Press, 2000); C. Richard King, ed., *Native Athletes in Sport and Society: A Reader* (Lincoln: University of Nebraska Press, 2005); Matthew Sakiestewa Gilbert, "Marathoner Louis Tewanima and the Continuity of Hopi Running, 1908–1912," *Western Historical Quarterly* 43 (Autumn 2012): 324–346; Matthew Sakiestewa Gilbert, "Hopi Footraces and American Marathons, 1912–1930," *American Quarterly* 62, no. 1 (March 2010): 77–101; Matthew Bentley, "The Rise of Athletic Masculinity at the Carlisle Indian School, 1904–1913," *International Journal of the History of Sport* 29, no. 10 (August 2012): 1466–1489; Sally Jenkins, *The Real All Americans: The Team That Changed a Game, a People, a Nation* (New York: Doubleday, 2007); David Wallace Adams, "More Than a Game: The Carlisle Indians Take to the Gridiron, 1893–1917," *Western Historical Quarterly* 32 (Spring 2001): 25–53; Matthew Bentley, "Playing White Men: American Football and Manhood at the Carlisle Indian School, 1893–1904," *Journal of the History of Childhood and Youth* 3, no. 2 (Spring 2010): 187–209; Ray Gamache, "Sport as Cultural Assimilation: Representations of American Indian Athletes in the Carlisle School Newspaper," *American Journalism* 26, no. 2 (Spring 2009): 7–37.

24. On Jim Thorpe, see Kate Buford, *Native American Son: The Life and Sporting Legend of Jim Thorpe* (New York: Knopf, 2010); Jack Newcombe, *The Best of the Athletic Boys: The White Man's Impact on Jim Thorpe* (New York: Doubleday, 1975); Robert W. Wheeler, *Jim Thorpe: World's Greatest Athlete* (Norman: University of Oklahoma Press, 1979); Bill Crawford, *All American: The Rise and Fall of Jim Thorpe* (Hoboken, N.J.: John Wiley & Sons, 2004); Mark Rubinfeld, "The Mythical Jim Thorpe: Re/presenting the Twentieth Century American Indian," *International Journal of the History of Sport* 23, no. 2 (2006): 167–189.

25. Oriard, *Reading Football*, 234–247. On the history of American Indian education and boarding schools, see Brenda J. Child, *Boarding School Seasons: American Indian Families, 1900–1940* (Lincoln: University of Nebraska Press, 1998); David Wallace Adams, *Education for Extinction: American Indians and the Boarding-School Experience, 1875–1928* (Lawrence: University Press of Kansas, 1995); K. Tsianina Lomawaima, *They Called It Prairie Light: The Story of Chilocco Indian School* (Lincoln: University of Nebraska Press, 1995); Jon Reyhner and Jeanne Eder, *American Indian Education: A History* (Norman: University of Oklahoma Press, 2006); Matthew Sakiestewa Gilbert, *Education Beyond the Mesas: Hopi Students at Sherman Institute, 1902–1929* (Lincoln: University of Nebraska Press, 2010); Hayes Peter Mauro, *The Art of Americanization at the Carlisle Indian School* (Albuquerque: University of New Mexico Press, 2011); Clyde Ellis, *To Change Them Forever: Indian Education at the Rainy Mountain Boarding School, 1893–1920* (Norman: University of Oklahoma Press, 2008); Jacqueline Fear-Segal, *White Man's Club: Schools, Race, and the Struggle for Indian Acculturation* (Lincoln: University of Nebraska Press, 2009).

26. Deloria, *Indians in Unexpected Places*, 120.

27. Victoria Paraschak, "Doing Race, Doing Gender: First Nations, 'Sport,' and Gender Relations," in *Sport and Gender in Canada*, ed. Kevin Young and Philip White (Don Mills. Ont.: Oxford University Press, 2007), 137–154.

28. James J. Buss, e-mail message to the author, August 22, 2013.

29. A number of tribally recognized Natives did attend institutions of higher education in the late nineteenth and early twentieth centuries, including at the University of Illinois. Yet the limited nature of these opportunities made their attendance a special occurrence rather than a common experience.

30. To undertake an exploration of physical culture, popular culture, and identity politics, three complementary literatures must be read side by side: critical sport studies, popular culture, and Indian mascotry. Critical sport studies—derived from the famous 1963 work of C. L. R. James's analysis of cricket, *Beyond a Boundary*, and the British School of Cultural

Studies—was embraced in the United States in the early 1990s. Read in opposition to sport studies, which often focused on event-based narratives that served more to document the game than critique its meaning, critical sports studies owes much of its rise to the postmodern theoretical school. Postmodern theorists, including Martin Heidigger, Jacques Derrida, Michel Foucault, Jean François Lyotard, and Jean Baudrillard, created the opportunity to read sport not as a simple event but as a text that could reveal the ways in which particular individuals, institutions, and societies constituted notions of race, identity, power, gender, and nation. For more on the history of colonialism and sport, see C. L. R. James, *Beyond a Boundary* (Durham, N.C.: Duke University Press, 1993). For a complete discussion of the evolution of the historical profession and its ties to various theoretical philosophies, see Peter Novick, *The Noble Dream: The "Objectivity" Question and the American Historical Profession* (New York: Cambridge University Press, 1988). For an exploration of sport history as postmodern, see Murray G. Phillips, ed., *Deconstructing Sport History: A Postmodern Analysis* (Albany: State University Press of New York, 2006), 16.

31. For an extensive discussion of the theories of cosmopolitanism, see Gerard Delanty, "The Cosmopolitan Imagination: Critical Cosmopolitanism and Social Theory," *British Journal of Sociology* 57 (1): 25–47. I argue for cultural cosmopolitanism as it specifically seeks to address the relations between individual and institutional identities within a specific historical expression. Minstrelsy, a form of cultural entertainment composed of skits, vaudeville acts, songs, and dancing, was often performed by whites in blackface prior to the Civil War. Postwar, often African Americans performed in blackface while whites expanded their performances to include performing in redface (Indian-themed) and yellow-face (Chinese- or Asian-themed). For more on minstrelsy and blackface specifically, see Dan Cockrell, *Demons of Disorder: Early Blackface Minstrels and Their World* (New York: Cambridge University Press, 1997); Eric Lott, *Love and Theft: Blackface Minstrelsy and the American Working Class* (New York: Oxford University Press, 1993); Hans Nathan, *Dan Emmett and the Rise of Early Negro Minstrelsy* (Norman: University of Oklahoma Press, 1962); Howard L. Sacks and Judith Sacks, *Way Up North in Dixie: A Black Family's Claim to the Confederate Anthem* (Washington, D.C.: Smithsonian Institution Press, 1993); Karen Sotiropoulos, *Staging Race: Black Performers in Turn of the Century America* (Cambridge, Mass.: Harvard University Press, 2006); Robert C. Toll, *Blacking Up: The Minstrel Show in Nineteenth-Century America* (New York: Oxford University Press, 1974).

32. An uneasy brand of cosmopolitanism marked by continual performances of belonging that were dependant on the continual enforcement of boundaries between "us" and "them," this mapping built the quintessential "modern" man and "modern" institution simultaneously. For more on modernity and cosmopolitanism, see Gerard Delanty, *Modernity and Postmodernity: Knowledge, Power, and the Self* (New York: Sage, 2000); Significantly, Delanty points out that modernity is not a product of Westernization but rather is present in societies and cultures as a series of processes and interactions. For a discussion of modernity within the Native context, see Joel Pfister, *Individuality Incorporated: Indians and the Multicultural Modern* (Durham, N.C.: Duke University Press, 2004).

33. Daniel J. Boorstin, *The Image: A Guide to Pseudo-Events in America* (New York: Vintage, 1992). Boorstin's use of commodity fetishism is based on the work of Theodor Adorno, *Negative Dialectics*, trans. E. B. Ashton (New York: Routledge, 1990).

34. Jean Baudrillard, *Simulations*, trans. Paul Foss, Paul Patton, and Philip Beitchman (London: Semiotext[e] Press, 1983), 95. See also Stuart Hall, *Representation: Cultural Representations and Signifying Practices* (New York: Sage and Open University, 1997); Jean Baudrillard, *Simulacra and Simulations*, trans. Sheila Faria Glaser (Ann Arbor: University of Michigan Press, 1995).

35. Guy Debord posited in his 1994 work, *The Society of the Spectacle*, that spectacle "is not a collection of images; rather, it is a social relationship between people that is mediated by images." See Guy Debord, *The Society of the Spectacle* (New York: Zone Books, 1999), 12. A Marxist study of television as spectacle, Debord's theorization of spectacle has particular importance with the cosmopolitan world of mascot production. Higher education situated collegiate sport as a site of spectacle in order to convey what its constituent community needed to have: young, white, male athletic bodies engaged with its national projects. Richard Schechner offers a parallel, but more complex, understanding of space and spectacle. He argues that "a theater is a place whose only or main use is to stage or enact performances." Fundamentally cultural, these spaces were transformed in places of gathering, performing, and dispersing that is particularly theatrical in nature. In underscoring both the demarcation of space into place through performance and the pattern of community activity, Schechner provides a useful construct for considering the layering of spectacle. See Richard Schechner, *Performance Studies: An Introduction*, 2nd ed. (New York: Routledge, 2006).

36. Jacques Derrida, *Différance*, in *Identity: A Reader*, ed. Paul du Gay, Jessica Evans, and Peter Redman (New York: Sage, 2001), 89.

37. Philip J. Deloria, *Playing Indian* (New Haven, Conn.: Yale University Press, 1988), 184. In concentrating on the physical performance of Indianness, Deloria positions physical "play" as an organizing concept of his exploration. Despite that recognition of the physical body as a vital element in the performance of Indianness, he neglects to explore sport (and particularly college sport) as a venue of cultural production. His 2006 monograph, *Indians in Unexpected Places*, recognized athletics as a venue of cultural production through his ethnography of his grandfather's experiences as an Indian athlete. In capturing Indian athletes "playing" Indian, Deloria challenged the notion that Indians could not appropriate various Indian identities for their own purposes. See also Deloria, *Indians in Unexpected Places*, 109–135.

38. See Carol Spindel, *Dancing at Halftime: Sports and the Controversy over Native American Mascots* (New York: New York University Press, 2000); C. Richard King and Charles Freuhling Springwood, eds., *Team Spirits: The Native American Mascot Controversy* (Lincoln: University of Nebraska Press, 2001). Spindel traces her journey to understand her place within the University of Illinois community. Devoted to placing the first-person narrative in the forefront, Spindel argues that contemporary discussions of the sports mascots issue rely on historical tropes that marginalize Native American individuals. Spindel rightly reads these images as part of a larger focus within popular culture in the period from 1880 to 1920. The difficulty with *Dancing at Halftime* lies in its rendering of Native American images as unchanging and the motivations of the individuals who are constructing them as uncomplicated. The author glosses over the complexities of these representations, their continued post-1920s production, and their dissemination, and largely fails to capture these images as part of a transnational dialogue on collegiate sport. King and Springwood's compendium *Team Spirits* offers a contemporary positioning of Native American sports mascots as framed through the popular political context of late twentieth-century America. The collection as a whole reveals the importance of invented traditions, the construction of white identity in America, and modern activism within the Native American sports mascot experience. Yet, like Spindel's framework, the lack of comprehensive research that moves beyond the case-study approach necessitates further interrogation of the historical contextualization and development of analyses of mascots attentive to but not dominated by present political concerns.

39. For a complete listing of the historiography of Indian mascotry, consult the bibliography.

CHAPTER 1   KING FOOTBALL AND GAME-DAY SPECTACLE

1. On the role of colleges and communities, see Thomas Bender, *Intellect and Public Life: Essays on the Social History of Academic Intellectuals in the United States* (Baltimore: Johns Hopkins Press, 1993), 3–46.

2. On the Ivy League origins of college football, see Mark F. Bernstein, *Football: The Ivy League Origins of an American Obsession* (Philadelphia: University of Pennsylvania Press, 2001).

3. Oriard, *Reading Football*, 26. On the history of sport and higher education, see Rudolph, *American College and University*, 373–393; Ronald A. Smith, *Sports and Freedom: The Rise of Big-Time Intercollegiate Athletics* (New York: Oxford University Press, 1988). On college football specifically, see Watterson, *College Football*; John M. Carroll, *Red Grange and the Rise of Modern Football* (Urbana: University of Illinois Press, 1999); Robin Lester, *Stagg's University: The Rise, Decline, and Fall of Big-Time Football at Chicago* (Urbana: University of Illinois Press, 1995).

4. Harvard drew its rules from rugby, which it had played against McGill University of Montreal in 1874. On the origins of Harvard football, see Watterson, *College Football*, 18–19. On the history of Harvard University football and its rivalry with Yale, see Bernard M. Corbett and Paul Simpson, *The Only Game That Matters: The Harvard/Yale Rivalry* (New York: Crown, 2004).

5. It was not until 1876 that a subgroup of these schools came together to create a uniform set of rules under the auspices of the Intercollegiate Football Association. On the role of associations in American society, see Trachtenberg, *Incorporation of America*.

6. On Walter Camp and his role in transforming the game of football, see Oriard, *Reading Football*, 40–56.

7. Watterson, *College Football*, 19. On the rules of football throughout the late nineteenth century, see Walter Camp, *American Football* (New York: Harper & Brothers, 1891); Amos Alonzo Stagg and Henry L. Williams, *A Scientific and Practical Treatise on American Football for Schools and Colleges* (Hartford, Conn.: Press of the Case, Lockwood, & Brainard, 1893); Walter Camp and Lorin F. Daniel, *Football* (New York: Riverside Press, 1896).

8. John Pettigrew, *Brutes in Suites: Male Sensibility in America, 1890–1920* (Baltimore: Johns Hopkins University Press, 2007), 135–136.

9. Watterson, *College Football*, 21.

10. Ibid., 1.

11. Ibid., 24.

12. Orrin Leslie Elliott, *Stanford University: The First Twenty-Five Years* (Stanford, Calif.: Stanford University Press, 1937), 234–235; see also Watterson, *College Football*, 93–98.

13. Watterson, *College Football*, 147. On Frank Angell specifically, see Elliott, *Stanford University*, 223–242.

14. Watterson, *College Football*, 148.

15. Edith R. Mirrielees, *Stanford: The Story of a University* (New York: G. P. Putnam's Sons, 1959), 146. On David Starr Jordan, see Edward McNall Burns, *David Starr Jordan: Prophet of Democracy* (Palo Alto, Calif.: Stanford University Press, 1953); Kevin Starr, *Americans and the California Dream, 1850–1915* (New York: Oxford University Press, 1973), 307–344.

16. "To Offset English Football in West," *New York Times*, March 11, 1909.

17. Watterson, *College Football*, 84. On the 1905 crisis and attempts to institute reform, see John S. Watterson, "The Gridiron Crisis of 1905: Was It Really a Crisis?" *Journal of Sport History* 27, no. 2 (Summer 2000): 291–298.

18. The critique of college football and its relationship to student athletes will sound familiar to many who follow contemporary debates on the role of athletics in higher education.

On the role of sport and its relationship to higher education, see Murray Sperber, *Beer and Circus: How Big-Time College Sport Is Crippling Undergraduate Education* (New York: Henry Holt, 2000); Andrew Zimbalist, *Unpaid Professionals* (Princeton, N.J.: Princeton University Press, 2010); Charles T. Clotfelter, *Big-Time Sports in American Universities* (Cambridge: Cambridge University Press, 2011); Ingrassia, *Rise of the Gridiron University*. On the history of athletic reform, see Ronald A. Smith, *Pay for Play: A History of Big-Time College Athletic Reform* (Urbana: University of Illinois Press, 2010).

19. Watterson, *College Football*, 86. On the myth of the frontier and American expansion, see Richard Slotkin, *The Fatal Environment: The Myth of the Frontier in the Age of Industrialization, 1800–1890* (New York: Macmillan, 1985); Richard Slotkin, *Gunfighter Nation: Myth of the Frontier in Twentieth-Century America* (Norman: University of Oklahoma Press, 1998). On Turner's frontier thesis, see Frederick Jackson Turner, "Significance of the Frontier in American History," in *The Frontier in American History* (1920; repr., New York: Dover, 1996), 1–38. On a more contemporary assessment of Turner's frontier thesis, see John Mack Faragher, *Rereading Frederick Jackson Turner: The Significance of the Frontier in American History and Other Essays* (New York: Henry Holt, 1994).

20. The Big Nine refers to the following schools in 1906: University of Illinois, Indiana University, University of Iowa, University of Michigan, University of Minnesota, Northwestern University, Purdue University, University of Wisconsin, and University of Chicago.

21. Watterson, *College Football*, 88; Minutes of the First Chicago Conference, January 19, 1906, Michigan Historical Collections, Ann Arbor.

22. Intercollegiate Athletic Association of the United States, *Proceedings of the First Annual Meeting Held at New York City, New York December 29, 1905* [New York: Intercollegiate Athletic Association of the United States, 1906], in Paul Stagg, "The Development of the National Collegiate Athletics Association in Relationship to Intercollegiate Athletics in the United States" (Ph.D. diss., New York University, 1946), 23. See also Watterson, *College Football*, 68–79; Smith, *Pay for Play*, 42–51.

23. Oriard, *King Football*, 3.

24. Watterson, *College Football*, 2.

25. Ibid., 3; "War Football," *New York Times*, November 23, 1919. On physical culture and war prior to the twentieth century, see Russell L. Johnson, *Warriors into Workers: The Civil War and the Formation of the Urban-Industrial Society in a Northern City* (New York: Fordham University Press, 2003), 169–171, 222–224.

26. Watterson, *College Football*, 143.

27. *Historical Statistics of the United* States, 210, in Oriard, *King Football*, 6.

28. Jesse Frederick Steiner, *Americans at Play* (1933; repr., New York: Arno Press and the New York Times, 1970), 88–90; see also Oriard, *King Football*, 7.

29. "9,796 Students—Why Are They Here?" *Daily Illini*, May 11, 1927.

30. David O. Levine, *American College and the Culture of Aspiration, 1915–1940* (Ithaca, N.Y.: Cornell University Press, 1986), 117. It is significant that although there is a rise in collegiate enrollment, there is also a parallel shift in the case of the University of Illinois away from students with farming backgrounds. "The proportion of children of businessmen, scientific professionals, government workers, and skilled laborers increased." Ibid., 131.

31. Oriard, *King Football*, 1; see also Harris, *King Football*.

32. Harris, *King Football*, 17.

33. Ibid.

34. The sense of alienation and disillusionment expressed by Harris along with other supposed verbal and written "attacks" on Columbia University's administration led to his

expulsion and an intervention by the American Civil Liberties Union (ACLU) to get him reinstated. While Harris's removal from the university is one extreme case, hundreds of other Americans were questioning the role that football played at colleges and universities across America.

35. Watterson, *College Football*, 146. On Notre Dame football, see Murray Sperber, *Shake Down the Thunder: The Creation of Notre Dame Football* (New York: Henry Holt, 1993).

36. Watterson, *College Football*, 146.

37. "Two Towns Bet $100,000 Upon 'Ringer' Game: Rivals Sought Aid of College Stars," *Chicago Daily Tribune*, January 29, 1922; "Citizens Stack Results with College Players," *Daily Illini*, January 29, 1922.

38. "How the Players Arrived," *Chicago Daily Tribune*, January 29, 1922.

39. Watterson, *College Football*, 152.

40. "Taylorville Backer Airs Big Ten Charges," *Chicago Daily Tribune*, February 2, 1922.

41. Harris, *King Football*, 139.

42. Ibid.

43. "All Time Trustee List," American Football Coaches Association, http://www.afca.com/ViewArticle.dbml?DB_OEM_ID=9300&KEY=&ATCLID=639366.

44. Watterson, *College Football*, 146.

45. Steven W. Pope, *Patriotic Games: Sporting Traditions in the American Imagination, 1876–1926* (New York: Oxford University Press, 1997), 157.

46. John Tunis, "The Great God Football," *Harper's* 157 (1928), 741.

47. Ibid., 742.

48. Ibid., 744.

49. Ibid., 741–742.

50. Ibid., 745.

51. Tunis romanticizes the early days when football was supposedly simple and did not involve fund-raising, boosters, and complicated pageantry. Calling football a "first-class octopus" that smothered the university before it was aware of its existence, Tunis overlooks the complicit nature of the university in originating modern football in exponentially expanding teams, adopting bands and cheerleaders, and paying coaches to establish first-class programs all prior to the "modern era" of football. The simple game that Tunis desired to celebrate lasted only briefly after 1876. More significant, Tunis's octopus, which he thought had devoured the educational mission of the university, was already fully grown by World War I.

52. Tunis, "Great God Football," 746.

53. Ibid., 747.

54. On the roots of the Progressive era, see Paul Boyer, *Urban Masses and Moral Order in America, 1820–1920* (Cambridge, Mass.: Harvard University Press, 1978); Robert M. Crunden, *Ministers of Reform: The Progressives' Achievement in American Civilization, 1889–1920* (1982; repr., Urbana: University of Illinois Press, 1984); Richard F. Hofstader, *The Age of Reform: From Bryan to F.D.R.* (1955; repr., New York: Vintage Press, 1960). On Progressivism more generally, see Wiebe, *Search for Order*, 164–195; Shelton Stromquist, *Reinventing the "People": The Progressive Movement, the Class Problem, and the Origins of Modern Liberalism* (Urbana: University of Illinois Press, 2006). On Progressive era reform and football specifically, see Ingrassia, *Rise of the Gridiron University*, 40–70.

55. Tunis, "Great God Football," 746.

56. Carroll, *Red Grange*, 43. On Red Grange and his role in college football, see Red Grange and Ira Morton, *The Red Grange Story: An Autobiography Told to Ira Morton* (Urbana: University of Illinois Press, 1993).

57. Carroll, *Red Grange*, 4.

58. Watterson, *College Football*, 152–155.

59. The tension between college and professional football was a hallmark of the 1920s. Structurally, despite the published concerns of the college associations, the college and professional games shared the same ills. On the contrast between collegiate and professional football, see Oriard, *King Football*, 200–201, 204, 206–208, 213–216. On the rise of professional football, see Robert W. Peterson, *Pigskin: The Early Years of Pro Football* (Oxford: Oxford University Press, 1996).

60. Ingrassia, *Rise of the Gridiron University*, 139. On the development of stadiums, see Raymond Schmidt, *Shaping College Football: The Transformation of an American Sport, 1919–1930* (Syracuse, N.Y.: Syracuse University Press, 2007), 39–61; Watterson, *College Football*, 143–157; Oriard, *King Football*, 6–7; Robert M. Soderstrom, *The Big House: Fielding H. Yost and the Building of Michigan Stadium* (Ann Arbor, Mich.: Huron River Press, 2005). On the technology of reinforced concrete, see Frederick W. Taylor and Sanford E. Thompson, *A Treatise on Concrete Plain and Reinforced: Materials, Construction, and Design of Concrete and Reinforced Concrete* (New York: John Wiley, 1905).

61. *The Story of the Stadium*, Stadium Drive Publications, University of Illinois, University of Illinois Archives.

62. Ibid. Note the remark as an example of how colonizers discounted indigenous history because it did not come to them in neatly bound books. Instead, the oral traditions and material histories of tribes were perceived as nonintellectual.

63. Raphaelson's role here becomes all the more intriguing given that he had just returned from a hiatus where he had composed "The Day of Atonement," a short story of the relationship between a Jewish cantor and his son, inspired by Al Jolson, whom Raphaelson had seen perform. "The Day of Atonement" was transformed into a Broadway play and then the screenplay for the 1927 film *The Jazz Singer*. On Samson Raphaelson, see Neal Gabler, *An Empire of Their Own: How Jews Invented Hollywood* (New York: Crown, 1988).

64. Robert S. Sampson, "Red Illini: Dorothy Day, Samson Raphaelson, and Rayna Simons at the University of Illinois, 1914–1916," *Journal of Illinois History* 5, no. 3 (Autumn 2002): 189.

65. Clarence Welsh, *University of Illinois Memorial Stadium*, Stadium Drive Publications, University of Illinois, University of Illinois Archives.

66. Ibid.

67. "Stadium Mass Meet Explains Expected Duties," *Daily Illini*, April 1, 1921, 1.

68. *Story of the Stadium*.

69. On the pivotal decade of the 1920s in football, see Raymond Schmidt, *Shaping College Football: The Transformation of an American Sport, 1919–1930* (Syracuse, N.Y.: Syracuse University Press, 2007).

70. Harris, *King Football*, 164; "Football: Mid-Season," *Time*, November 17, 1930.

71. "Football: Mid-Season."

72. Ibid.

73. Ibid.

CHAPTER 2   AN INDIAN VERSUS A COLONIAL LEGEND

1. While Leutwiler's initiative in taking to the field has been well documented by scholars and the University of Illinois alike, the role of the UPenn figure "Benjamin Franklin" or, alternately in Illinois narratives, "William Penn," has received little attention. On the history of the University of Illinois mascot, see Spindel, *Dancing at Halftime*; King and Springwood, *Team Spirits*; Brenda Farnell, "The Fancy Dance of Racializing Discourse," *Journal of Sport and Social Issues* 28, no. 1 (2004): 30.

2. Carol Spindel, Personal Papers, in author's possession (hereafter cited as Spindel Papers).

3. Spindel, *Dancing at Halftime*, 81.

4. Yale University claims itself as the first college in the United States to have a mascot for its athletic teams with the purchase of a bulldog in 1889 named Handsome Dan. In fact, the UPenn football team posed in 1895 with a live dog, and other football teams quickly began to appropriate animals as mascots. On mascots and nicknames, see Roy E. Yarbaugh, *Mascots: The History of Senior College and University Mascots Nicknames* (Philadelphia: Bluff University Communications, 1998); Cullen Vane, *College Nicknames: The Ultimate Guide* (San Jose, Calif.: Strike Three, 2011); Peter J. Fornier, *The Handbook of Mascots and Nicknames* (Leesburg, Fla.: Raja Associates, 2003); Mark T. Jenkins, *Nickname Mania: The Best of College Nicknames and Mascots and the Stories Behind Them* (Omaha, Neb.: Admark Communications, 1997).

5. Princeton University claims that John Orangeman was constructed as a representation of John Harvard, the founding father of Harvard University. It is unclear whether this assertion is true given the lack of evidence available. On the history of Princeton University, see Don Oberdorfer, *Princeton University* (Princeton, N.J.: Princeton University Press, 1995); James Axtell, *The Making of Princeton University: From Woodrow Wilson to the Present* (Princeton, N.J.: Princeton University Press, 2006).

6. Patricia H. Rodgers, Charles Sullivan, and the Cambridge Historical Commission, *A Photographic History of Cambridge* (Cambridge, Mass.: MIT Press, 1984), quoted in American Landscape and Architectural Design, 1850–1920, Library of Congress, American Memory, http://memory.loc.gov/ammem/award97/mhsdhtml/harvardbldgs.html#hbft4.

7. "John the Orangeman Dead," *New York Times*, August 13, 1906, 7.

8. Henry Fielding, *The Story of John the Orange-man: Being a Short Sketch of the Life of Harvard's Popular Mascot* (Cambridge, Mass.: John Wilson and Son–University Press, 1891), 33.

9. Ibid., 34–35. Lovett's attendance, while generating enthusiasm and support for Harvard, was not a constructed spectacle of racialized performance per se. Instead, it would be more appropriate to consider Lovett a preferred fan or cheerleader versus a mascot. However, his engagement with the spectacle surrounding football demonstrates the ways men of the community aligned themselves with football spectacle.

10. Bruce A. Kimball, "The Langdell Problem: Historicizing the Century of Historiography, 1906–2000s," *Law and History Review* 22, no. 2 (Summer 2004), http://www.history cooperative.org/journals/lhr/22.2/kimball.html; Samuel Batchelder, "Wanted!—College Characters," in *Bits of Harvard History* (Cambridge, Mass.: Harvard University Press, 1924), 262, 287–288, 296.

11. The "Orangeman" who was integrated into the grandstand had to be white because to allow a nonwhite access to the enclave of the grandstand would be to denigrate the whiteness of Harvard University and its fans. On whiteness and the Irish, see Noel Ignatiev, *How the Irish Became White* (New York: Routledge Press, 1996); David R. Roediger, *The Wages of Whiteness: Race and the Making of the American Working Class* (New York: Verso Books, 1991).

12. I would like to thank Adrian Burgos for his suggestions regarding the conceptualization of Lovett's status.

13. Max Weber, P. R. Baehr, and G. C. Wells, *The Protestant Ethic and the "Spirit" of Capitalism* (New York: Penguin Classics, 2002.)

14. Adrian Burgos Jr., *Playing America's Game: Baseball, Latinos, and the Color Line* (Berkeley: University of California Press, 2007), 59. Importantly, the division lines between collegiate sport and professional sport were extremely blurred during the post–Civil War period. Many professional athletes participated simultaneously in collegiate sport and vice versa. Further, the coaches, teams, and traveling sport circuits often converged. See also *The Sporting News*, November 4, 1893, quoted in ibid., 61.

15. *The Sporting News*, August 25, 1888, quoted in ibid., 61.

16. Peter Levine, *A. G. Spalding and the Rise of Baseball: The Promise of American Sport* (New York: Oxford University Press, 1985), 101–102. Duval was included on the tour in spite of protest by Anson. The historical record is obviously silent on Duval's feelings about the performance, yet it would be hard to imagine a lack of a sense of exploitation on his part. See also Jerry Malloy, "Out at Home," in *The National Pastime*, ed. John Thorn (New York: Warner Books, 1987), 24.

17. Levine, *A. G. Spalding*, 104.

18. Jeffrey Powers-Beck, "Chief: The American Indian Integration of Baseball, 1897–1945," *American Indian Quarterly* 25, no. 4 (2001): 508.

19. Ibid.

20. Ellen J. Staurowsky, "An Act of Honor or Exploitation? The Cleveland Indians' Use of the Louis Francis Sockalexis Story," *Sociology of Sport Journal* 15 (1998): 305.

21. "Indian Students Not Dying," *New York Times*, January 5, 1890, 3; "Suicide Was 105 Years Old," *New York Times*, January 8, 1900, 5. James Carey, a prominent communications theorist, has explored the role of newspapers as performance. He argues that newspapers are not "information acquisition, though such acquisition occurs, but of dramatic action in which the reader joins a world of contending forces as an observer at play." I consider the production and consumption of newspapers, as Carey does, a performance of identity and frameworks of meaning. On newspapers as communication, see James Carey, *Communication as Culture: Essays on Media and Society* (New York: Routledge, 1992).

22. Lester Leutwiler, "Chief Illiniwek Tradition," 1974, in Spindel Papers.

23. David I. MacLeod, *Building Character in the American Boy: The Boy Scouts, the YMCA, and Their Forerunners* (Madison: University of Wisconsin Press, 1983), 3–4.

24. Not surprisingly, the BSA began in the United States in 1910 under the auspices of leaders in the YMCA, who worked to further imperial projects at home and abroad. Conjoined, the YMCA and the BSA joined narratives of economic production, namely labor and markets, with governance to produce and encourage citizens who could compete alongside older European nations. As a result, the perceived barbarianism of foreigners at home and abroad reinforced the virtuous "civilized" white American. On nativism and American imperialism through cultural belonging, see Matthew Frye Jacobson, *Barbarian Virtues: The United States Encounters Foreign Peoples at Home and Abroad, 1876–1917* (New York: Hill and Wang, 2000).

25. Emily Mieras, "Tales from the Other Side of the Bridge: YMCA Manhood, Social Class, and Social Reform in Turn-of-the-Century Philadelphia," *Gender & History* 17, no. 2 (2005): 409–440.

26. Thomas Winter, *Making Men, Making Class: The YMCA and Workingmen, 1877–1920* (Chicago: University of Chicago Press, 2002).

27. MacLeod, *Building Character*, 146. Importantly, the roots of the BSA lay in elite efforts to control middle-class youth. Chicago publisher William Bryce recruited Edgar Robinson, senior secretary of the YMCA Committee on Boys' Work; Ernest Thompson Seton, founder of the Woodcraft Indians; and Dan Beard, founder of the Sons of Daniel Boone, to oversee the formation of the first American chapter. Boyce sought a congressional charter, which would have clearly spelled out the ties of American citizenship to social educational programs for boys. While Boyce ultimately failed to secure the charter, he was able to recognize the usefulness of YMCA organizers and resources for the nascent organization.

28. Ibid., 147.

29. Ibid., 149.

30. Ibid., 130.

31. Brian Morris, "Ernest Thompson Seton and the Origins of the Woodcraft Movement," *Journal of Contemporary History* 5, no. 2 (1970): 187.

32. MacLeod, *Building Character*, 131.

33. Morris, "Ernest Thompson Seton," 185.

34. MacLeod, *Building Character*, 131.

35. Ibid., 132.

36. Ibid.

37. E. S. Martin, "A Double-Barrelled Social Agency: The Boy Scouts of America," *Social Forces* 4 (September 1925): 94–97.

38. Ann Leutwiler-Brandenberg, communication with Carol Spindel, n.d., in Spindel Papers.

39. Like any other Harvard student, Elbert Hubbard almost certainly was aware of Lovett and his role as a fan.

40. Nellie Snyder Yost, *A Man as Big as the West* (Boulder, Colo: Pruitt, 1979), 19.

41. Ibid., 59–60.

42. Ibid., 35.

43. Ibid., 61.

44. Ibid., 66. Hubbard's introduction to the American West reads as a cautionary tale. During their first night at the boardinghouse, Hubbard was awakened by the landlady who called them to the window to see a shooting at the saloon across the street. He was "wildly excited by it all."

45. Ibid., 71.

46. Ibid., 35.

47. Ibid., 106. Hubbard's emotional affinity for Indian dance suggested a level of lifelong dedication that was undoubtedly genuine. Yet Hubbard fails to understand the nuance and contextualization associated with these dances. In altering the gestures, the meaning of the performance changes. Many dances are highly ritualized, and to shift the sequence of the performance or the slightest gesture can suggest an entirely different series of meanings.

48. Ibid., 107.

49. Ibid., 109. The ways in which Leutwiler, Hubbard, and others participated in international travel and/or the consumption of international commodities (including news stories, novels, and travelogues) contributed to the anxiety of modern life where it seemed as if all corners of the world were closely intertwined. American fascination with the global shaped local expressions of identity. The purchase and display of exotic goods from Asia, of couture from Paris, and of global commodities allowed men and women to illustrate a particular brand of cultural knowledge that allowed the exotic to affirm class and race. In the same way, having young boys familiarize themselves with the global, through travel and knowledge consumption, allowed for the affirmation of American ascendancy where white men and women were both the product of and driving force behind the nation. On the American fascination with global and transnational culture, see Kristin Hoganson, *Consumers' Imperium: The Global Production of American Domesticity, 1865–1920* (Chapel Hill: University of North Carolina Press, 2007); Thomas Bender, *A Nation among Nations: America's Place in World History* (New York: Hill and Wang, 2006).

50. Yost, *Man as Big as the West*, 114.

51. Ibid., 116–117.

52. Ibid., 119.

53. Ibid., 118. The actions and programs these Indian boys experienced remain unexplored. Were they willing participants or merely curiosities?

54. Ibid., 119.

55. Richard White, *The Middle Ground: Indians, Empires, and Republics in the Great Lakes Region, 1650–1815* (New York: Cambridge University Press, 1991), 22. "Catlinite" refers to the stone material from which the pipe was constructed. These pipes took a variety of shapes and were not necessarily associated with political or social rituals. "Calumet" refers to the highly

decorated stem that graced the pipe. For a thorough discussion of the variety of pipes and the nuances of the calumet ceremony, see Ian W. Brown, "The Calumet Ceremony in the Southeast and Its Archeological Manifestations," *American Antiquity* 54, no. 2 (April 1989): 311–331.

56. Reuben Gold Thwaites, ed., *Father Louis Hennepin's A New Discovery of a Vast Country in America* (facsimile ed., Toronto: Coles, 1974 reprint of 1903 ed.), 125, quoted in White, *Middle Ground*, 21.

57. Focusing on Chief Illiniwek as a sports mascot has eroded the larger cultural context of performances of historical revision and memory that were being undertaken in local and national venues, including Urbana High School. Leutwiler's adoption of the Chief Illiniwek persona was not a response to inquiries by the UPenn band who hoped to utilize their articulated personae of "Benjamin Franklin" during a halftime skit as other scholars have suggested. Leutwiler adopted an untitled persona two years earlier that formed the basis for the chief during experiences as a Boy Scout and for performances at his alma mater, Urbana High School. On the origins of Leutwiler's performance at Urbana, see Leutwiler-Brandenberg, communication with Carol Spindel.

58. On the history of the University of Pennsylvania, see George E. Thomas and David B. Brownlee, *Building America's First University: An Historical and Architectural Guide to the University of Pennsylvania* (Philadelphia: University of Pennsylvania Press, 2000).

59. The mascot "Benjamin Franklin" was immediately replaced in Illinois narratives both contemporarily by Leutwiler and the student paper in favor of the mascot "William Penn." Scholars have continued this misidentification and, in doing so, have missed the suggestive nature of the replacement of Benjamin Franklin with William Penn. By 1900, William Penn was being used on university memorabilia and in campus promotional literatures at the University of Pennsylvania, yet at the same moment, Benjamin Franklin was appearing at sporting matches as the university mascot. The conjoined representations of William Penn, as the colonial founder, and Benjamin Franklin, as the University of Pennsylvania founder, suggest an elaborately constructed convergence where UPenn legitimated its existence through historical genealogies of founding and state formation. The first encounter between the chief portrayed by Leutwiler and the UPenn mascot demonstrated an immediate act of revision, where Benjamin Franklin as the mascot was immediately read as William Penn. Why did Illinois band members, including Leutwiler, alter the embodied persona? Further, did that alteration shift the meaning of the performance? I argue here that the substitution continued a long-term practice of eliding the historical consequences of colonial conquest. On the history of conquest in Pennsylvania, see James H. Merrell, *Into the American Woods: Negotiators on the Pennsylvania Frontier* (New York: Norton, 2000).

60. James O'Neil Spady, "Colonialism and the Discursive Antecedents of *Penn's Treaty with the Indians*," in *Friends and Enemies in Penn's Woods: Indians, Colonists, and the Racial Construction of Pennsylvania*, ed. William A. Pencak and Daniel K. Richter (University Park: Pennsylvania State University Press, 2004), 19. See also Francis Jennings, "Thomas Penn's Oath," *American Journal of Legal History* 8, no. 4 (October 1964): 303–313.

61. Spady, "Colonialism," 18.

62. Ibid., 19.

63. Shari M. Huhndorf, *Going Native: Indians in the American Cultural Imagination* (Ithaca, N.Y.: Cornell University Press, 2001), 11.

64. Leutwiler, "Chief Illiniwek Tradition."

65. These performances are, in Baudrillard's terminology, "reality, image, echo, appearance." See Baudrillard, *Simulations*, 95. See also Hall, *Representation*; Baudrillard, *Simulacra and Simulations*.

CHAPTER 3   AND THE BAND PLAYED NARRATIVES
OF AMERICAN EXPANSION

1. The tension between the educational aspects of the University of Illinois band and its theatrical performances at halftime performance created a peculiar notion of ownership by band
members of the Chief Illiniwek persona. It is important to note here that there seems to be a shift
in the perceived role of the band by the broader university community in the mid-twentieth
century from an educational organization to an entertainment purveyor.

2. Leutwiler-Brandenberg, communication with Carol Spindel.

3. Who selected the music for Leutwiler's first University of Illinois performance? Was it
Raymond Dvorak, the assistant band director who taught Leutwiler at Urbana High School?
Was it the bandleader, Albert Austin Harding, who controlled the band's musical repertoire? Or
was it Leutwiler himself? While the historical record remains silent, it is quite possible to con-
clude that each or all of the three could have been involved in the selection of the three pieces.

4. The Paris High School Football Team was not affiliated with the Paris, Illinois, high school.
Instead, the designation "High School" connotes that the athletes are older adolescents and
young men from the local area.

5. Cary Clive Burford, *We're Loyal to You, Illinois: The Story of the University of Illinois Bands
under Albert Austin Harding for 43 Years, Superimposed upon Glimpses of University History during the Half-Century of Harding Leadership on Campus* (Danville, Ill.: Interstate, 1952), 66–77.
For an in-depth examination of the early University of Illinois bands, see Peter James Griffin,
"A History of the Illinois Industrial University/University of Illinois Band, 1867–1908" (Ph.D.
diss., University of Illinois at Urbana-Champaign, 2004).

6. Jerry Thomas Haynie, "The Changing Role of the Band in American Colleges and
Universities, 1900–1968" (Ph.D. diss., George Peabody College for Teachers of Vanderbilt
University, 1971), 232.

7. The role of "the March King," John Philip Sousa, a mentor and personal friend of Albert
Austin Harding and the University of Illinois band, and his influence on university bands have
been chronicled in depth by the University of Illinois, which maintains the Sousa Archives: A
Center for American Music. The archive contains exhaustive primary and secondary materials on Sousa and his career. Most recently, Paul Edmund Bierley's *The Incredible Band of John
Philip Sousa* (Urbana: University of Illinois Press, 2006) captures eloquently the dimensions
of Sousa's musical and personal life through oral history, archival research, and compositional
analysis. It would be tantalizing to say that the mode of the sports themselves may suggest
some of the division: football as a rigid, formulaic undertaking with disciplined athletes
marking yardage down the field versus baseball, with its exciting plays and dramatic home
runs. Yet it is more likely that baseball was more familiar to fans. Football was still a relatively
young sport and was not imbued with the same social rituals as baseball with its barnstorming leagues, which created carnival-like atmospheres where residents could gather to watch
touring teams and local players. Football was just beginning to transform itself from its rural-
Ohio factory team beginnings into a dominant national sport at a moment when baseball was
solidifying its importance in the national ethos. Importantly, while football would follow the
developmental pattern of baseball, at the turn of the twentieth century baseball dominated
as the "national pastime." As a result, when considering the articulations of race outlined
throughout this book, it is important to consider baseball and football as conjoined sites of
representation. Baseball and football teams often shared the same field and the same athletes
well into the twentieth century.

8. Haynie, "Changing Role of the Band," 232.

9. Ibid. The Purdue band was reported to have formed the letter "P" in 1907, while the
University of Illinois is able to formally document the formation of the letter "I" in November

1909 without the use of pistol shots, whistles, or any other signal from the drum major. This integration directly suggests the limited meaning of football competition in the opening decade of the twentieth century: football was an opportunity for honorable competition between matched foes. Honoring the opposition with tribute lettering alleviated the tense nature of the competition itself. It was a guise for the combat action itself and provided a needed measure of gentlemanly reconciliation between the institutions. Again, this is a familiar articulation within the narratives of what a white middle-class young man should represent.

10. "Illinois Loyalty," Illinois Songs and Music, 1903–1958, Box 2, University of Illinois, University of Illinois Archives. See also Burford, *We're Loyal to You, Illinois*, 122.

11. "Illinois Loyalty" drew from "We're Loyal to You, Brown," a casual phrase Guild originated while attending Brown University. Guild formed an immediate friendship with Harding upon his arrival at Illinois and frequently sat in on band rehearsals as a cornet player. With a common interest in music, Guild consulted Harding on his evolving piano composition. "Guild played and I listened and made suggestions," Harding remembered. "My contribution was encouragement and advisory counsel. I may have provided that gentle pat on the back, that little forward push, but the song remains the conception, the ideal of a college song, of Thatcher Howland Guild." Although Harding downplayed his involvement in the creation of "Illinois Loyalty," he transcribed Guild's piano score and turned it into a full-fledged band composition.

12. Burford, *We're Loyal to You, Illinois*, 128.

13. "Illinois Loyalty"; Thatcher Howland Guild, *We're Loyal to You, Illinois* (New York: Melrose Music, 1906), in Burford, *We're Loyal to You, Illinois*, 179.

14. Women were fans, not athletes themselves, in their understanding, despite an increasing number of women enrolling in the university supporting informal and formal sporting teams in basketball, tennis, and gymnastics. On the role of women and sport in the historical context, see Susan Birrell and C. L. Cole, eds., *Women, Sport, and Culture* (Champaign, Ill.: Human Kinetics, 1994); Jennifer Hargreaves, *Sporting Feminisms: Critical Issues in the History and Sociology of Women's Sport* (New York: Routledge, 1994); Nancy Struna, "Gender and Sporting Practice in Early America, 1750–1810," *Journal of Sport History* 18 (Spring 1991): 10–30; Roberta Park, "The Attitude of Leading New England Transcendentalists toward Healthful Exercise, Active Recreation, and Proper Care of the Body: 1830–1860," *Journal of Sport History* 4 (Spring 1977): 34–50; Roberta Park, "'Embodied Selves': The Rise and Development of Concern for Physical Education, Active Games, and Recreation for American Women, 1776–1865," *Journal of Sport History* 5 (Summer 1978): 5–41; Cindy L. Himes, "The Female Athlete in American Society, 1860–1940" (Ph.D. diss., University of Pennsylvania, 1986); Martha H. Verbrugge, *Able-Bodied Womanhood: Personal Health and Social Change in Nineteenth-Century Boston* (Oxford: Oxford University Press, 1988). On women's place in college football in particular, see Oriard, *Reading Football*, 247–273.

15. Watterson, *College Football*, 99–100. Women initially were integrated into college football via their roles as wives, mothers, and even cheerleaders. With the increasing tension over women's feminist goals, they were marginalized and largely limited in the ways they could involve themselves with the game.

16. "Oskey wow-wow" is the phrase used in "Illinois Loyalty" while "Oskee-wow-wow" refers to the song created in 1908 by Howard R. Green and Howard Hill as part of a university-wide contest. While many scholars have used the later spelling to refer to the previous, it is important to recognize the difference between the two compositions. On "Oskey wow-wow," see Burford, *We're Loyal to You, Illinois*, 171. See also Spindel, *Dancing at Halftime*, 72.

17. This was vital in the early twentieth century as men struggled with anxieties wrought by the shifting constructions of masculinity and manliness. For more on masculinity and manliness, see Bederman, *Manliness and Civilization*; Mark C. Carnes, "Middle-Class Men and the Solace of Fraternal Ritual," in Mark C. Carnes and Clyde Griffin, *Meanings for Manhood: Constructions of Masculinity in Victorian America* (Chicago: University of Chicago Press, 1990), 37–66.

18. "Oskee-Wow-Wow," Illinois Songs and Music, 1903–1958, Box 2, University of Illinois, University of Illinois Archives. See also Burford, *We're Loyal to You, Illinois*, 171, 181.

19. "Hail to the Orange," Illinois Songs and Music, 1903–1958, Box 2, University of Illinois, University of Illinois Archives.

20. Although originally donated to, licensed by, and included in the fraternity songbook of Sigma Alpha Epsilon, "Hail to the Orange" was largely divorced from its fraternity roots because of its use by the entire Illinois community.

21. "Oskee-Wow-Wow."

22. Ibid.

23. Ibid. The historical record regarding the commission of the two performances is conflicted. Leutwiler believed that both King and Alford were commissioned, while the University of Illinois notes that only Alford was commissioned. See also Louis A. Garippo, *A Report to the Board of Trustees: The Chief Illiniwek Dialogue Report*, "History of the Chief," Section IV, http://www.uillinois.edu/trustees/dialogue/report_files/IV.html.

24. Leutwiler-Brandenberg, communication with Carol Spindel, 5.

25. "Pride of the Illini," in A. Austin Harding Collection, Box 99, Folder 7, n.d., University of Illinois, University of Illinois Archives.

26. Thomas Hatton, *Karl L. King: An American Bandmaster* (Evanston, Ill.: Instrumentalist, 1975), 29–56. On circuses and American fascination, see Janet M. Davis, *The Circus Age: Culture and Society under the American Big Top* (Chapel Hill: University of North Carolina Press, 2002); Maureen Brundale and Mark Schmitt, *The Bloomington-Normal Circus Legacy: The Golden Age of Aerialists* (Charleston, S.C.: History Press, 2013).

27. Hatton, *Karl L. King*, 35–36. On the Barnum and Bailey Circus, see Jerry Apps, *Ringlingville USA: The Stupendous Story of Seven Siblings and Their Stunning Circus Success* (Madison: Wisconsin Historical Society Press, 2005).

28. Deloria, *Indians in Unexpected Places*, 183–223.

29. Gordon M. Carver, "Sells-Floto Circus 1914–15," in *Bandwagon*, ed. Fred D. Pfenning Jr. (Columbus, Ohio: Journal of the Circus Historical Society, November–December, 1975), 22–29. On William A. "Buffalo Bill" Cody and the history of his Wild West show, see Louis S. Warren, *Buffalo Bill's America: William Cody and the Wild West Show* (New York: Alfred A. Knopf, 2005); Don Russell, *The Lives and Legends of Buffalo Bill* (Norman: University of Oklahoma Press, 1960); Joy S. Kasson, *Buffalo Bill's Wild West: Celebrity, Memory, and Popular History* (New York: Hill and Wang, 2000); Paul Reddin, *Wild West Shows* (Urbana: University of Illinois Press, 1990); Sarah J. Blackstone, *Buckskins, Bullets, and Business: A History of Buffalo Bill's Wild West* (Westport, Conn.: Greenwood, 1986). On images of Indians in Wild West shows, see L. G. Moses, *Wild West Shows and the Images of American Indians, 1883–1933* (Albuquerque: University of New Mexico Press, 1996); Linda Scarangella McNenly, *Native Performers in Wild West Shows: From Buffalo Bill to Euro Disney* (Norman: University of Oklahoma Press, 2012); Sam A. Maddra, *Hostiles? The Lakota Ghost Dance and Buffalo Bill's Wild West* (Norman: University of Oklahoma Press, 2006). On the international aspects of Native performance in Wild West shows, see Norman K. Denzin, *Indians on Display: Global Commodification of Native America in Performance, Art, and Museums* (Walnut Creek, Calif.: Left Coast Press, 2013); Robert W. Rydell and Rob Kroes, *Buffalo Bill in Bologna: The Americanization of the World, 1869–1922* (Chicago: University of Chicago Press, 2005).

30. Jess L. Gerardi, "Karl L. King: His Life and Music" (Ph.D. diss., University of Colorado, 1973), 29.

31. Blackstone, *Buckskins, Bullets, and Business*, 104. See also Michael Lee Masterson, "Sounds of the Frontier: Music in Buffalo Bill's Wild West" (Ph.D. diss., University of New Mexico, 1990), 4. Masterson's dissertation offers a tremendous analysis of the musical relationship between western European, Native American, African American, and American music that resulted in the "popular song."

32. John Burke, 1885, quoted in Masterson, "Sounds of the Frontier," 54.

33. James Anderson, "From Loony Coons to Tacos and Tequila: The Aesthetics of Race in Middle Class America" (lecture, University of Illinois at Urbana-Champaign, Spurlock Museum, March 31, 2009); Patrick Robert Warfield, "Salesman of Americanism, Globetrotter, and Musician: The Nineteenth-Century John Philip Sousa, 1854–1893" (Ph.D. diss., Indiana University, 2003).

34. Masterson, "Sounds of the Frontier," 138. The "Indian music formula" can be summarized for the nonspecialist as the use of "rhythms in straight eighth notes hitting accents on one and two in the bass and snare drum parts" with a concentration on the "white notes scale" of the piano from A to A, known as the sixth position of the major scale. Almost every major American western film has used this rhythm. See also Deloria, *Indians in Unexpected Places*, 183.

35. Allison Griffiths, "Science and Spectacle: Native American Representations in Early Cinema," in Bird, *Dressing in Feathers*, 79.

36. Burford, *We're Loyal to You, Illinois*, 182.

37. "March of the Illini," in A. Austin Harding Collection, Series 1, Box 127, Folder 2, University of Illinois, University of Illinois Archives.

38. William J. Schafer, "Ragtime Arranging for Fun and Profit: The Cases of Harry L. Alford and J. Bodewalt Lampe," *Journal of Jazz Studies* 3, no. 1 (Fall 1975): 106.

39. A survey of scores arranged include: "Down in Hindu Town," "China Baby," "Ghost Dance," "Hawaiian Blues," "Minstrel Show Parade," and "That Indian Rag," as well as the western-themed "Gold Dust" and "Hacienda."

40. On the history of American Indian assimilation, see Francis P. Prucha, *American Indian Policy in Crisis: Christian Reformers and the Indian, 1865–1890* (Norman: University of Oklahoma Press, 1976); Frederick Hoxie, *A Final Promise: The Campaign to Assimilate the Indians, 1880–1920* (1984; repr., Lincoln: University of Nebraska Press, 2001). More recently, C. Joseph Genetin-Pilawa's *Crooked Paths to Allotment: The Fight Over Federal Indian Policy after the Civil War* (Chapel Hill: University of North Carolina Press, 2012) offers a nuanced rebuttal to Prucha and Hoxie by showing how Native reformers and activists challenged assimilationist policies.

41. Harding was convinced "that all possibilities for college bands had not yet been exploited; that they should reflect the quality and dignity of the institutions they represented." See Harold B. Bachman, *The Biggest Boom in Dixie: The Story of Band Music at the University of Florida* (Gainesville, Fla.: Paramount Press, 1968), 8.

42. Burford, *We're Loyal to You, Illinois*, 532–533.

43. Ibid., 539.

44. Albert Austin Harding, A. Austin Harding Collection, 1895–1958, University of Illinois, University of Illinois Archives.

45. The ABA was the birthplace of a tremendous number of professional organizations for bands and their directors. At least five major professional organizations, including the National Band Association, were begun by ABA members. On the history and role of the ABA, see Captain William Stannard to Albert Austin Harding, August 1928, quoted in "The American Bandmasters Association History," American Bandmasters Association, http://americanbandmasters.org/history/

46. Hatton, *Karl L. King*, 157.

47. "Adding a Little Pep and Ginger," Northwestern University Archives, http://www.north western.edu/about/historic_moments/athletics/the_marching_band.html.

48. "The University of Wisconsin Marching Band History: Dvorak Era," University of Wisconsin Band, University of Wisconsin, http://web.archive.org/web/20080807121103/http://www.badgerband.com/history/dvorak.php.

49. Hatton, *Karl L. King*, 157.

CHAPTER 4   THE LIMITATIONS OF HALFTIME SPECTACLE

1. See Greg Hand et al., *Bearcats! The Story of Basketball at the University of Cincinnati* (Cincinnati: University of Cincinnati Bookstores, 1998). The University of Cincinnati adopted the athletic identity of "Baehr-cats" in honor of fullback Leonard K. "Teddy" Baehr on October 31, 1914. Competing against rival University of Kentucky and its "Wildcats," cheerleader Norman "Pat" Lyon chanted, "They may be Wildcats, but we have a Baehr-cat on our side." "Baehr-cat" was changed to "Bearcat" by a cartoonist in the November 3, 1914, edition of the student paper.

2. Founded in 1809 as part of the Northwest Ordinance and the Symmes Purchase, Miami University was established by elite northerners who had come to the Ohio Territory to settle the frontier, as was Cincinnati University. On the history of Miami University, see Curtis W. Ellison, *Miami University, 1809–2009: Bicentennial Perspectives* (Athens: Ohio University Press, 2009); Phillip R. Shriver, *Miami University: A Personal History*, ed. William Pratt (Oxford, Ohio: Miami University Press, 1998); Walter Havighurst, *Men of Old Miami, 1809–1873: A Book of Portraits* (New York: Putnam, 1974). On the history of the founding of the state of Ohio, see R. Douglas Hurt, *The Ohio Frontier: Crucible of the Old Northwest, 1720–1830* (Bloomington: Indiana University Press, 1996); Andrew R. L. Cayton, *Ohio: A History of a People* (Columbus: Ohio State University Press, 2002). On colonial expansion into the Ohio Valley, see James J. Buss, *Winning the West with Words: Language and Conquest in the Lower Great Lakes* (Norman: University of Oklahoma Press, 2011); White, *Middle Ground*.

3. Miami administrators refused to assent to an 1822 petition to the State General Assembly to merge the University of Cincinnati and Miami University. The annual athletic rivalries between the schools became an expression of the continual frustration between the two schools.

4. "Bearcats Come to Oxford Saturday Seeking Hides of Big Red-Skinned Warriors," *Miami Student*, January 11, 1928.

5. Ibid.

6. Nancy Shoemaker, *A Strange Likeness: Becoming Red and White in Eighteenth Century America* (New York: Oxford University Press, 2004), 129.

7. Ibid., 131. One Taensas headmen in 1725 identified his tribe to the French as "red men," while both Creeks and Cherokees one year later used "red" to differentiate themselves from Europeans they encountered. They also designated themselves as members of the same community, "red people." Importantly, the addition of "red" as a simple label to the already existing framework of black (or "negro") and white, which had been constructed within the framework of slavery and slave trading, marks the mid-eighteenth century as an important line of demarcation for Americans and their perceptions of race. The interplay between white and black has been written about extensively in contemporary historiography. For a traditional interpretation of racial hierarchy, see Winthrop Jordan, *The White Man's Burden: Historical Origins of Racism in America* (1974; repr., Oxford University Press, 2002).

8. Claudio Saunt, *A New Order of Things: Property, Power, and the Transformation of the Creek Indians, 1733–1816* (Cambridge: Cambridge University Press, 1999).

9. Shoemaker, *Strange Likeness*, 132. See also William Jones, "Episodes in the Culture-Hero Myth of the Sauks and Foxes," *Journal of American Folk-Lore* 14 (1901): 225–239.

10. Shoemaker, *Strange Likeness*, 135.

11. The binary nature of these demarcations was highly problematic given that many indigenous peoples intermarried with white colonizers.

12. James Axtell and William C. Sturtevant, "The Unkindest Cut, or Who Invented Scalping," *William and Mary Quarterly* 37, no. 3 (July 1980): 456.

13. H. P. Biggar, ed., *The Works of Samuel de Champlain* (Toronto: Publications of the Champlain Society, 1922–1936), 1:102–103, 108, in Axtell and Sturtevant, "Unkindest Cut," 459.

14. Gabriel Sagard, *The Long Journey to the Country of the Hurons*, ed. George M. Wrong, trans. H. H. Langton (Toronto: Champlain Society, 1939), 152, in Axtell and Sturtevant, "Unkindest Cut," 460.

15. Depictions of the rituals of scalp collection and display include Theodore de Bry's engraving of Jacques le Moyne's *Treatment of the Enemy Dead by Outina's Forces* (1591) and Alexandre De Batz's 1732 and 1735 Choctaw paintings. These paintings provide visual cues derived from original testimonials regarding scalping practices and rituals.

16. Axtell and Sturtevant, "Unkindest Cut," 470.

17. Theda Perdue, *Cherokee Women: Gender and Culture Change, 1700–1835* (Lincoln: University of Nebraska Press, 1998). Serving the purposes of colonists who were intent on expansion, the valuation of men higher than women relied on preconceived notions of the role of men in warfare by the Europeans. Europeans believed that only men waged warfare and as such did not value the role of women, who served as defenders of the village and provided supplies and goods to men to enable them to fight.

18. Again, Indians themselves were not needed to participate in these circuits; only an echo of their lives was essential to the performance. Actual Indians could destabilize the meaning and understandings that Miami University was relying on to communicate its desire for young, white, male citizens who could become students.

19. On the Miami name, see Miami University, *The Miami Connection*, brochure, June 15, 1991, Miami University Archives, Miami, Ohio; the Atchatchakangouens, a band of the Illinois division of the Algonquin-speaking Miami tribe, referred to themselves as "Twa-h-twa-h," an imitation of the alarm cry of the sandhill crane. Early French traders like Jean Nicolet in 1634 called these individuals the "Crane People," while the Chippewas referred to them as "Oumamik," or "peninsula dwellers." These contradictory titles were influenced by the transitory nature of the Miami tribe. Father Gabriel Dreuilettes, traveling in 1658, mentioned a band of Indians, probably Miami, living at the tip of Green Bay. Jesuit agent Jules Tailhan and New France royal agent Bacqueville de La Potherie refuted this, claiming that the Miami lived on a portage sixty miles north of Wisconsin Bay, or near the mouth of the Fox River. The large amount of territory covered by the seasonally moving tribe dictated these sightings. The Miami probably occupied the peninsula areas west, south, and east of lower Lake Michigan as well as southward from the Wabash Valley to the three rivers area of what is currently known as the Miami Valley. Father Claude Allouez, a Jesuit missionary, began recording these encounters and history in 1669. By 1673, Jesuit missionary Father Jacques Marquette, during a trip with two Miami warriors, had altered the Oumamik name to its French pronunciation, "me-aw'me." Through common usage and recording over time, the French spelling fell to the English "mi-am'-e," or Miami. This name replaced "Twa-h-twa-h" and remains the formal name to this day. See also Bert Anson, *The Miami Indians* (Norman: University of Oklahoma Press, 1999), 3; Karen Alexander, "Miami Tribe of Oklahoma: Past, Present, Future," Miami Tribe, Miami University Nickname and Mascot Papers, Miami University Archives, 1 HST Box 1; Harvey Lewis Carter, *The Life and Times of Little Turtle: First Sagamore of the Wabash* (Urbana: University of Illinois Press, 1987), 20; Shriver, *Miami University*, 32.

20. Miami University, *Recensio*, 1915, Miami University, Miami University Archives.

21. From 1908 onward, female athletes were awarded an "M" by the Girls' Athletic Association, later the Women's Athletics Association, for sports as varied as volleyball, soccer, tennis, field hockey, baseball, and basketball. I draw attention to this distinction as it underscores the vibrant masculinity deployed as part of men's athletics identity and as part of the larger articulation of white middle-class male identity as racialized. While female athletes could be "M" women and enjoy athletic success, they were not described as "red-skinned warriors" intent on scalping their opponents.

22. The Origin of the Designated Name for the Miami University Athletic Teams, October 9, 1981, Box 10, Walter Havighurst Collection, Miami University, Miami University Archives. There is no record of Upham's ever approaching the board of trustees to formalize Games's supposed suggestion. See also Miami University, Office of the Student Body, "Miami University and the 'Redskins': An Analysis," March 11, 1993, Miami University Archives (hereafter cited as "Redskins": An Analysis). Coach Charles Pittser, Miami University football coach, also claimed to originate the appellation "Redskins" for its athletic teams. He purportedly called his athletes "Redskins" in 1931. Importantly, both Pittser's and Games's speculation were recollections justified, legitimized, and authenticated over thirty years after production. There is no currently available archival evidence to support Coach Charles Pittser's claim, nor is their corroborating evidence for Frank Games's. No university or student publication used the name "Redskins" until 1933, two years following Games's graduation and Pittser's alleged designation. Further, the 1930 alumni newsletter does not specifically name "Redskins" as the athletic name.

23. Miami University, "M Book," 1933, Miami University Archives.

24. Miami University, *Recensio*, 1933, Miami University Archives.

25. "Redskins": An Analysis, 9.

26. Miami University, *Alumni Newsletter*, 1930, Miami University Archives.

27. Anson, *Miami Indians*, 19.

28. Ibid., 21.

29. In perspective, the University of Illinois was the third largest institution in the United States with over 12,700 students on its campus at the same time. "1927–1928 & 1928–1929 Enrollment by Curricula," Enrollment Tables, 1911–1930, University of Illinois Archives, 25/3/810, Urbana, University of Illinois, http://archives.library.illinois.edu/erec/University%20Archives/2503810/1928–29%20%26%201929–30%20Enrollment%20by%20Curricula.pdf.

30. The use of "Dakota" was drawn from colonial encounters with Indian peoples in the area that became the Dakota Territory in 1861. "In the seventeenth century, when the French first came into Sioux country, they referred to them by an Ottawa term that the French wrote as 'Nadouessioux.' Eventually, this was shortened to 'Sioux.'" Jeffrey Ostler, *The Plains Sioux and U.S. Colonialism from Lewis and Clark to Wounded Knee* (New York: Cambridge University Press, 2004), 21. See also Raymond J. DeMallie, "Kinship and Biology in Sioux Culture," in *North American Indian Anthropology: Essays on Society and Culture*, ed. Rayond J. DeMallie and Alfonso Ortiz (Norman: University of Oklahoma Press, 1994), 130; Raymond J. DeMallie, "Sioux until 1850," in *Handbook of North American Indians*, vol. 13, *Plains*, ed. Raymond J. DeMallie (Washington, D.C.: Smithsonian Insitution, 2001), pt. 2, 718, 749–750. As the historian Jeffrey Ostler notes, "the Sioux formally referred to themselves as Oceti Sakowin (Seven Council Fires) and, depending on dialect, as Dakota or Lakota, a word signifying friendship or 'allied.'" Moving into the area stretching from western Minnesota through North and South Dakota to Montana and Wyoming in the eighteenth century, Sioux peoples spoke three distinct dialects (Lakota, Nakota, and Dakota) and were organized into politically autonomous groups that were often in flux. "Dakota" generally referred to a group of

Native peoples recognized as the "Santees," or eastern band of Sioux speakers. The "Santees," or Dakotas, recognized four bands within the larger unit: Mdewakantonwan, Wahepeton, Sissetonwan, and Wahpekute. The Santees lived in semipermanent villages ranging from Minnesota to the northern Rocky Mountains in Montana and south through the northwestern part of Nebraska. By the turn of the nineteenth century, "Lakota" referred to the "Teton" (western) Sioux, which included the Ogala, Brule, Hunkpapa, Minneconjou, Sans Arc, Black Kettle, and Teton bands. The Nakota included the Yankton and Yanktonai (central) Sioux. While UND students may have been identifying their community as "allied," the use of "Dakota" as a marker of communal identity was laden with implicit tensions. Settlers had been actively grappling with the state's Indian populace, and the process of colonization had been fraught with violent confrontation and broken promises. See Ostler, *Plains Sioux*, 21; DeMallie, "Kinship and Biology in Sioux Culture," 718, 749–750; Loretta Fowler, *The Columbia Guide to American Indians of the Great Plains* (New York: Columbia University Press, 2003), 13.

Founded on October 2, 1883, one of the "brightest, crispest, freshest, most palpably wholesome days of the most glorious autumn that even Dakota ever saw," one mile west of Grand Forks, the University of North Dakota was welcomed by music, prayer, and speeches that rang out over the windy, chilly prairie. The seventh territorial governor, Nehemiah Ordway; former surveyor-general of the Dakota territories and current superintendent of public instruction General William Henry Harrison Beadle; and other luminaries gathered with a small group of citizens to witness the laying of the cornerstone of the University of North Dakota. Passed by the Territorial Assembly of the Dakota territories on February 27, 1883, the University of North Dakota "shall be to provide the means of acquiring a thorough knowledge of the various branches of learning connected with scientific, industrial and professional pursuits . . . and also instruction in the fundamental laws of the United States, and of this Territory, in what regards the rights and duties of citizens." Following the national pattern of utilizing educational institutions as a means of inculcating young men, the University of North Dakota was, at its core, a response to the dramatic change being felt within the Dakota territories. See *Grand Forks Herald*, in Louis George Geiger, *University of the Northern Plains: A History of the University of North Dakota, 1883–1958* (Grand Forks: University of North Dakota Press, 1958), 3–7; see also "An Act Establishing a Territorial University at Grand Forks, Dakota," University of North Dakota History, University of North Dakota, http://www.und.nodak.edu/history/.

31. Geiger, *University of the Northern Plains*, 3–7.

32. Ibid.

33. Ibid., 180.

34. The breakdown was 2,576 whites versus 2,261 Indians. Of the total 4,837 inhabitants, 1,774 were foreign-born. U.S. Department of Commerce, Bureau of the Census, Census, 1860, http://www2.census.gov/prod2/decennial/documents/1860a-14.pdf. See also U.S. Department of Commerce, Bureau of the Census, Decennial Census, 1870, http://www2.census.gov/prod2/decennial/documents/1870a-03.pdf; U.S. Department of Commerce, Bureau of the Census, Census, 1880, http://www2.census.gov/prod2/decennial/documents/1880a_v1-07.pdf.

35. U.S. Department of Commerce, Bureau of the Census, Census, 1880, http://www2.census.gov/prod2/decennial/documents/1880a_v1-07.pdf.

36. Geiger, *University of the Northern Plains*, 9–10.

37. *Dacotah*, 1906, University of North Dakota, University of North Dakota Archives; see also *Dacotah*, 1912, University of North Dakota, University of North Dakota Archives. Prior to 1912, the *Dacotah* was published sporadically and rarely used Indian imagery or motifs. Only the cover of the 1906 *Dacotah* featured an Indian motif: a frontal portrait of an Indian from the shoulders up surrounded by a circle. With no accompanying text either on the cover

or throughout the yearbook itself, the graphic signals a recognition of the use of the term "*Dacotah*" as Indian in origin but significantly differs from what is presented in later editions. The lack of an elaborately detailed historical narrative of the relationship between the Dakota Indians and UND suggests that students were just beginning to be actively invested in constructing narratives of racial hierarchy and white inheritance that privileged the existence of UND and its students. A convergence of the relative youth of the university as well as the lack of distance from the violent conflict undertaken by the Sioux in the former Dakota territories, the 1906 edition could not have depicted Indians as part of the historical past with UND as the inheritor of the land. In effect, this was a less-developed use of narratives of conquest, the past and the future, within the rhetoric of community building.

38. *Dacotah*, 1926, foreword, University of North Dakota, University of North Dakota Archives. The supposed meeting between Dakota Indians and students seems to be the first such meeting recorded by universities as they created Indian-themed spectacles. The notion that a tribe could assent or authorize a university to use its identity for commercial purposes would become a major issue in contemporary challenges to the use of Native American tribal names and imagery for athletic identities.

39. Ostler, *Plains Sioux*, 63–84.

40. President Abraham Lincoln commuted or pardoned all but thirty-nine.

41. For an in-depth examination of Custer and the Battle of Little Big Horn, see Ostler, *Plains Sioux*; Jeffrey Ostler and Robert Utley, *Cavalier in Buckskin: George Armstrong Custer and the Western Military Front* (Norman: University of Oklahoma Press, 2001). For an in-depth examination of the mythology of Custer, see Brian W. Dippie, *Custer's Last Stand: The Anatomy of an American Myth* (Lincoln: University of Nebraska, 1994); Slotkin, *Fatal Environment*.

42. "First Account of the Custer Massacre," *Bismarck Tribune Extra*, July 6, 1876. Digital edition available from: http://history.nd.gov/archives/06July1876TribuneExtra.pdf.

43. R. David Edmunds, Frederick E. Hoxie, and Neal Salisbury, *The People: A History of Native America* (Boston: Houghton Mifflin, 2007), 339.

44. Ostler, *Plains Sioux*, 313–337.

45. Estimates of the number of dead and wounded at Wounded Knee vary greatly. Ostler lists 270 to 300 of Big Foot's group dead or fatally wounded, with 170–200 of these noted as being women and children. See Ostler, *Plains Sioux*, 338–343. Sioux and military sources both confirm that victims littered the grounds up to three miles from the site of the initial encounter. This confirms survivors' accounts, which depict women and children being chased by soldiers across the badlands.

46. Edmunds, Hoxie, and Salisbury, *People*, 339; see also Ostler, *Plains Sioux*, 338–360.

47. Ostler, *Plains Sioux*, 351.

48. L. Frank Baum, "Editorial," *Saturday Pioneer* (Aberdeen, S.D.), December 20, 1890.

49. L. Frank Baum, "Editorial," *Saturday Pioneer* (Aberdeen, S.D.), January 3, 1891.

50. "A Colorful Name for 'Nodaks' Found," *Dakota Student*, September 23, 1930, 2.

51. The *Dakota Student* newspaper served as an organizing force for efforts to change the school name and symbol. Of the editorials and articles published in the September 23 and 30 editions, only a few lines present negative views on the possible change. Each of these lines is buried with larger numbers of articles offering support for the change. Tellingly, Alvin Austin, the *Student* editor, later said, "I personally wrote those letters to the editor as well as the laudatory editorials. Power of the Press?" A stinging critique written in private correspondence suggests the likely veracity of Austin's claim.

52. "Eleven U Faculty Members Favor Change in Pep Name," *Dakota Student*, September 30, 1930, 1.

53. Ibid.

54. Ibid.

55. Brenda Ling and Michelle Midstokke, "UND Fighting Sioux: Building Understanding and Respect or Showing Disrespect and Insensitivity?" University of North Dakota *Alumni Review*, March/April 2000.

56. "The Bystander," *Dakota Student*, September 30, 1930, 2.

CHAPTER 5   STUDENT INVESTMENT IN UNIVERSITY IDENTITIES

1. Oriard, *King Football*, 272.

2. Ingrassia, *Rise of the Gridiron University*, 149–150.

3. Stanford University opened October 1, 1891, as a tribute to Leland Stanford Jr., the deceased son of founder Leland Stanford and his wife, Jane. Unlike the University of Illinois or Miami University, which relied on state and government involvement in their origins, Stanford University was founded on the dream of former California governor Leland Stanford who, the night following his fifteen-year-old son's death, dreamed that his son appeared and spoke to him. When he awakened Stanford reportedly declared, "the children of California shall be our children." See Mirrielees, *Stanford*, 20.

4. Ingrassia, *Rise of the Gridiron University*, 150.

5. Board of Athletic Control, "Resolution on the Indian as Symbol," in *Minutes of the Board of Athletic Control* (Burlingame, Calif.: Stanford University, 1930), Stanford University Archives. Stanford had, like many colleges, including Illinois, utilized school colors as the primary markers of athletic belonging. The "cardinal red" color of Stanford University had been utilized in player's uniforms, but Stanford University had no iconography associated with its teams except designation of the level of athletic involvement, football being a major sport awarding an uppercase "S," whereas polo was a minor sport awarding a lowercase "s." In demarcating between major and minor sports, the university was clearly demonstrating its investment and perception of the value of the game itself. Football was perceived as a superior athletic event to polo. Athletes from major sports became "Block S" men and were able to jockey for social position because of these awards.

6. Petty, "Stanford Goes Indian," *Stanford Illustrated Review*, January 1931, 177.

7. Importantly, though, the racial hierarchy inherent within the equating of Indians to animals goes unexplored in almost every text on mascotry.

8. "Sandstone and Tile: Dr. Tom Williams," *Stanford Historical Society* 11, no. 4 (Summer 1987): 3.

9. Ibid., 4.

10. Ibid.

11. Ibid., 6–7.

12. Ibid., 7.

13. Don E. Liebendorfer, *The Color of Life Is Red: A History of Stanford Athletics, 1892–1972* (Palo Alto, Calif.: Department of Athletics, Stanford University, 1972), 314. Self-dubbed the "sculptor in buckskin," Proctor's role in the Stanford Indian ascent has been largely ignored.

14. Vivian A. Paladin, "A. Phimister Proctor: Master Sculptor of Horses," *Montana: The Magazine of Western History* 14, no. 1 (1964): 10–24. Most recognizable to today's audiences are *The Bucking Bronco* and *On the Warpath*, which reside in Denver and depict the century-old roles of cowboy and Indian. See also Katharine C. Ebner, ed., *Sculptor in Buckskin: The Autobiography of Alexander Phimister Proctor*, 2nd ed. (Norman: University of Oklahoma Press, 2009). Originally commissioned to produce six bronzes to grace the bridges over the lagoon at the Columbian Exposition, Proctor had, by January 1, 1893, rendered two polar bears, two jaguars, two elk, and two moose.

15. Peter H. Hassrick, *Wildlife and Western Heroes: Alexander Phimister Proctor, Sculptor* (Fort Worth, Tex.: Amon Carter Museum, 2003), 36.

16. Ibid., 37. While completing *Cowboy* established Proctor as the first American artist to create a sculptural work of a cowboy, *Indian* was not the first of its kind or the only Indian-themed sculpture at the fair. On the Columbian Exposition sculpture and art, see Robert Rydell and Carolyn Kinder Carr, eds., *Revisiting the White City: American Art at the 1893 World's Fair* (Washington, D.C.: Smithsonian Institution Press, 1993); Diane Dillon, "'The Fair as Spectacle': American Art and Culture at the 1893 World's Fair" (Ph.D. diss., Yale University, 1994); Melissa Dubakis, *Visualizing Labor in American Sculpture: Monuments, Manliness, and the Work Ethic, 1880–1935* (New York: Cambridge University Press, 1999). On the Columbia Exposition more generally, see Robert Rydell, *All the World's a Fair: Visions of Empire at American International Expositions, 1876–1916* (Chicago: University of Chicago Press, 1987), 38–71; Kasson, *Buffalo Bill's Wild West*, 93–122; David J. Bertuca, ed., *World's Columbian Exposition: A Centennial Bibliographic Guide.* Bibliographies and Indexes in American History, vol. 26 (Westport, Conn.: Greenwood, 1996); Donald L. Miller, *City of the Century: The Epic of Chicago and the Making of America* (New York: Simon and Schuster, 1996). On the exposition as a modern spectacle of urban planning, see Katherine Kia Tehranian, "The Chicago Columbian Exposition of 1893: A Symbol of Modernism," *Proceedings of the National Conference on American Planning History* 5 (1993): 500–511. On the exposition and the myth of the frontier, see Ladee Hubbard, "Mobility in America: The Myth of the Frontier and the Performance of National Culture at the Chicago World's Fair of 1893" (Ph.D. diss., University of California, Los Angeles, 2003). An entertaining fictionalized take is Erik Larson's *The Devil in the White City: Murder, Magic, and Madness at the Fair That Changed America* (New York: Crown, 2003).

17. That visual image of an Indian gazing upon the horizon is replicated throughout university publications during the 1920s and 1930s.

18. J. Harrison Mills, "Concerning Early Art in Colorado," Western History Collection, Denver Public Library, Denver, 1916, in Hassrick, *Wildlife and Western Heroes*, 21. It is interesting that Mills draws a parallel between Proctor and Benjamin West. West's 1771 painting *William Penn's Treaty with the Indians* depicted the very ritual that the University of Illinois would reenact with the University of Pennsylvania in establishing Leutwiler's "Indian." Proctor's statuary would play a similar role within the origin of the Stanford Indian.

19. Hassrick, *Wildlife and Western Heroes*, 44.

20. In traveling the American West to gather inspiration and participate in hunts, Proctor was not alone. Ralph Hubbard, Leutwiler's Boy Scout mentor, had lived in and traveled throughout the West.

21. "Varsity Coaches Drill Cardinals for Olympic Game," *Daily Palo Alto*, October 2, 1922. The origins of the Indian head symbol used on the blanket remain vague. Beyond a brief mention in Don Liebendorfer's Stanford history *The Color of Life Is Red*, there is little to which to trace the origins of the use of the Indian head. Until 1923, Stanford was overwhelmingly referred to by its team color, cardinal, with the male athletes themselves being referred to as "cards." Contrary to popularly publicized narratives, the use of Indian terminology to refer to Stanford teams did not begin until after Williams's attempted introduction of the Indian symbol and the hiring of Glenn "Pop" Warner, the famous former coach of the University of Pittsburgh and the Carlisle Indian School, in 1924. See also Margo Baumgarten Davis and Roxanne Nilan, *The Stanford Album* (Palo Alto, Calif.: Stanford University Press, 1989), 223.

22. "More about Commercialism," *Daily Palo Alto*, April 26, 1923.

23. "Alumnus Gives Hint to Improve Stanford Spirit," *Daily Palo Alto*, March 14, 1923.

24. A site of resistance to the desires of the community being promoted via this circuit of athletics and sport mascotry, the failure of Stanford students to adopt the Indian name and logo suggests an intervention in the idea of top-down dominance where individuals could not exert resistance against institutional or community meanings.

25. Alexander Phimister Proctor, *Alexander Phimister Proctor: Sculptor in Buckskin* (Norman: University of Oklahoma Press, 1971), 177. Proctor needed a studio for the winter. His New York studio was being sublet by sculptor Frederick MacMonnies, so his brother helped him secure a barn in Los Alto, a few miles from Palo Alto. Surprisingly, though, almost nothing is written in his autobiography or in biographies about his involvement in the Stanford University and Palo Alto communities beyond his lease of space at the university. Significantly, the lack of attention to Proctor's role in the formation of the Indian mascot also suggests the efforts to appeal to lower-class forms of entertainment with middle-class institutions of education. That one of the most well known artists of the period was involved in the creation of a popular symbol with almost no mention demonstrates the ways in which the links between highbrow aesthetics have been ignored in studies of the middle class.

26. Liebendorfer, *Color of Life Is Red*, 25.

27. Of Irish–Sac and Fox descent on his paternal line and French-Potawatomi on his mother's, Thorpe was raised among the Sac and Fox Indians of Oklahoma on a prosperous 1,200-acre farm. Noted in the 1887 report by the Sac and Fox agent that the Thorpe family was among the 15 percent that wore "civilized clothes," Thorpe and his siblings, including his twin brother, Charlie, were educated at the Sac and Fox Agency boarding school initially. Enrolled in the Haskell Institute in 1898 and Garden Grove School by 1903, Jim Thorpe's interest in assimilationist programs echoed that of many young men of the period: a lack of interest coupled with a tendency to "run away" to rejoin family.

28. "FSU Team's Now Seminoles," *Tallahassee Daily Democrat*, November 9, 1947.

29. Bill McGrotha, *Seminoles! The First Forty Years* (Tallahassee, Fla.: Tallahassee Democrat, 1987), 44.

30. Ibid.

31. Ibid.

32. Ibid.

33. *The Seminole*, University of Florida, 1910.

34. Ibid., 49.

35. Ibid. Creeks and Cherokees rallied to challenge the citizenship law of 1901 that mandated that all Indians in Indian territories would become U.S. citizens, thereby dissolving their Indian nations. Lone Wolf, of the Kiowas, refused to cooperate with federal authorities, going so far as to file suit in federal courts to enjoin the secretary of the interior from selling surplus Indian lands under the Jerome Agreement. Sioux, under the leadership of Chief Red Cloud, used lobbyists and legal appeals to challenge U.S. authority to determine the value of the Black Hills. In part, Rader's failure to recognize nonviolent resistance to American rule was part of the continuing construction of colonial practices of subjugation that was an innate production of this circuit of cultural cosmopolitanism. More simply, Indian survival into the twentieth century was portrayed as people lingering in far-off lands where they avoided white settlements and society.

36. Ibid.

37. In pleading for a portion of the Everglades to be set aside, Rader recognized the importance of land and land-use policies for Indian peoples. Yet in overlooking the possible repatriation of lands in northern Florida and Georgia to the Seminoles in favor of the Everglades, Rader neglects to recognize the larger claim that could be made about the Seminoles: their demise was not a result of clinging to old traditions and customs but instead was a direct result of colonial violence between warring nations: Creek, Seminole, American, Spanish, and English. Rader likely avoids this position as it would necessitate recognizing that the Seminoles were, in fact, not unconquered peoples but instead a confederation of peoples deeply influenced by the systematic disenfranchisement at the hands of Spanish, English, and American colonizers.

38. James W. Covington, *The Seminoles of Florida* (Gainesville: University of Florida Press, 1993), 3.

39. Ibid., 5.

40. Saunt, *New Order of Things*, 33–34. Importantly, these permanent settlements sit squarely within Gainesville, Florida.

41. Ibid., 35. The term *"cimarrones"* is defined as "free people" by the Seminole Tribe of Florida, while scholars, including Claudio Saunt, equate the term to the word "runaway." Saunt also provides an explanation of the term "Seminole" as a translation of the Muskogee words *"ishti semoli,"* meaning "wild men."

42. Ibid.

43. Ibid.

44. Covington, *Seminoles of Florida*, 26.

45. Ibid., 51.

46. Ibid., 53.

47. Osceola plays a significant part in the articulation of Florida State University athletic identity beginning in 1978.

48. *Seminole*, University of Florida, 1910, 2.

49. There is significant complexity to the history of the origins of the Florida Gator mascot that is beyond the scope of examination here. The August 19, 1948, *Florida Times-Union* recounts the remembrances of Austin Miller, a University of Virginia student whose father owned a Gainesville soda fountain and stationery store. On a trip to Charlottesville to visit his son, Phillip Miller visited the Michie Company, which manufactured pennants and banners for athletic powerhouses Yale and Princeton. Austin Miller chose the name "Alligators" as the alligator was both native to Florida and had not been adopted by any other school. "I had no idea it would stick, or even be popular with the student body," Miller said. "We wanted to get the Michie firm started on the pennants as quickly as possible, though, so they would be available in time for the opening of the 1908 school term." Michie's supplied Miller's store blue banners measuring six by three feet depicting various positions of the alligator, including one with the now familiar alligator head. A 1928 letter to the *Gainesville Sun* contradicted Miller's recounting. The first captain of the Florida football team, Ray Corbett, charged that the "Gators" nickname was derived from substitute center Neal "Bo-Gator" Storter. Storter, a "Florida Legend" according to 1912 senior class president Thomas Bryant, was the grandson of an Alabama migrant who operated a trading post visited by the Seminoles in Everglade (later Everglade City, south of Naples, Florida) and served as a local shipping merchant. On the variety of origin stories, see Carl Van Ness, "UF's First Gators," *UF Today* (University of Florida Alumni Association, September 2000), 35–39; *Florida Times-Union*, August 2, 1948; Bachman, *Biggest Boom in Dixie*, 27.

50. "The Gator Nickname," University of Florida, University of Florida Archives.

51. "1905–1909," Florida State University, http://www.fsu.edu/~fsu150/history/history_03_1905a.html.

52. Similar concerns at Miami University led to women's intercollegiate basketball being abolished in 1912. See "Miami University History of Women's Athletics," 25 Years of Women's Athletics at Miami University, Miami University, http://www.lib.muohio.edu/epub/wsports/hist.html.

53. "1920–1930," Florida State University, http://www.fsu.edu/~fsu150/history/history_03_1905c.html.

54. "1930–1940," Florida State University, http://www.fsu.edu/~fsu150/history/history_03_1905d.html.

55. Robin J. Sellars, *Femina Perfecta: The Genesis of Florida State University* (Tallahassee: Florida State University Foundation, 1995), 245; see also *Florida Flambeau*, October 2, 1936.

56. Sellars, *Femina Perfecta*, 245; see also *Florida Flambeau*, March 17, 1939; *Jacksonville Journal*, May 12, 1939.

57. "1947–1959," Florida State University, http://www.fsu.edu/~fsu150/history/history_ 04_1947a.html.

58. Old Miss Traditions, Ole Miss Sports, http://www.olemisssports.com/ViewArticle .dbml?DB_OEM_ID=2600&ATCLID=541582.

59. Joshua I. Newman, "The Colonel's Secret Recipe?: Reconsidering the Cultural and Corporate Logics of the South's Sporting Symbolic," in author's possession.

60. "University Adopts New Nickname- Rebels," *Mississippian*, 1936, in Newman, "Colonel's Secret Recipe?"

61. The origins of "Colonel Reb" are disputed. In one popular narrative, "Colonel Reb" is modeled after African American vendor Blind Jim Ivy. See Joshua I. Newman, "Army of Whiteness? Colonel Reb and the Sporting South's Cultural and Corporate Symbolic," *Journal of Sport and Social Issues* 31, no. 4 (November 2007): 315–339; Nadine Cohodas, *The Band Played Dixie: Race and the Liberal Conscience at Ole Miss* (New York: Free Press, 1997).

62. For a complete discussion of Civil War remembrances, see Michael Kammen, *Mystic Chords of Memory* (New York: Knopf, 1991), 101–131; David Blight, *Race and Reunion: The Civil War in American Memory* (Cambridge, Mass.: Harvard University Press, 2001); Tony Horwitz, *Confederates in the Attic: Dispatches from the Unfinished Civil War* (New York: Vintage Books, 1998).

63. Dana Ste. Claire, *Cracker: The Cracker Culture in Florida History*, 2nd ed. (Daytona Beach, Fla.: Museum of Arts and Sciences, 1998), 24–34. See also Grady McWhiney, *Cracker Culture: Celtic Ways in the Old South* (Tuscaloosa: University of Alabama Press, 1988); Frank L. Owsley, *Plain Folk in the Old South* (Baton Rouge: Louisiana State University Press, 1949).

64. Ste. Claire, *Cracker*, 48.

65. Ibid., 50.

66. It is important to differentiate between all poor white southerners and those with "cracker" culture. Not all poor southerners lived isolated, self-sufficient nomadic lives, nor did all "crackers" live an unprosperous life.

67. Ste. Claire, *Cracker*, 55.

68. Julian M. Pleasants, "Frederic Remington in Florida," *Florida Historical Quarterly* 61, no. 1 (July 1977): 1–12.

69. Riess, *Touching Base*, 15; see also Tim Darnell, *The Crackers: Early Days of Atlanta Baseball* (Athens, Ga.: Hill Street Press, 2003).

70. Sharing Ponce de Leon Park with the Atlanta Crackers, a semipro team named the "Cubs" was reorganized as a result of the inclusion of black serviceman in a 1918 Atlanta Crackers game. Renamed by Birmingham fans, in 1919 the Negro League professional team from Atlanta adopted the name Atlanta Crackers directly from the white team who shared their field. A fixture in the *Atlanta Daily World*, the Atlanta Crackers baseball team ushered in the integration of athletic space in segregated Atlanta. In one notable March 1944 encounter, the *World* headlined: "Georgia Indians Will Make Bow to Baseball Fans This Season." Considerations of the Atlanta Crackers are vital to understanding how African Americans leveraged co-option of southern identity for their own purposes, yet the existence of the Atlanta Crackers is not essential for understanding how Florida State students formed their identity.

71. Marseille Dell Donne, Florida State University Seal, Florida State University Handbook, 1948.

72. McGrotha, *Seminoles!*, 44.

6   INDIAN BODIES PERFORMING ATHLETIC IDENTITY

1. Carl Stephens, *Illini Years: A Picture History of the University of Illinois, 1868–1950* (Urbana: University of Illinois Press, 1950), 100.

2. "Princess Illiniwek, Idelle Sith," October 26, 1943, Box ATH 1–2, Folder ATH 1–2 Chief Illiniwek Stith, Idelle, 1943 Negative Number: 9869, Record Series 39/2/22, University of Illinois Archives, http://www.library.illinois.edu/archives/archon/?p=digitallibrary/digitalcontent&id=462.

3. Spindel, *Dancing at Halftime*, 117.

4. Ibid., 118–119.

5. "Campus Night Club Returns with New, Entertaining Show," *Daily Illini*, November 28, 1942.

6. "The Party Line," *Daily Illini*, October 31, 1943.

7. Milcy Sloboda, "Idelle Stith Dons Chief's Moccasins to Keep Another Tradition Alive," *Daily Illini*, October 27, 1943.

8. "V-12 Marching Band to Play Today," *Daily Illini*, October 7, 1944, 7.

9. "Holthaus Is Named Chief Illiniwek by Mark Hindsley," *Daily Illini*, October 9, 1941, 1; "Sixth Chief Illiniwek to Perform Today," *Daily Illini*, October 10, 1942.

10. "Illinois Seeks Man to Fill Illiniwek's War Regalia," *Daily Illini*, September 17, 1941, 1. I have italicized *real* to underscore the language of authenticity being used by the university.

11. "New Illiniwek Is 'Real McCoy,'" A. Austin Harding Collection, Series 2, Box 139, Folder 10, n.d., University of Illinois Archives; "Yourself and Others," *Daily Illini*, October 18, 1939, 2.

12. Miami University, *Miami Tomahawk* 1, no. 1 (February 1946), 2.

13. Ibid., 6.

14. Michael A. Sheyahshe, *Native Americans in Comic Books: A Critical Study* (Jefferson, N.C.: McFarland, 2008).

15. Kevin Breen, "Native American Heroes in the Comics," Blue Corn Comics, http://www.bluecorncomics.com/kbreen.htm.

16. Miami University, *Miami Tomahawk* 1, no. 2 (March 1946), 3.

17. Ibid.

18. Ibid.

19. Miami University, *Miami Tomahawk*, 1, no. 11 (December 1946), 6.

20. Miami University, *Miami Tomahawk*, 3, no. 9 (October 1948), cover.

21. Western Reserve University, now Case Western Reserve University, ran a university-wide contest to choose its athletic mascot in 1921–1922. Nominated names included: Tornadoes, Northern Blizzards, Catamounts, Thunderbolts, Greyhounds, Lynx, Wild Cats, Marathons, Warriors, Wampuns, and Martians. "Pioneers" was selected and was used until 1928, when the "Red Cat" was selected after Marietta (Ohio) College challenged its use of "Pioneers." "Team Colors, Mascots, Names," Case Western Reserve University, http://www.case.edu/its/archives/Sports/teams.htm.

22. "Indians" was the first Marshall athletic identity used before 1910. After 1910, Marshall was referred to as the "Big Green" after its school colors until the selection of the "Thundering Herd" in the late 1920s. "Marshall University Traditions," Marshall University Athletics, http://herdzone.cstv.com/trads/mars-trads.html.

23. It is important to highlight here that the inclusion of comedic representations is not constituted as a site of resistance to mascots themselves. The comedic is seen here as a way of reinforcing belonging with the community by relieving anxieties—in this case, the anxiety of post–World War II America and the massive upheavals felt by young men and women across America and the sense of chaos stimulated by the returning flood of students to campus.

24. John D'Emilio and Estelle B. Freedman, *Intimate Matters: A History of Sexuality in America* (New York: Harper & Row, 1988), 277.

25. Harris, *King Football*, 139.

26. W. Losh, ed., *Dacotah*, University of North Dakota, 1942.

27. N. Christianson, ed., *Dacotah*, University of North Dakota, 1935.

28. Ibid.

29. M. Sarles and F. Hass, eds., *Dacotah*, University of North Dakota, 1937.

30. Christianson, *Dacotah*.

31. R. S. Kunkel, ed., *Dacotah*, University of North Dakota, 1938.

32. In 1942, as Sammy came to life, students at the "Band Blare" dressed in blackface for the campus audience.

33. Herbert D. Seiter, *Prince Lightfoot: Indian from the California Redwoods* (Del Norte County, Calif.: Troubador Press, 1959), 12.

34. Ibid.

35. Charles Fruehling Springwood, "Playing Indian and Fighting (for) Mascots: Reading the Complications of Native American and Euro-American Alliances," in King and Springwood, *Team Spirits*, 305; Chris Eddy, "In Praise of Prince Lightfoot," *Stanford Magazine* (Palo Alto, Calif.: Stanford Alumni Organization), May/June 2001, http://www.stanfordalumni.org/news/magazine/2001/mayjun/upfront/lettoed.html.

36. A. J. Bledsoe, "1881 History: Del Norte County, California," *Humbolt Times* (Eureka, Calif.: Humbolt Press, 1971), in Thomas Buckley, "Yurok Realities in the Nineteenth and Twentieth Centuries" (Ph.D. diss., University of Chicago, 1982), 16.

37. Seiter, *Prince Lightfoot*, 14.

38. In drawing attention to the limits of Williams's performance, I do not mean to suggest that Williams should have had a more developed sense of consciousness of Indian stereotypes, nor do I assign responsibility to Williams himself in leveraging the Sioux stereotype for his own use.

CONCLUSION

1. David Glassberg, *American Historical Pageantry: The Uses of Tradition in the Early Twentieth Century* (Chapel Hill: University of North Carolina Press, 1990), 284.

2. Board of Trustees of Stanford University, *The Stanford Presidency* (Stanford, Calif: Stanford University, 2005), DVD.

3. S. L. Price, "Indian Wars," *Sports Illustrated*, August 17, 2005, http://sportsillustrated.cnn.com/2005/magazine/08/17/indian.wars030402/.

4. "American Indian Opinion Leaders," *Indian Country Today*, August 7, 2001, http://indiancountrytodaymedianetwork.com/ictarchives/2001/08/07/american-indian-opinion-leaders-american-indian-mascots-84807.

5. Ben Nuckols, "AP-GFK Poll," Associated Press Newswire, May 2, 2013, http://ap-gfkpoll.com/featured/our-latest-story-2.

6. Revenue for the National Football League in 2011–2012 was estimated at $9.5 billion. Cork Gaines, "SPORTS CHART OF THE DAY: NFL Revenue Is Nearly 25% More Than MLB," *Business Insider*, October 9, 2012, http://www.businessinsider.com/sports-chart-of-the-day-nfl-revenue-still-dwarfs-other-major-sports-2012-10.

BIBLIOGRAPHY

I list here a limited bibliography of writings that have been in use in the completion of this book. While it is by no means exhaustive of every work available, it does recognize the broad disciplinary intersections that inform this book. In particular, I highlight the contextual historical and theoretical material that forms the core underpinnings of my analysis. For ease of readers who might attempt to retrace my research, I provide the bibliography with two subcategories: archival collections and all other materials no matter their type.

ARCHIVAL COLLECTIONS

Florida State University Special Collections and University Archives
Alumni Association Records
Bernard F. Sliger Collection
Department of Athletics
Doak Campbell Papers, 1935–1972
Florida State College for Women/Florida State University
Florida State University Media Relations Files
Florida State University Seminole Mascot Files
Florida State University Student Government Association Records
Florida State University Student Publications
Heritage Protocol Photograph Collection
Memorabilia
Robert Manning Strozier Speeches and Addresses
Student Affairs
William George Dodd Papers

Miami University Archives
Alumni Affairs/Development
Board of Trustees
Digital Archive
Faculty: James Rodabaugh
Intercollegiate Athletics
Miami University, General A–Z
Pictures/Artifacts/Maps/Plans
President: 1965–81, Phillip R. Shriver
Public Information
Reference
Student Affairs: Miami Tribe
Student Life
Vertical Files: Mascot

Stanford University

Arthur Leland Miller Papers
Associated Students of Stanford University
Board of Athletic Control Records, 1916–1954
Board of Control: Graduate Manager of Athletics Records, 1904–1915
David Starr Jordan Papers
Department of Athletics
Department of Athletics: Physical Education and Recreation: Media Relations Records
Department of Athletics, Physical Education and Recreation Photograph Albums,
     1923–1977
Historical Photograph Collection, 1887–ca. 1996
Marching Band
Native American Cultural Center Library
Photographs and Ephemera
President's Office
Stanford Alumni Association
Stanford Athletics Photograph Collection, 1929–1973
Stanford Athletics Scrapbook, 1925–1930
Stanford Band
Stanford University Football Programs
Stanford University Publications
Stanford University Special Collections and University Archives
Stanford University Student Life
Student Letters and Memoirs
Thomas M. Williams, MD Papers, 1871–1947
Women's Physical Education Department Records, 1928–1982
Women's Recreation Association

University of Illinois Archives
(includes the Sousa Archives and Center for American Music)

A. Austin Harding Collection
Alumni Association
Applied Health Sciences: Dean's Office: George A. Huff Papers, 1883–1947
Chief Illiniwek
College of Media: Division of University Broadcasting
College of Media: Journalism Department: Jay Rosenstein Papers, 1997
Digital Images and Records
Division of Intercollegiate Athletics
Fine and Applied Arts: University Bands
Fine and Applied Arts: University Bands: John Philip Sousa Music and Personal Papers,
     ca. 1880–1932
Fine and Applied Arts: University Bands: Mark H. Hindsley Papers, 1920–1983
Fine and Applied Arts: University Bands: Raymond F. Dvorak Papers, 1922–1934
Fine and Applied Arts: University Bands: University Bands Collection, ca. 1840–1997
Public Information
Student Affairs
Student Affairs: Office of the Dean of Students, Fred H. Turner Papers, 1918–1975
Videotapes

University of North Dakota
Department of American Indian Studies
Office of the President

University of North Dakota Chester Fritz Library, Elwyn B. Robinson
Department of Special Collections, University Archives
Alumni Association
Department of Athletics
Memorabilia
Music Department Records
Papers of Kendall Baker
Papers of William Julison: Sports–1890–1988
President's Office Records
Sioux Logo and Nickname Collection
Student Affairs
Student Organizations
Student Organizations: Golden Feather Club Records
Student Papers: Edward J. Franta Papers
Student Papers: Mary Elizabeth Ewing Scrapbook
Student Publications: Dakota Student
Student Publications and Yearbooks
University Band

ALL OTHER MATERIALS

Adams, David Wallace. *Education for Extinction: American Indians and the Boarding-School Experience, 1875–1928.* Lawrence: University Press of Kansas, 1995.

———. "More Than a Game: The Carlisle Indians Take to the Gridiron, 1893–1917." *Western Historical Quarterly* 32 (Spring 2001): 25–53.

Addonizio, S. "Osceola's Public Life: Two Images of the Seminole Hero." *Dimensions of Native America: The Contact Zone* (1998): 90–95.

Adelman, Melvin L. *A Sporting Time: New York City and the Rise of Modern Athletics, 1820–1870.* 1986. Reprint, Urbana: University of Illinois Press, 1990.

Adorno, Theodor W. *Negative Dialectics.* New York: Routledge, 1990.

Alexander, Bryant Keith. *Performing Black Masculinity: Race, Culture, and Queer Identity.* Lanham, Md.: AltaMira Press, 2006.

Allen, Thornton W., ed. *Intercollegiate Song Book: Alma Mater and Football Songs of the American Colleges.* New York: Intercollegiate Song Book, 1927.

American Football Coaches Association. "All Time Trustee List." http://www.afca.com/ViewArticle.dbml?DB_OEM_ID=9300&ATCLID=639656.

Anderson, Benedict. *Imagined Communities: Reflections on the Origin and Spread of Nationalism.* London: Verso Editions/NLB, 1983.

Anderson, James. "From Loony Coons to Tacos and Tequila: The Aesthetics of Race in Middle-Class America." Lecture, Spurlock Museum, University of Illinois at Urbana-Champaign, March 31, 2009. http://cas.illinois.edu/Events/ViewPublicEvent.aspx?Guid=DB10F22C-F640-4BC8-8D38-705FB807E490.

Anderson, Karen L. *Chain Her by One Foot: The Subjugation of Women in Seventeenth-Century New France.* New York: Routledge, 1991.

Andrews, David L., Daniel S. Mason, and Michael L. Silk, eds. *Qualitative Methods in Sports Studies*. Oxford: Berg, 2005.

Anson, Bert. *The Miami Indians*. Norman: University of Oklahoma Press, 2000.

Apps, Jerry. *Ringlingville USA: The Stupendous Story of Seven Siblings and Their Stunning Circus Success*. Madison: Wisconsin Historical Society Press, 2005.

Axtell, J., and W. Sturtevant. "The Unkindest Cut of All, or Who Invented Scalping." *William and Mary Quarterly* (July 1980): 451–472.

Ayers, Edward L. *The Promise of the New South: Life after Reconstruction*. New York: Oxford University Press, 1992.

Baca, L. R. "Native Images in Schools and the Racially Hostile Environment." *Journal of Sport and Social Issues* 28, no. 1 (2004): 71–78.

Bachman, Harold B. *The Biggest Boom in Dixie: The Story of Band Music at the University of Florida*. Gainesville: University Press of Florida, 1968.

Bailyn, Bernard, Robert Daliek, David Davis, David Donald, and John Thomas. *The Great Republic: A History of the American People*. Lexington, Mass.: D. C. Heath, 1985.

Baker, Houston A., Jr. *Modernism and the Harlem Renaissance*. Chicago: University of Chicago Press, 1987.

Banks, D., Laurel R. Davis, Synthia Sydnor Slowikowski, and L. A. Wenner. "Tribal Names and Mascots in Sports." *Journal of Sport and Social Issues* 17, no. 1 (1993): 5–8.

Barthes, Roland. "Myth Today." In *Mythologies*. Trans. Annette Lavers and C. Smith. New York: Hill and Wang, 1972.

Bastille, Gretchen M. *Native American Representations: First Encounters, Distorted Images, and Literary Appropriations*. Lincoln: University of Nebraska Press, 2001.

Batchelder, Samuel. "Wanted!—College Characters." In *Bits of Harvard History*. Cambridge, Mass.: Harvard University Press, 1924.

Batchelor, Ray. *Henry Ford: Mass Production, Modernism and Design*. Manchester: Manchester University Press, 1995.

Baudrillard, Jean. *Simulations*. Trans. Paul Foss, Paul Patton, and Philip Beitchman. New York: Semiotext(e), 1983.

———. *Simulacra and Simulations*. Trans. Sheila Faria Glaser. Ann Arbor: University of Michigan Press, 1995.

Beard, Daniel Carter. *Hardly a Man Is Now Alive: The Autobiography of Dan Beard*. New York: Doubleday, Doran, 1939.

Bederman, Gail. *Manliness and Civilization: A Cultural History of Gender and Race in the United States, 1880–1917*. Chicago: University of Chicago Press, 1995.

Beidler, Peter G. *Native Americans in the Saturday Evening Post*. Lanham, Md.: Scarecrow Press, 2000.

Bell, Elizabeth. *Theories of Performance*. Los Angeles: Sage, 2008.

Bender, Thomas. *Intellect and Public Life: Essays on the Social History of Academic Intellectuals in the United States*. Baltimore: Johns Hopkins University Press, 1993.

Bentley, Matthew. "Playing White Men: American Football and Manhood at the Carlisle Indian School, 1893–1904." *Journal of the History of Childhood and Youth* 3, no. 2 (Spring 2010): 187–209.

———. "The Rise of Athletic Masculinity at the Carlisle Indian School, 1904–1913." *International Journal of the History of Sport* 29, no. 10 (August 2012): 1466–1489.

Benton, Michael P. *Ethnic and Racial Consciousness*. 2nd ed. London: Longman Press, 1997.

Berkhofer, Robert F. *The White Man's Indian: Images of the American Indian from Columbus to the Present*. New York: Knopf, 1978.

Bernstein, Mark F. *Football: The Ivy League Origins of an American Obsession*. Philadelphia: University of Pennsylvania Press, 2001.

Bertuca, David J., ed. *World's Columbian Exposition: A Centennial Bibliographic Guide.* Bibliographies and Indexes in American History, vol. 26. Westport, Conn.: Greenwood, 1996.

Best, Gary D. *The Nickel and Dime Decade: American Popular Culture during the 1930s.* Westport, Mass.: Praeger, 1993.

Bierley, Paul E. *The Incredible Band of John Philip Sousa.* Urbana: University of Illinois Press, 2006.

Biggar, H. P., and H. Percival. *The Works of Samuel de Champlain.* Toronto: University of Toronto Press, 1971.

Bird, S. Elizabeth, ed. *Dressing in Feathers: The Construction of the Indian in American Popular Culture.* Boulder, Colo.: Westview Press, 1996.

Birrell, Susan, and C. L. Cole, eds. *Women, Sport, and Culture.* Champaign, Ill.: Human Kinetics, 1994.

Black, Jason E. "The 'Mascotting' of Native America: Construction, Commodity, and Assimilation." *American Indian Quarterly* 26, no. 4 (2002): 605–622.

Blackstone, Sarah J. *Buckskins, Bullets, and Business: A History of Buffalo Bill's Wild West.* Westport, Conn.: Greenwood Press, 1986.

Bledsoe, A. J. *1881 History: Del Norte County, California.* Eureka, Calif.: Humboldt Press, 1881.

Blight, David W. *Race and Reunion: The Civil War in American Memory.* Cambridge, Mass.: Harvard University Press, 2002.

Bloom, John. *To Show What an Indian Can Do: Sports at Native American Boarding Schools.* Minneapolis: University of Minnesota Press, 2000.

Bloom, John, and Michael Nevin Willard. *Sports Matters: Race, Recreation, and Culture.* New York: New York University Press, 2002.

Board of Athletic Control. *Minutes of the Board of Athletic Control.* Palo Alto, Calif.: Stanford University, 1930.

Bodmer, Karl. *Karl Bodmer's North American Prints.* Lincoln: University of Nebraska Press, 2004.

Boorstin, Daniel J. *The Image: A Guide to Pseudo-Events in America.* New York: Vintage, 1992.

Booth, Douglas. *The Field: Truth and Fiction in Sport History.* London: Routledge, 2005.

Borchers, Albert Webber. *Chief Illiniwek.* Champaign, Ill.: W. Borchers, 1979.

Bordewich, Fergus. M. *Killing the White Man's Indian: Reinventing Native Americans at the End of the Twentieth Century.* New York: Doubleday, 1996.

Bourke, W. "'You're Dixie's Football Pride': American College Football and the Resurgence of Southern Identity." *Identities* 10, no. 4 (2003): 477–494.

Boyer, Paul. *Urban Masses and Moral Order in America, 1820–1920.* Cambridge, Mass.: Harvard University Press, 1978.

Breen, Kevin. "Native American Heroes in the Comics." *Blue Corn Comics.* http://www.bluecorncomics.com/kbreen.htm.

Broacher, John Seiler, and Willis Rudy. *Higher Education in Transition: A History of American Colleges and Universities.* New York: Transaction, 1997.

Brown, Ian W. "The Calumet Ceremony in the Southeast and Its Archaeological Manifestations." *American Antiquity* 54, no. 2 (April 1989): 311–331.

Brown, J. "The Clyde A. Erwin High School Mascot Controversy." Ph.D. diss., Western Carolina University, 2007.

Brown, Jennifer S. H. *Strangers in Blood: Fur Trade Company Families in Indian Country.* Norman: University of Oklahoma Press, 1996.

Brown, K. A. "Native American Team Names and Mascots: Disparaging and Insensitive or Just a Part of the Game?" *Sports Law Journal* 9 (2002): 115–263.

Brownell, Susan. *The 1904 Anthropology Days and Olympic Games: Sport, Race, and American Imperialism*. Lincoln: University of Nebraska Press, 2008.

Brundale, Maureen, and Mark Schmitt, *The Bloomington-Normal Circus Legacy: The Golden Age of Aerialists*. Charleston, S.C.: History Press, 2013.

Buckley, Thomas. "Yurok Realities in the Nineteenth and Twentieth Centuries." Ph.D. diss., University of Chicago, 1982.

Buford, Cary Clive. *We're Loyal to You, Illinois: The Story of the University of Illinois Bands under Albert Austin Harding for 43 Years, Superimposed upon Glimpses of University History during the Half-Century of Harding Leadership on Campus*. Danville, Ill.: Interstate, 1952.

Buford, Kate. *Native American Son: The Life and Sporting Legend of Jim Thorpe*. New York: Knopf, 2010.

Burgos, Adrian. *Playing America's Game: Baseball, Latinos, and the Color Line*. Berkeley: University of California Press, 2007.

Burk, Robert F. *Much More Than a Game: Players, Owners and American Baseball since 1921*. Chapel Hill: University of North Carolina Press, 2001.

Burns, Edward McNall. *David Starr Jordan: Prophet of Democracy*. Palo Alto, Calif.: Stanford University Press, 1953.

Buss, James J. *Winning the West with Words: Language and Conquest in the Lower Great Lakes*. Norman: University of Oklahoma Press, 2011.

Cahill, Cathleen D. "Native Men, White Women, and Marriage in the Indian Service." *Frontiers: A Journal of Women Studies*, 29, nos. 2–3 (2008): 106–145.

Camp, Walter. *American Football*. New York: Harper & Brothers, 1891.

Camp, Walter, and Lorin F. Daniel. *Football*. New York: Riverside Press, 1896.

Carey, James W. *Communication as Culture: Essays on Media and Society*. New York: Routledge, 1992.

Carnes, Mark C., and Clyde Griffin. *Secret Ritual and Manhood in Victorian America*. New Haven, Conn.: Yale University Press, 1989.

———. *Meanings for Manhood: Constructions of Masculinity in Victorian America*. Chicago: University of Chicago Press, 1990.

Carroll, John M. *Red Grange and the Rise of Modern Football*. Urbana: University of Illinois Press, 1999.

Carter, Harvey Lewis. *The Life and Times of Little Turtle: First Sagamore of the Wabash*. Urbana: University of Illinois Press, 1987.

Carver, Gordon M. "Sells-Floto Circus 1914–15." In *Bandwagon*, ed. Fred D. Pfenning Jr. Columbus, Ohio: Journal of the Circus Historical Society, November–December, 1975.

Case Western Reserve University. "Team Colors, Mascots, Names." http://www.case.edu/its/archives/Sports/teams.htm.

Cayton, Andrew R. L. *Ohio: A History of a People*. Columbus: Ohio State University Press, 2002.

The Chief: A Historical Documentary on Chief Illiniwek. Champaign, Ill.: The Chief Illiniwek Educational Foundation, 2000.

The Chief's Last Dance? Champaign, Ill.: Honor the Chief Society, 2007.

Child, Brenda J. *Boarding School Seasons: American Indian Families, 1900–1940*. Lincoln: University of Nebraska Press, 1998.

Churchill, Winston S. *Great Contemporaries*. New York: W. W. Norton, 1991.

Clark, D. A. T. "Indigenous Voice and Vision as Commodity in a Mass-Consumption Society." *American Indian Quarterly* 29 (2005): 228–238.

Clarkson, G. "Racial Imagery and Native Americans: A First Look at the Empirical Evidence behind the Indian Mascot Controversy." *Cardozo Journal of International and Comparative Law* 11 (2003): 393–407.

Clotfelter, Charles T. *Big-Time Sports in American Universities.* Cambridge: Cambridge University Press, 2011.

Cockrell, Dan. *Demons of Disorder: Early Blackface Minstrels and Their World.* New York: Cambridge University Press, 1997.

Cohodas, Nadine. *The Band Played Dixie: Race and the Liberal Conscience at Ole Miss.* New York: Free Press, 1997.

"College Yell." *Quarterly Journal of the University of North Dakota* 13 (1923): 379.

Connolly, M. R. "What's in a Name? A Historical Look at Native American–Related Nicknames and Symbols at Three US Universities." *Journal of Higher Education* (2000): 515–547.

Coombe, Rosemary J. "Embodied Trademarks: Mimesis and Alterity on American Commercial Frontiers." *Cultural Anthropology* (1996): 202–224.

Corbett, Bernard M., and Paul Simpson. *The Only Game That Matters: The Harvard/Yale Rivalry.* New York: Crown, 2004.

Cott, Nancy F. *The Grounding of Modern Feminism.* New Haven, Conn.: Yale University Press, 1987.

Covington, James W. *The Seminoles of Florida.* Gainesville: University Press of Florida, 1993.

Crawford, Bill. *All American: The Rise and Fall of Jim Thorpe.* Hoboken, N.J.: John Wiley & Sons, 2004.

Creamer, Robert W. *Babe: The Legend Comes to Life.* New York: Simon and Schuster, 1974.

Cross, Coy F. *Justin Smith Morrill: Father of the Land-Grant Colleges.* East Lansing: Michigan State University Press, 1999.

Crue, C. A. "White Racism/Redface Minstrels: Regimes of Power in Representation." Ph.D. diss., University of Illinois at Urbana-Champaign, 2002.

Crunden, Robert M. *Ministers of Reform: The Progressives' Achievement in American Civilization, 1889–1920.* 1982. Reprint, Urbana: University of Illinois Press, 1984.

Culhane, J. *The American Circus: An Illustrated History.* New York: Holt, 1990.

Darnell, Tim. *The Crackers: Early Days of Atlanta Baseball.* Athens, Ga.: Hill Street Press, 2003.

Davis, A. L. "A History of the American Bandmasters Association." Ph.D. diss., Arizona State University, 1987.

Davis, James C. *Commerce in Color: Race, Consumer Culture, and American Literature, 1893–1933.* Ann Arbor: University of Michigan Press, 2007.

Davis, Janet M. *The Circus Age: Culture and Society under the American Big Top.* Chapel Hill: University of North Carolina Press, 2002.

Davis, Laurel R. "Protest against the Use of Native American Mascots: A Challenge to Traditional American Identity." *Journal of Sport and Social Issues* 17, no. 1 (1993): 9–22.

Davis, Margo Baumgarten, and Roxanne Nolan. *The Stanford Album: A Photographic History, 1885–1945.* Stanford, Calif.: Stanford University Press, 1989.

Debord, Guy. *Society of the Spectacle.* 5th ed. New York: Zone Books, 1999.

Deford, Frank. *Big Bill Tilden: The Triumph and the Tragedy.* New York: Simon and Schuster, 1976.

Delaney, Michelle Anne, and National Museum of American History (U.S.). *Buffalo Bill's Wild West Warriors: A Photographic History by Gertrude Käsebier.* Washington, D.C.: Smithsonian National Museum of American History, 2007.

Delanty, Gerard. *Modernity and Postmodernity: Knowledge, Power, and the Self.* New York: Sage, 2000.

———. "The Cosmopolitan Imagination: Critical Cosmopolitanism and Social Theory." *British Journal of Sociology* 57, no. 1 (2006): 25–47.

Deloria, Philip Joseph. *Playing Indian.* New Haven, Conn.: Yale University Press, 1999.

————. *Indians in Unexpected Places*. Lawrence: University Press of Kansas, 2004.

DeMallie, Raymond J. "Kinship and Biology in Sioux Culture." In *North American Indian Anthropology: Essays on Society and Culture*, ed. Rayond J. DeMallie and Alfonso Ortiz. Norman: University of Oklahoma Press, 1994.

————. "Sioux until 1850." In *Handbook of North American Indians. Vol. 13, Plains*, ed. Raymond J. DeMallie, pt. 2. Washington, D.C.: Smithsonian Insitution, 2001.

D'Emilio, John, and Estelle B. Freedman. *Intimate Matters: A History of Sexuality in America*. New York: Harper & Row–Perennial, 1992.

Demming, Michael. *Mechanic Accents: Dime Novels and Working-Class Culture in America*. New York: Verso, 1987.

Denzin, Norman K. *Indians on Display: Global Commodification of Native America in Performance, Art, and Museums*. Walnut Creek, Calif.: Left Coast Press, 2013.

Dewey, E. H. "Football and the American Indians." *New England Quarterly* 3, no. 4 (1930): 736–740.

Dillon, Diane. "'The Fair as Spectacle': American Art and Culture at the 1893 World's Fair." Ph.D. diss., Yale University, 1994.

Dimitriadis, Greg. *Performing Identity/Performing Culture: Hip Hop as Text, Pedagogy, and Lived Practice*. New York: P. Lang, 2001.

Dippie, Brian W. *Custer's Last Stand: The Anatomy of an American Myth*. Lincoln: University of Nebraska Press, 1994.

Drinnon, Richard. *Facing West: The Metaphysics of Indian-Hating and Empire-Building*. Norman: University of Oklahoma Press, 1997.

Dubakis, Melissa. *Visualizing Labor in American Sculpture: Monuments, Manliness, and the Work Ethic, 1880–1935*. New York: Cambridge University Press, 1999.

Dubin, Margaret D. *Native America Collected: The Culture of an Art World*. Albuquerque: University of New Mexico Press, 2001.

du Gay, Paul, Jessica Evans, and Peter Redman, eds. *Identity: A Reader*. New York: Sage, 2001.

Eastman, Benjamin. *America's Game(s): A Critical Anthropology of Sport*. London: Routledge, 2008.

Eastman, Charles A., and E. L Blumenschein. *Indian Boyhood*. New York: Dover, 1971.

Ebner, Katharine C., ed. *Sculptor in Buckskin: The Autobiography of Alexander Phimister Proctor*. 2nd ed. Norman: University of Oklahoma Press, 2009.

Eddy, Edward D., Jr. *Colleges for Our Land and Time: The Land-Grant Idea in American Education*. New York: Harper, 1957.

Edmunds, R. David, Frederick E. Hoxie, and Neal Salisbury. *The People: A History of Native America*. Boston: Houghton Mifflin, 2007.

Elliott, Michael A. *Custerology: The Enduring Legacy of the Indian Wars and George Armstrong Custer*. Chicago: University of Chicago Press, 2007.

Elliott, Orrin Leslie. *Stanford University: The First Twenty-Five Years*. Stanford, Calif: Stanford University Press, 1977.

Ellis, Clyde. *To Change Them Forever: Indian Education at the Rainy Mountain Boarding School, 1893–1920*. Norman: University of Oklahoma Press, 2008.

Faragher, John Mack. *Rereading Frederick Jackson Turner: The Significance of the Frontier in American History and Other Essays*. New York: Henry Holt, 1994.

Farnell, Brenda. "The Fancy Dance of Racializing Discourse." *Journal of Sport and Social Issues* 28, no. 1 (2004): 30–55.

————. "Zero-Sum Game: An Update on the Native American Mascot Controversy at the University of Illinois." *Journal of Sport and Social Issues* 28, no. 2 (2004): 212–215.

Fass, Paula S. *The Damned and the Beautiful: American Youth in the 1920s*. New York: Oxford University Press, 1977.

Fear-Segal, Jacqueline. *White Man's Club: Schools, Race, and the Struggle for Indian Acculturation.* Lincoln: University of Nebraska Press, 2009.

Fielding, Henry. *The Story of John the Orange-man: Being a Short Sketch of the Life of Harvard's Popular Mascot.* Cambridge, Mass.: John Wilson and Son–University Press, 1891.

Fletcher, Matthew L. M. "The Legal Fiction of Gridiron Cowboys and Indians." *Indigenous Peoples' Journal of Law, Culture & Resistance,* no. 2 (2005): 11–27.

Florida Senate. *Florida Senate Journal,* 1850.

Florida State University. "1905–1909." *Sesquicentennial Celebration History.* http://www.fsu.edu/~fsu150/history/history_03_1905a.html.

———. "1920–1930." *Sesquicentennial Celebration History.* http://www.fsu.edu/~fsu150/history/history_03_1905c.html.

———. "1930–1940." *Sesquicentennial Celebration History.* http://www.fsu.edu/~fsu150/history/history_03_1905d.html.

———. "1947–1959." *Sesquicentennial Celebration History.* http://www.fsu.edu/~fsu150/history/history_03_1905d.html.

———. "About Florida State." *History.* http://www.fsu.edu/about/history.html.

———. "Buckman Bill." *Sesquicentennial Celebration History.* http://www.fsu.edu/~fsu150/history/history_03_1905d.html.

Foner, Eric. *Reconstruction: America's Unfinished Revolution, 1863–1877.* New York: Harper & Row, 1988.

Fornier, Peter J. *The Handbook of Mascots and Nicknames.* Leesburg, Fla.: Raja Associates, 2003.

Foster, Susan Leigh. *Choreographing History.* Bloomington: Indiana University Press, 1995.

Fowler, Loretta. *The Columbia Guide to American Indians of the Great Plains.* New York: Columbia University Press, 2003.

Freedman, Russell. *Scouting with Baden-Powell.* New York: Holiday House, 1967.

Fryberg, Stephanie Ann. "Really? You Don't Look Like an American Indian: Social Representations and Social Group Identities." Ph.D. diss., Stanford University, 2003.

Fryberg, Stephanie, and H. R. Markus. "On Being American Indian: Current and Possible Selves." *Self and Identity* 2, no. 4 (2003): 325–344.

Fryberg, Stephanie, H. R. Markus, D. Oyserman, and J. M. Stone. "Of Warrior Chiefs and Indian Princesses: The Psychological Consequences of American Indian Mascots." *Basic and Applied Social Psychology* 30, no. 3 (2008): 208–218.

Fuller, Linda K. *Sport, Rhetoric, and Gender: Historical Perspectives and Media Representations.* New York: Palgrave Macmillan, 2006.

Gabler, Neal. *An Empire of Their Own: How Jews Invented Hollywood.* New York: Crown, 1988.

Gamache, Ray. "Sport as Cultural Assimilation: Representations of American Indian Athletes in the Carlisle School Newspaper." *American Journalism* 26, no. 2 (Spring 2009): 7–37.

Garber, Jan. *More College Medleys.* Hollywood, Calif.: Capitol Records, 1948.

Garippo, Louis A. *A Report to the Board of Trustees: The Chief Illiniwek Dialogue Report.* Urbana: University of Illinois, 2000.

Garoian, Charles R. *Spectacle Pedagogy: Art, Politics, and Visual Culture.* Albany: State University of New York Press, 2008.

Gaudio, Michael. *Engraving the Savage: The New World and Techniques of Civilization.* Minneapolis: University of Minnesota Press, 2008.

Geertz, Clifford. *The Interpretation of Cultures.* New York: Basic Books, 1984.

Geiger, Louis George. *University of the Northern Plains: A History of the University of North Dakota, 1883–1958.* Grand Forks: University of North Dakota Press, 1958.

General Assembly of Florida. "An Act to Provide for the Location of the Two Seminaries of Learning to Be Established in This State." In *Acts and Resolutions Adopted by the General Assembly of Florida.* Tallahassee, Fla.: Charles E. Dyke, 1859.

Genetin-Pilawa, C. Joseph. *Crooked Paths to Allotment: The Fight Over Federal Indian Policy after the Civil War*. Chapel Hill: University of North Carolina Press, 2012.

Gerardi, Jess Louis. "Karl L. King: His Life and His Music." Ph.D. diss., University of Colorado, 1973.

Giddens, Anthony. *The Third Way: The Renewal of Social Democracy*. Cambridge: Polity Press, 1998.

Gilbert, Matthew Sakiestewa. *Education Beyond the Mesas: Hopi Students at Sherman Institute, 1902–1929*. Lincoln: University of Nebraska Press, 2010.

———. "Hopi Footraces and American Marathons, 1912–1930." *American Quarterly* 62, no. 1 (March 2010): 77–101.

———. "Marathoner Louis Tewanima and the Continuity of Hopi Running, 1908–1912." *Western Historical Quarterly* 43 (Autumn 2012): 324–346.

Glassberg, David. *American Historical Pageantry: The Uses of Tradition in the Early Twentieth Century*. Chapel Hill: University of North Carolina Press, 1990.

Glenn, James Lafayette. *My Work among the Florida Seminoles*. Orlando: University Press of Florida, 1982.

Goddard, I. "'I Am a Red-Skin': The Adoption of a Native American Expression (1769–1826)." *Native American Studies* 19, no. 2 (2005): 1–20.

Gonzalez, John. "In-group/Out-group Dynamics of Native American Mascot Endorsement." Ph.D. diss., University of North Dakota, 2005.

Grange, Red, and Ira Morton. *The Red Grange Story: An Autobiography Told to Ira Morton*. Urbana: University of Illinois Press, 1993.

Green, Reyna. "The Tribe Called Wannabee: Playing Indian in America and Europe." *Folklore* 99, no. 1 (1988): 30–55.

Griffin, Peter James. "A History of the Illinois Industrial University/University of Illinois Band, 1867–1908." Ph.D. diss., University of Illinois at Urbana-Champaign, 2004.

Gruber, Carol S. *Mars and Minerva: World War I and the Uses of the Higher Learning in America*. Baton Rouge: Louisiana State University Press, 1975.

Guild, Thacher Howland. *We're Loyal to You, Illinois*. New York: Melrose Bros. Music, 1906.

———. *The Illinois Loyalty Song: A Song of the University of Illinois*. Chicago: Melrose Bros. Music, 1907.

Guiliano, Jennifer E. "Red Card: The Role of Native Americans as Sports Mascots at Miami University." Master's thesis, Miami University, 2002.

———. "An American Spectacle: College Mascots and the Performance of Tradition." Ph.D. diss., University of Illinois at Urbana-Champaign, 2010.

Guttmann, Allen. *From Ritual to Record: The Nature of Modern Sports*. New York: Columbia University Press, 1978.

———. *Games and Empires: Modern Sports and Cultural Imperialism*. New York: Columbia University Press, 1996.

Hall, Donald E. *Muscular Christianity: Embodying the Victorian Age*. Cambridge: Cambridge University Press, 1994.

Hall, Stuart. *Representation: Cultural Representations and Signifying Practices*. New York: Sage and Open University, 1997.

Hamilton, Henry W. *Remington Schuyler's West: Artistic Visions of Cowboys and Indians*. Pierre: South Dakota State Historical Society Press, 2004.

Hand, Greg. "History of the Bearcat Mascot." *About UC*, June 30, 2000.

Handler, Richard. "Authenticity." *Anthropology Today* 2, no. 1 (1986): 2–4.

Handler, Richard, and J. Innekin. "Tradition, Genuine or Spurious." *Journal of American Folklore* 97, no. 385 (1984): 273–290.

Hanson, Glenn. "Reflecting the Community through the Yearbook." *English Journal* 35, no. 2 (February 1946): 90–94.

Hargreaves, Jennifer. *Sporting Feminisms: Critical Issues in the History and Sociology of Women's Sport.* New York: Routledge, 1994.

Harris, Reed. *King Football: The Vulgarization of the American College.* New York: Vanguard Press, 1932.

Hassrick, Peter H. *Wildlife and Western Heroes: Alexander Phimister Proctor, Sculptor.* Fort Worth, Tex.: Amon Carter Museum, 2003.

Hatton, Thomas J. *Karl L. King: An American Bandmaster.* Evanston, Ill.: Instrumentalist, 1975.

Havighurst, Walter. *The Miami Years, 1809–1959.* New York: Putnam, 1958.

Hawley, Ellis W. *The Great War and the Search for the Modern Order: A History of the American People and Their Institutions, 1917–1933.* Prospect Heights, Ill.: Waveland Press, 1992.

Haynie, Jerry Thomas. "The Changing Role of the Band in American Colleges and Universities, 1900 to 1968." Ph.D. diss., Peabody College for Teachers of Vanderbilt University, 1971.

Hays, Robert G. *A Race at Bay: New York Times Editorials on "the Indian Problem," 1860–1900.* Carbondale: Southern Illinois University Press, 1997.

———. *Editorializing "the Indian Problem": The New York Times on Native Americans, 1860–1900.* Carbondale: Southern Illinois University Press, 2007.

Helmberger, Pat Stave. *Indians as Mascots in Minnesota Schools.* Burnsville, Minn.: Friends of the Bill of Rights Foundation, 1999.

Hemmer, J. J. "Exploitation of American Indian Symbols: A First Amendment Analysis." *American Indian Quarterly* 32, no. 2 (2008): 121–140.

Hennepin, Louis, Reuben Gold Thwaites, and V. H. Paltsits. *A New Discovery of a Vast Country in America.* Chicago: A. C. McClure, 1903.

The Heritage of Miami University. Oxford, Ohio: Miami University Audio Visual Service, 1981.

Herzberg, Bob. *Savages and Saints: The Changing Image of American Indians in Westerns.* Jefferson, N.C.: McFarland, 2008.

Hilger, Michael. *From Savage to Nobleman: Images of Native Americans in Film.* Lanham, Md.: Scarecrow Press, 1995.

Himes, Cindy L. "The Female Athlete in American Society, 1860–1940." Ph.D. diss., University of Pennsylvania, 1986.

Hirth, Floyd J. *Illini Fight Song.* Chicago, 1938. University of Illinois Archives.

Hobsbawm, Eric J., and Terence Ranger. *The Invention of Tradition.* Cambridge: Cambridge University Press, 1983.

Hodes, Martha. *White Women, Black Men: Illicit Sex in the Nineteenth-Century South.* New Haven, Conn.: Yale University Press, 1997.

Hofmann, Sudie. "The Elimination of Indigenous Mascots, Logos, and Nicknames: Organizing on College Campuses." *American Indian Quarterly* 29, nos. 1/2 (Winter 2005): 156–177.

Hofstader, Richard F. *The Age of Reform: From Bryan to F.D.R.* 1955. Reprint, New York: Vintage Press, 1960.

Hoganson, Kristin L. *Consumers' Imperium: The Global Production of American Domesticity, 1865–1920.* Chapel Hill: University of North Carolina Press, 2007.

Holt, Thomas C. "Marking: Race, Race-Making, and the Writing of History." *American Historical Review* 100, no. 1 (February 1995): 1–20.

Hoose, Phillip M. *Necessities: Racial Barriers in American Sports.* New York: Random House, 1989.

Horwitz, Tony. *Confederates in the Attic: Dispatches from the Unfinished Civil War.* New York: Vintage Books, 1999.

Howe, Dan Walker. *What Hath God Wrought: The Transformation of America, 1815–1848.* New York: Oxford University Press, 2007.

Hoxie, Frederick E. *A Final Promise: The Campaign to Assimilate the Indians, 1880–1920.* 1984. Reprint, Lincoln: University of Nebraska Press, 2001.

Hubbard, Ladee. "Mobility in America: The Myth of the Frontier and the Performance of National Culture at the Chicago World's Fair of 1893." Ph.D. diss., University of California, Los Angeles, 2003.

Huhndorf, Shari M. *Going Native: Indians in the American Cultural Imagination.* Ithaca, N.Y.: Cornell University Press, 2001.

Hurt, R. Douglas. *The Ohio Frontier: Crucible of the Old Northwest, 1720–1830.* Bloomington: Indiana University Press, 1996.

If the Name Has to Go. Grand Forks, N.D.: Quiet Coyote Video Productions, 2004.

Ignatiev, Noel. *How the Irish Became White.* New York: Routledge, 1995.

Ingrassia, Brian. *The Rise of the Gridiron University: Higher Education's Uneasy Alliance with Big-Time Football.* Lawrence: University Press of Kansas, 2012.

Intercollegiate Athletic Association of the United States. *Proceedings of the First Annual Meeting Held at New York City, New York December 29, 1905.* New York: Intercollegiate Athletic Association of the United States, 1906.

In Whose Honor? Champaign, Ill.: New Day Films for Smoking Munchkins Video, 2005.

Jacobs, Donald Trent. *Unlearning the Language of Conquest: Scholars Expose Anti-Indianism in America: Deceptions That Influence War and Peace, Civil Liberties, Public Education, Religion and Spirituality, Democratic Ideals, the Environment, Law, Literature, Film, and Happiness.* Austin: University of Texas Press, 2006.

Jacobs, Michelle Renee. *Framing Pseudo-Indian Mascots: The Case of Cleveland.* Kent, Ohio: Kent State University Press, 2007.

Jacobson, Matthew Frye. *Barbarian Virtues: The United States Encounters Foreign Peoples at Home and Abroad, 1876–1917.* New York: Hill and Wang, 2000.

———. *Roots Too: White Ethnic Revival in Post–Civil Rights America.* Cambridge, Mass.: Harvard University Press, 2006.

James, C. L .R. *Beyond a Boundary.* Durham, N.C.: Duke University Press, 1993.

Jaska, N. "Louis Sockalexis: An Analysis of Media Coverage Given to Baseball's First Native American." Bachelor's thesis, University of North Carolina, 2003.

Jay, G. S. "'White Man's Book No Good': D. W. Griffith and the American Indian." *Cinema Journal* 39, no. 4 (2000): 3–26.

Jenkins, Mark T. *Nickname Mania: The Best of College Nicknames and Mascots and the Stories Behind Them.* Omaha, Neb.: Admark Communications, 1997.

Jenkins, Sally. *The Real All Americans: The Team That Changed a Game, a People, a Nation.* New York: Doubleday, 2007.

Jennings, F. "Thomas Penn's Loyalty Oath." *American Journal of Legal History* 8 (1964): 303–313.

Jensen, Robert. *The Heart of Whiteness: Confronting Race, Racism, and White Privilege.* San Francisco: City Lights, 2005.

Johnson, James W. *The Wow Boys: A Coach, a Team, and a Turning Point in College Football.* Lincoln: University of Nebraska Press, 2006.

Johnson, Russell L. *Warriors into Workers: The Civil War and the Formation of the Urban-Industrial Society in a Northern City.* New York: Fordham University Press, 2003.

Jolivétte, Andrew. *Cultural Representation in Native America.* Lanham, Md.: AltaMira Press, 2006.

Jones, W. "Episodes in the Culture-Hero Myth of the Sauks and Foxes." *Journal of American Folklore* 14, no. 55 (1901): 225–239.

Jordan, Winthrop. *The White Man's Burden: Historical Origins of Racism in America.* 1974. Reprint, Oxford University Press, 2002.

Jumper, Betty Mae. *A Seminole Legend: The Life of Betty Mae Tiger Jumper.* Gainesville: University Press of Florida, 2001.

Kahn, Roger. *A Flame of Pure Fire: Jack Dempsey and the Roaring 20s.* New York: Houghton Mifflin Harcourt, 1999.

Kammen, Michael G. *Mystic Chords of Memory: The Transformation of Tradition in American Culture.* New York: Knopf, 1991.

Kashatus, William C. *Money Pitcher: Chief Bender and the Tragedy of Indian Assimilation.* University Park: Pennsylvania State University Press, 2006.

Kaspar, Beth Marie. "Unpacking the Siwash Stories: Encoding the Narrative Texts of George Fitch." Bachelor's thesis, Knox College, 1997.

Kasson, Joy S. *Buffalo Bill's Wild West: Celebrity, Memory, and Popular History.* New York: Hill and Wang, 2000.

Kilpatrick, Jacquelyn. *Celluloid Indians: Native Americans and Film.* Lincoln: University of Nebraska Press, 1999.

Kimball, Bruce A. "The Langdell Problem: Historicizing the Century of Historiography, 1906–2000s." *Law and History Review* 22, no. 2 (Summer 2004). http://www.historycooperative.org/journals/lhr/22.2/kimball.html.

Kimmel, Michael. *Manhood in America: A Cultural History.* New York: Free Press, 1996.

King, C. Richard. *Colonial Discourses, Collective Memories, and the Exhibition of Native American Cultures and Histories in the Contemporary United States.* New York: Garland, 1998.

———. "Defensive Dialogues: Native American Mascots, Anti-Indianism, and Educational Institutions." *SIMILE: Studies in Media & Information Literacy Education* 2, no. 1 (2002): 1–12.

———. "Estrangements: Native American Mascots and Indian-Black Relations." In *Confounding the Color Line: The Indian-Black Experience in North America*, ed. James Brooks. Lincoln: University of Nebraska Press, 2002.

———. "De/Scribing Squ* w: Indigenous Women and Imperial Idioms in the United States." *American Indian Culture and Research Journal* 27, no. 2 (2003): 1–16.

———. "Borrowing Power." *CR: The New Centennial Review* 4 (2004): 189–209.

———. "Preoccupations and Prejudices: Reflections on the Study of Sports Imagery." *Anthropologica* 46 (2004): 29–36.

———. "This Is Not an Indian: Situating Claims about Indianness in Sporting Worlds." *Journal of Sport and Social Issues* 28, no. 1 (2004): 3–10.

———, ed. *Native Athletes in Sport and Society: A Reader.* Lincoln: University of Nebraska Press, 2005.

———. "On Being a Warrior: Race, Gender, and American Indian Imagery in Sport." *International Journal of the History of Sport* 23, no. 2 (2006): 315–330.

———. *Native Americans and Sport in North America: Other People's Games.* London: Routledge, 2008.

King, C. Richard, and Charles Fruehling Springwood, eds. *Team Spirits: The Native American Mascots Controversy.* Lincoln: University of Nebraska Press, 2001.

King, C. Richard, D. J. Leonard, and K. W. Kusz. "Fighting Spirits: The Racial Politics of Sports Mascots." *Journal of Sport and Social Issues* 24, no. 3 (2000): 282–304.

———. "Playing Indian: Why Native American Mascots Must End." *Chronicle Review* 9 (2001).

———. "White Power and Sport: An Introduction." *Journal of Sport and Social Issues* 31, no. 1 (2007): 3–10.

King, C. Richard, Ellen J. Staurowsky, Lawrence Baca, Laurel R. Davis, and Cornel Pewewardy. "Of Polls and Race Prejudice: *Sports Illustrated*'s Errant Indian Wars." *Journal of Sport and Social Issues* 26, no. 4 (2002): 381–402.

Krech, Shepard. *The Ecological Indian: Myth and History*. New York: W. W. Norton, 1999.

Krech, Shepard, and B. A. Hail. *Collecting Native America, 1870–1960*. Washington, D.C.: Smithsonian Institution Press, 1999.

Lanctot, Neil. *Negro League Baseball: The Rise and Ruin of a Black Institution*. Philadelphia: University of Pennsylvania Press, 2004.

Lansing, Michael. "Plains Indian Women and Interracial Marriage in the Upper Missouri Trade, 1804–1868." *Western Historical Quarterly* 31 (2000): 413–433.

LaRocque, Angela. "Psychological Distress between American Indian and Majority Culture College Students Regarding the Use of the Fighting Sioux Nickname and Logo." Ph.D. diss., University of North Dakota, 2004.

Larson, Erik. *The Devil in the White City: Murder, Magic, and Madness at the Fair That Changed America*. New York: Crown, 2003.

Lears, T. J. Jackson. *No Place of Grace: Antimodernism and the Transformation of American Culture, 1880–1920*. Chicago: University of Chicago Press, 1994.

———. *Rebirth of a Nation: The Making of Modern America, 1877–1920*. New York: HarperCollins, 2009.

Leavelle, T. N. "'Bad Things' and 'Good Hearts': Mediation, Meaning, and the Language of Illinois Christianity." *Church History* 76, no. 2 (2007): 363–394.

Lester, Robin. *Staff's University: The Rise, Decline, and Fall of Big-Time Football at Chicago*. Urbana: University of Illinois Press, 1995.

Levine, David O. *The American College and the Culture of Aspiration, 1915–1940*. Ithaca, N.Y.: Cornell University Press, 1986.

Levine, Lawrence. *Highbrow/Lowbrow: The Emergence of Cultural Hierarchy in America*. Cambridge, Mass.: Harvard University Press, 1988.

Levine, Peter. *A. G. Spalding and the Rise of Baseball: The Promise of American Sport*. New York: Oxford University Press, 1986.

Liebendorfer, Don E. *The Color of Life Is Red: A History of Stanford Athletics, 1892–1972*. Palo Alto, Calif.: Department of Athletics, Stanford University, 1972.

Lipsitz, George. *Time Passages: Collective Memory and American Popular Culture*. Minneapolis: University of Minnesota Press, 1990.

Lomawaima, K. Tsianina. *They Called It Prairie Light: The Story of Chilocco Indian School*. Lincoln: University of Nebraska Press, 1995.

Lopenzina, Drew. "'Good Indian': Charles Eastman and the Warrior as Civil Servant." *American Indian Quarterly* 27, no. 3 (2003): 727–757.

Lott, Eric. *Love and Theft: Blackface Minstrelsy and the American Working Class*. New York: Oxford University Press, 1995.

Lowen, Rebecca S. *Creating the Cold War University: The Transformation of Stanford*. Berkeley: University of California Press, 1997.

Lucas, Christopher J. *American Higher Education*. New York: Palgrave Macmillan, 1996.

Luschen, G. "The Interdependence of Sport and Culture." *International Review for the Sociology of Sport* 2, no. 1 (1967): 127–141.

MacCambridge, Michael. *America's Game: The Epic Story of How Pro Football Captured a Nation*. New York: Random House, 2004.

MacCauley, Clay. *The Seminole Indians of Florida*. Gainesville: University Press of Florida, 2000.

Macleod, David I. "Act Your Age: Boyhood, Adolescence, and the Rise of the Boys Scouts of America." *Journal of Social History* 16, no. 2 (Winter 1982): 3–20.

———. *Building Character in the American Boy, 1870–1920: The Boy Scouts, the YMCA, and Their Forerunners.* Madison: University of Wisconsin Press, 1983.

Maddra, Sam A. *Hostiles? The Lakota Ghost Dance and Buffalo Bill's Wild West.* Norman: University of Oklahoma Press, 2006.

Malloy, Jerry. "Out at Home: Baseball Draws the Color Line." *National Pastime* 2 (1983): 14–28.

Mandelbaum, Michael. *The Meaning of Sports: Why Americans Watch Baseball, Football, and Basketball, and What They See When They Do.* New York: Public Affairs, 2004.

Manley, Walter, W. *The Supreme Court of Florida and Its Predecessor Courts, 1821–1917.* Gainesville: University Press of Florida, 1997.

Manley, Walter W. II, Edgar Canter Brown, and Eric W. Rise. "Progressive Era Perspectives." In *The Supreme Court of Florida and Its Predecessor Courts, 1821–1917.* Gainesville: University Press of Florida, 1998.

Marchand, Roland. *Advertising the American Dream: Making Way for Modernity, 1920–1940.* Berkeley: University of California Press, 1985.

Marcus, Alan I. "If All the World Were Mechanics and Farmers: American Democracy and the Formative Years of Land-Grant Colleges." *Ohio Valley History* 5, no. 1 (Spring 2005): 23–37.

Marshall University. "Marshall University Traditions." *Marshall University Traditions.* http://herdzone.cstv.com/trads/mars-trads.html.

Martin, E. S. "A Double-Barrelled Social Agency: The Boy Scouts of America." *Social Forces* (1925): 94–97.

Masterson, Michael Lee. "*Sounds of the Frontier: Music in Buffalo Bill's Wild West.*" Ph.D. diss., University of New Mexico, 1990.

Matthiessen, Peter. *In the Spirit of Crazy Horse.* New York: Viking Press, 1983.

Mauro, Hayes Peter. *The Art of Americanization at the Carlisle Indian School.* Albuquerque: University of New Mexico Press, 2011.

McCrady, David G. *Living with Strangers: The Nineteenth-Century Sioux and the Canadian-American Borderlands.* Lincoln: University of Nebraska Press, 2006.

McGerr, Michael. *A Fierce Discontent: The Rise and Fall of the Progressive Movement in America.* New York: Oxford University Press, 2003.

McGrotha, Bill. *Seminoles! The First Forty Years.* Tallahassee, Fla.: Tallahassee Democrat, 1987.

McNenly, Linda Scarangella. *Native Performers in Wild West Shows: From Buffalo Bill to Euro Disney.* Norman: University of Oklahoma Press, 2012.

McWhiney, Grady. *Cracker Culture: Celtic Ways in the Old South.* Tuscaloosa: University of Alabama Press, 1988.

Mechling, Jay. *On My Honor: Boy Scouts and the Making of American Youth.* Chicago: University of Chicago Press, 2001.

Meek, B. A. "And the Injun Goes 'How!': Representations of American Indian English in White Public Space." *Language in Society* 35, no. 1 (2006): 93–128.

Merrell, James H. *Into the American Woods: Negotiations on the Pennsylvania Frontier.* New York: W. W. Norton, 2000.

Meyer, Carter Jones, and Diana Royer. *Selling the Indian: Commercializing and Appropriating American Indian Cultures.* Tucson: University of Arizona Press, 2001.

Miami University. "Miami University History of Women's Intercollegiate Athletics." *Miami University History of Women's Intercollegiate Athletics,* 1999. http://www.lib.muohio.edu/epub/wsports/hist.html.

Miami University, Office of the Student Body. *Miami University and the "Redskins": An Analysis.* Miami University, March 11, 1993. Miami University Archives.

Miami University and James MacBride. *Laws Passed by the Ohio Legislature, Establishing Miami University and the Ordinances, Passed by the President & Trustees of the Miami University.* Hamilton, Ohio: Printed by Keen & Stewart for J. M'Bride, 1814.

Michigan, State of. *Michigan Civil Rights Commission Report on Use of Nicknames, Logos, and Mascots Depicting Native American People in Michigan Educational Institutions.* Lansing, Mich.: Department of Civil Rights, Civil Rights Commission, 1988.

Mieras, Emily. "Tales from the Other Side of the Bridge: YMCA Manhood, Social Class, and Social Reform in Turn-of-the-Twentieth-Century Philadelphia." *Gender and History* 17, no. 2 (2005): 409–440.

Mihesuah, Devon A. *American Indians: Stereotypes and Realities.* Atlanta: Clarity, 1996.

Milanich, Jerald T. *Florida's Indians from Ancient Times to the Present.* Gainesville: University Press of Florida, 1998.

Miller, Charles L., and George R. Hamell. "A New Perspective on Indian-White Contact: Cultural Symbols and Colonial Trade." *Journal of American History* 73, no. 2 (1986): 311–328.

Miller, Donald L. *City of the Century: The Epic of Chicago and the Making of America.* New York: Simon and Schuster, 1996.

Miller, Jackson B. "'Indians,' 'Braves,' and 'Redskins': A Performative Struggle for Control of an Image." *Quarterly Journal of Speech* 85, no. 2 (1999): 188–202.

Miller, Nathan. *New World Coming: The 1920s and the Making of Modern America.* New York: Scribner, 2003.

Mills, Billy Helphrey, and National Coalition on Racism in Sports and Media. *American Indian Forum on Racism in Sports and Media.* St. Paul, Minn.: National Coalition on Racism in Sports and Media, 2001.

Minutes of the First Chicago Conference. Ann Arbor, Mich., January 19, 1906. Michigan Historical Collections.

Mirrielees, Edith Ronald. *Stanford: The Story of a University.* New York: Putnam, 1960.

———. *Stanford Mosaic: Reminiscences of the First Seventy Years at Stanford University.* Palo Alto, Calif.: Stanford University Press, 1962.

Mitchell, John Pearce. *Stanford University, 1916–1941.* Palo Alto, Calif.: Stanford University Press, 1958.

Moor, Liz. "'The Buzz of Dressing': Commodity Culture, Fraternity and Football Fandom." *South Atlantic Quarterly* 105, no. 2 (2006): 327–347.

Moore, Albert Allan. "The Development of Intercollegiate Athletics at Miami University, Oxford, Ohio." Master's thesis, Miami University, 1949.

Moore, MariJo. *Genocide of the Mind: New Native American Writing.* New York: Thunder's Mouth Press/Nation Books, 2003.

Moore, Robert J. *Native Americans, a Portrait: The Art and Travels of Charles Bird King, George Catlin, and Karl Bodmer.* New York: Stewart, Tabori & Chang, 1997.

Morgan, William John. *Why Sports Morally Matter.* New York: Routledge, 2006.

Morris, B. "Ernest Thompson Seton and the Origins of the Woodcraft Movement." *Journal of Contemporary History* 5, no. 2 (1970): 183–194.

Moses, L. G. *Wild West Shows and the Images of American Indians, 1883–1933.* Albuquerque: University of New Mexico Press, 1996.

Mott, Margaret M. "A Bibliography of Song Sheets: Sports and Recreations in American Popular Songs: Part I." *Notes* 6, no. 3 (June 1949): 379–418.

———. "A Bibliography of Song Sheets Sports and Recreations in American Popular Songs: Part II." *Notes* 7, no. 4 (September 1950): 522–561.

Mulroy, Kevin. *Freedom on the Border: The Seminole Maroons in Florida: The Indian Territory— Coahuila and Texas.* Lubbock: Texas Tech University Press, 1993.

Nathan, Hans. *Dan Emmett and the Rise of Early Negro Minstrelsy.* Norman: University of Oklahoma Press, 1962.

Nelson, Dana D. *National Manhood: Capitalist Citizenship and the Imagined Fraternity of White Men.* Durham, N.C.: Duke University Press, 1998.

Nevins, Allan. *The Origins of the Land-Grant Colleges and State Universities.* Washington, D.C.: Civil War Centennial Commission, 1962.

Newcombe, Jack. *The Best of the Athletic Boys: The White Man's Impact on Jim Thorpe.* New York: Doubleday, 1975.

Newman, Joshua I. "Army of Whiteness? Colonel Reb and the Sporting South's Cultural and Corporate Symbolic." *Journal of Sport and Social Issues* 31, no. 4 (2007): 315–339.

News-Gazette (Champaign, Ill.). *Fighting Illini Basketball: A Hardwood History.* Champaign, Ill.: Sports Publishing, 2000.

———. *100 Years of University of Illinois Basketball.* Champaign, Ill.: News-Gazette, 2004.

———. *Chief Illiniwek: A Tribute to an Illinois Tradition.* Rev. and updated commemorative ed. Champaign, Ill.: News-Gazette, 2007.

Novick, Peter. *The Noble Dream: The "Objectivity" Question and the American Historical Profession.* New York: Cambridge University Press, 1988.

Oberdeck, Kathryn J. *The Evangelist and the Impresario: Religion, Entertainment, and Cultural Politics in America, 1884–1914.* Baltimore: Johns Hopkins University Press, 1999.

Oberdorfer, Don. *Princeton University.* Princeton, N.J.: Princeton University Press, 1995.

Oltusky, Rose J. *Fight, Illini! The Stadium Song.* Champaign, Ill.: Students Supply Store, 1921.

Oriard, Michael. *Dreaming of Heroes: American Sports Fiction, 1868–1980.* Chicago: Nelson Hall Press, 1980.

———. *Reading Football: How the Popular Press Created an American Spectacle.* Cultural Studies of the United States. Chapel Hill: University of North Carolina Press, 1993.

———. *King Football: Sport and Spectacle in the Golden Age of Radio and Newsreels, Movies and Magazines, the Weekly and the Daily Press.* Chapel Hill: University of North Carolina Press, 2001.

Ostler, Jeffrey. *The Plains Sioux and U.S. Colonialism from Lewis and Clark to Wounded Knee.* New York: Cambridge University Press, 2004.

Ostler, Jeffrey, and Robert Utley. *Cavalier in Buckskin: George Armstrong Custer and the Western Military Front.* Norman: University of Oklahoma Press, 2001.

Owsley, Frank Lawrence. *Plain Folk of the Old South.* Baton Rouge: Louisiana State University Press, 1949.

Oxendine, Joseph B. *American Indian Sports Heritage.* 2nd ed. Lincoln: University of Nebraska Press, 1995.

Paladin, Vivian A. "A. Phimister Proctor: Master Sculptor of Horses." *Montana: The Magazine of Western History* 14, no. 1 (1964): 10–24.

Paraschak, Victoria. "Doing Race, Doing Gender: First Nations, 'Sport,' and Gender Relations." In *Sport and Gender in Canada,* ed. Kevin Young and Philip White. Don Mills, Ont.: Oxford University Press, 2007.

Parezo, Nancy J. *Anthropology Goes to the Fair: The 1904 Louisiana Purchase Exposition.* Lincoln: University of Nebraska Press, 2007.

Park, Roberta. "The Attitude of Leading New England Transcendentalists toward Healthful Exercise, Active Recreation, and Proper Care of the Body: 1830–1860." *Journal of Sport History* 4 (Spring 1977): 34–50.

———. "'Embodied Selves': The Rise and Development of Concern for Physical Education, Active Games, and Recreation for American Women, 1776–1865." *Journal of Sport History* 5 (Summer 1978): 5–41.

Parker, Andrew, and Eve Kosofsky Sedgwick, eds. *Performativity and Performance.* New York: Routledge, 1995.

Pearce, Roy Harvey. *Savagism and Civilization: A Study of the Indian and the American Mind.* Baltimore: Johns Hopkins University Press, 1965.

Peers, Laura L. *Playing Ourselves: Interpreting Native Histories at Historic Reconstructions.* Lanham, Md.: AltaMira Press, 2007.

Pencak, William A., and Daniel K. Richter. *Friends and Enemies in Penn's Woods: Indians, Colonists, and the Racial Construction of Pennsylvania.* University Park: Pennsylvania State University Press, 2004.

Perdue, Theda. *Cherokee Women: Gender and Culture Change, 1700–1835.* Lincoln: University of Nebraska Press, 1998.

———. *"Mixed Blood" Indians: Racial Construction in the Early South.* Athens: University of Georgia Press, 2003.

Perry, P. "White Means Never Having to Say You're Ethnic: White Youth and the Construction of 'Cultureless' Identities." *Life in America: Identity and Everyday Experience* (2004): 339–358.

Peterson, Robert W. *Pigskin: The Early Years of Pro Football.* Oxford: Oxford University Press, 1996.

Pettegrew, John. *Brutes in Suits: Male Sensibility in America, 1890–1920.* Baltimore: Johns Hopkins University Press, 2007.

Pfister, Joel. *The Yale Indian: The Education of Henry Roe Cloud.* Durham, N.C.: Duke University Press, 2009.

Phillips, Murray G., ed. *Deconstructing Sport History: A Postmodern Analysis.* Albany: State University of New York Press, 2006.

Pleasants, Julian M. "Frederic Remington in Florida." *Florida Historical Quarterly* (1977): 1–12.

———. *Gator Tales: An Oral History of the University of Florida.* Gainesville: University Press of Florida, 2006.

Poole, Gary Andrew. *The Galloping Ghost: Red Grange, an American Football Legend.* Boston: Houghton Mifflin, 2008.

Pope, Steven W. *Patriotic Games: Sporting Traditions in the American Imagination, 1876–1926.* New York: Oxford University Press, 1997.

Powel, Harford. *Walter Camp, the Father of American Football: An Authorized Biography.* Boston: Little, Brown, 1926.

Powers-Beck, Jeffrey. "'Chief': The American Indian Integration of Baseball, 1897–1945." *American Indian Quarterly* 25, no. 4 (2001): 508–538.

———. *The American Indian Integration of Baseball.* Lincoln: University of Nebraska Press, 2009.

Proctor, Alexander Phimister. *Alexander Phimister Proctor, Sculptor in Buckskin: An Autobiography.* Norman: University of Oklahoma Press, 1971.

———. *Wildlife and Western Heroes: Alexander Phimister Proctor, Sculptor.* Fort Worth, Tex.: Amon Carter Museum, 2003.

Pronger, Brian. *The Arena of Masculinity: Sports, Homosexuality, and the Meaning of Sex.* New York: St. Martin's Press, 1990.

Prucha, Francis P. *American Indian Policy in Crisis: Christian Reformers and the Indian, 1865–1890.* Norman: University of Oklahoma Press, 1976.

Putney, Clifford. *Muscular Christianity: Manhood and Sports in Protestant America, 1880–1920.* Cambridge, Mass.: Harvard University Press, 2001.

Racism or Respect? Chief Illiniwek, Dignified Symbol or Racist Mascot? Champaign, Ill.: Progressive Resource/Action Cooperative & People Against Racism, 1996.

Rapoport, Ron. *The Immortal Bobby: Bobby Jones and the Golden Age of Golf.* Hoboken, N.J.: John Wiley & Sons, 2005.

Reddin, Paul. *Wild West Shows.* Urbana: University of Illinois Press, 1999.

Reyhner, Jon, and Jeanne Eder. *American Indian Education: A History.* Norman: University of Oklahoma Press, 2006.

Riess, Steven A. *City Games: The Evolution of American Urban Society and the Rise of Sports.* Urbana: University of Illinois Press, 1989.

———. *Touching Base: Professional Baseball and American Culture in the Progressive Era.* Urbana: University of Illinois Press, 1999.

Roach, J. "Mardi Gras Indians and Others: Genealogies of American Performance." *Theatre Journal* 44, no. 4 (1992): 461–483.

Roberts, Randy. *Jack Dempsey: The Manassa Mauler.* Baton Rouge: Louisiana State University Press, 1980.

Rodgers, Patricia H., Charles Sullivan, and the Cambridge Historical Commission. *A Photographic History of Cambridge.* Cambridge, Mass.: MIT Press, 1984, quoted in *American Landscape and Architectural Design, 1850–1920,* Library of Congress, American Memory. http://memory.loc.gov/ammem/award97/mhsdhtml/harvardbldgs. html#hbft4.

Roediger, David R. *The Wages of Whiteness: Race and the Making of the American Working Class.* London: Verso, 1991.

———. *Working toward Whiteness: How America's Immigrants Became White: The Strange Journey from Ellis Island to the Suburbs.* New York: Basic Books, 2005.

Rotundo, E. Anthony. *American Manhood: Transformations in Masculinity from the Revolution to the Modern Era.* New York: Basic Books, 1993.

Rubin, Joan Shelley. *The Making of Middlebrow Culture.* Chapel Hill: University of North Carolina Press, 1992.

Rubinfeld, Mark. "The Mythical Jim Thorpe: Re/presenting the Twentieth-Century American Indian." *International Journal of the History of Sport* 23, no. 2 (2006): 167–189.

Rudolph, Frederick. *The American College and University: A History.* 1962. Reprint, Athens: University of Georgia Press, 1990.

Russell, Don. *The Lives and Legends of Buffalo Bill.* Norman: University of Oklahoma Press, 1960.

Rydell, Robert W. *All the World's a Fair: Visions of Empire at American International Expositions, 1876–1916.* Chicago: University of Chicago Press, 1987.

———. *World of Fairs: The Century-of-Progress Expositions.* Chicago: University of Chicago Press, 1993.

———. *Fair America: World's Fairs in the United States.* Washington, D.C.: Smithsonian Institution Press, 2000.

———. *Buffalo Bill in Bologna: The Americanization of the World, 1869–1922.* Chicago: University of Chicago Press, 2005.

Rydell, Robert, and Carolyn Kinder Carr, eds., *Revisiting the White City: American Art at the 1893 World's Fair.* Washington, D.C.: Smithsonian Institution Press, 1993.

Sacks, Howard L., and Judith Rose Sacks. *Way Up North in Dixie: A Black Family's Claim to the Confederate Anthem.* Washington, D.C.: Smithsonian Institution Press, 1993.

Sagard, Gabriel. *The Long Journey to the Country of the Hurons.* Ed. George M. Wrong. Trans. H. H. Langton. Toronto: Champlain Society, 1939.

Said, Edward W. *Power, Politics, and Culture: Interviews with Edward W. Said.* New York: Vintage Books, 2002.

———. *Orientalism.* New York: Vintage Books, 2003.

Sammons, Jeffrey T. *Beyond the Ring: The Role of Boxing in American Society.* Champaign: University of Illinois Press, 1989.

Sampson, Robert S. "Red Illini: Dorothy Day, Samson Raphaelson, and Rayna Simons at the University of Illinois, 1914–1916." *Journal of Illinois History* 5, no. 3 (Autumn 2002): 170–196.

Sansing, D. G. *The University of Mississippi: A Sesquicentennial History.* Jackson: University Press of Mississippi, 1999.

Saunt, Claudio. *A New Order of Things: Property, Power, and the Transformation of the Creek Indians, 1733–1816.* Cambridge: Cambridge University Press, 1999.

"Savages and Saints: The Changing Image of American Indians in Westerns." http://www.amazon.com/Savages-Saints-Changing-American-Indiands/dp/0786434465/ref=sr_1_1?ie=UTF8&s=books&qid=1257986230&sr=1-1.

Schafer, William J. "Ragtime Arranging for Fun and Profit: The Cases of Harry L. Alford and J. Bodewalt Lampe." *Journal of Jazz Studies* 3, no. 1 (Fall 1975): 103–117.

Schechner, Richard. *Performance Theory.* London: Routledge, 2003.

———. *Performance Studies: An Introduction.* 2nd ed. New York: Routledge, 2006.

Scheckel, Susan. *The Insistence of the Indian: Race and Nationalism in Nineteenth-Century American Culture.* Princeton, N.J.: Princeton University Press, 1998.

Schmidt, Raymond. *Shaping College Football: The Transformation of an American Sport, 1919–1930.* Syracuse, N.Y.: Syracuse University Press, 2007.

Seiter, Herbert D. W. *Prince Lightfoot: Indian from the California Redwoods.* Del Norte County, Calif.: Troubador Press, 1959.

Sellars, Robin J. *Femina Perfecta: The Genesis of Florida State University.* Tallahassee: Florida State University Foundation, 1995.

Seton, Ernest Thompson. *The Book of Woodcraft and Indian Lore: With Over 500 Drawings.* Garden City, N.Y.: Doubleday, Page, 1921.

Shanley, Kathryn W., and S. Ortiz. "The Indians America Loves to Love and Read: American Indian Identity and Cultural Appropriation." *American Indian Quarterly* 21, no. 4 (1997): 675–702.

Sheyahshe, Michael A. *Native Americans in Comic Books: A Critical Study.* Jefferson, N.C.: McFarland, 2008.

Shindo, Charles. *1927 and the Rise of Modern America.* Lawrence: University Press of Kansas, 2010.

Shoemaker, Nancy. *A Strange Likeness: Becoming Red and White in Eighteenth-Century North America.* New York: Oxford University Press, 2004.

Shriver, Phillip R. *Years of Wisdom: The Collected Works of Phillip R. Shriver.* Oxford, Ohio: Miami University Press, 1981.

———. "Founding Miami." Lecture, Miami University, September 9, 1998.

———. *Miami University: A Personal History.* Ed. Willaim Pratt. Oxford, Ohio: Miami University Press, 1998.

Sigelman, L. "Hail to the Redskins? Public Reactions to a Racially Sensitive Team Name." *Sociology of Sport Journal* 15, no. 4 (1998): 317–325.

Sleeper-Smith, Susan. *Indian Woman and French Men: Rethinking Cultural Encounter in the Western Great Lakes.* Amherst: University of Massachusetts Press, 2001.

Slotkin, Richard. *The Fatal Environment: The Myth of the Frontier in the Age of Industrialization, 1800–1890.* New York: HarperCollins, 1985.

———. *Gunfighter Nation: The Myth of the Frontier in Twentieth-Century America.* Norman: University of Oklahoma Press, 1998.

Slowikowski, Synthia Sydnor. "Cultural Performance and Sport Mascots." *Journal of Sport and Social Issues* 17, no. 1 (1993): 23–33.

Smith, G. "School Team Names in Washington State." *American Speech* (1997): 172–182.

Smith, Ronald A. *Sports and Freedom: The Rise of Big-Time Intercollegiate Athletics.* New York: Oxford University Press, 1988.

———. *Pay for Play: A History of Big-Time College Athletic Reform.* Urbana: University of Illinois Press, 2010.

Soderstrom, Robert M. *The Big House: Fielding H. Yost and the Building of Michigan Stadium.* Ann Arbor, Mich.: Huron River Press, 2005.

Sotiropoulos, Karen. *Staging Race: Black Performers in Turn of the Century America.* Cambridge, Mass.: Harvard University Press, 2006.

Spady, James O'Neil. "Colonialism and the Discursive Antecedents of *Penn's Treaty with the Indians.*" In *Friends and Enemies in Penn's Woods: Indians, Colonists, and the Racial Construction of Pennsylvania,* ed. William A. Pencak and Daniel K. Richter. University Park: Pennsylvania State University Press, 2004.

Sperber, Murray. *Shake Down the Thunder: The Creation of Notre Dame Football.* New York: Henry Holt, 1993.

———. *Beer and Circus: How Big-Time College Sport Is Crippling Undergraduate Education.* New York: Henry Holt, 2000.

Spindel, Carol. *Dancing at Halftime: Sports and the Controversy Over American Indian Mascots.* New York: New York University Press, 2000.

Springwood, Charles Fruehling. *Beyond the Cheers: Race as Spectacle in College Sport.* New York: State University of New York Press, 2001.

———. "'I'm Indian Too!': Claiming Native American Identity, Crafting Authority in Mascot Debates." *Journal of Sport and Social Issues* 28, no. 1 (2004): 56–70.

Springwood, Charles Fruehling, and C. Richard King. "Race, Power, and Representation in Contemporary American Sport." *Multiculturalism in the United States: Current Issues, Contemporary Voices* (2000): 161–175.

Stangl, Jane Marie. "Naming and Social Privilege: A Century of (Mis)appropriating Siwash." Ph.D. diss., University of Iowa, 1999.

Starr, Kevin. *Americans and the California Dream, 1850–1915.* New York: Oxford University Press, 1973.

State ex rel. Moodie v. Bryan. 50 Fla. 293; 39 So. 929; 1905 Fla. LEXIS 231 (Supreme Court of Florida).

Staurowsky, Ellen J. "An Act of Honor or Exploitation? The Cleveland Indians' Use of the Louis Francis Sockalexis Story." *Sociology of Sport Journal* 15 (1998): 299–316.

———. "American Indian Imagery and the Miseducation of America." *Quest* 51, no. 4 (1999): 382–392.

———. "The Cleveland 'Indians': A Case Study in American Indian Cultural Dispossession." *Sociology of Sport Journal* 17, no. 4 (2000): 307–330.

———. "Privilege at Play: On the Legal and Social Fictions That Sustain American Indian Sport Imagery." *Journal of Sport and Social Issues* 28, no. 1 (2004): 11–29.

———. "Getting Beyond Imagery: The Challenges of Reading Narratives about American Indian Athletes." *International Journal of the History of Sport* 23, no. 2 (2006): 190–212.

———. "'You Know, We Are All Indian': Exploring White Power and Privilege in Reactions to the NCAA Native American Mascot Policy." *Journal of Sport and Social Issues* 31, no. 1 (2007): 61–76.

Ste. Claire, Dana. *Cracker: The Cracker Culture in Florida History.* 2nd ed. Daytona Beach, Fla.: Museum of Arts and Sciences, 1998.

Stedman, Raymond William. *Shadows of the Indian: Stereotypes in American Culture.* Norman: University of Oklahoma Press, 1982.

Steiner, Jesse Frederick. *Americans at Play*. 1933. Reprint, New York: Arno Press and the New York Times, 1970.

Stephens, Carl. *Illini Years: A Picture History of the University of Illinois, 1868–1950*. Urbana: University of Illinois Press, 1950.

Stocking, George W. *Race, Culture, and Evolution: Essays in the History of Anthropology*. Chicago: University of Chicago Press, 1982.

———. *Volksgeist as Method and Ethic: Essays on Boasian Ethnography and the German Anthropological Tradition*. Madison: University of Wisconsin Press, 1996.

Storey, John. *Inventing Popular Culture: From Folklore to Globalization*. Malden, Mass.: Blackwell, 2003.

The Story of John the Orange-Man; Being a Short Sketch of the Life of Harvard's Popular Mascot. Cambridge, Mass.: John Wilson and Son, 1891.

Stromquist, Shelton. *Reinventing the "People": The Progressive Movement, the Class Problem, and the Origins of Modern Liberalism*. Urbana: University of Illinois Press, 2006.

Strong, Pauline Turner. "Animated Indians: Critique and Contradiction in Commodified Children's Culture." *Cultural Anthropology* (1996): 405–424.

———. "The Mascot Slot: Cultural Citizenship, Political Correctness, and Pseudo-Indian Sports Symbols." *Journal of Sport and Social Issues* 28, no. 1 (2004): 79–87.

Struna, Nancy. "Gender and Sporting Practice in Early America, 1750–1810." *Journal of Sport History* 18 (Spring 1991): 10–30.

Tate, Loren. *A Century of Orange and Blue: Celebrating 100 Years of Fighting Illini Basketball*. Champaign, Ill.: Sports Publishing, 2004.

Taylor, Frederick Winslow. *Concrete, Plain and Reinforced*. 4th ed. New York: John Wiley & Sons, 1925.

Taylor, Michael. "Native American Images as Sports Team Mascots: From Chief Wahoo to Chief Illiniwek." Ph.D. diss., Syracuse University, 2005.

Tehranian, Katherine Kia. "The Chicago Columbian Exposition of 1893: A Symbol of Modernism." *Proceedings of the National Conference on American Planning History* 5 (1993): 500–511.

Thelen, David P. *Memory and American History*. Bloomington: Indiana University Press, 1990.

Thelin, John R. *A History of American Higher Education*. Baltimore: Johns Hopkins University Press, 2004.

Thomas, George E., and David B. Brownlee. *Building America's First University: An Historical and Architectural Guide to the University of Pennsylvania*. Philadelphia: University of Pennsylvania Press, 2000.

Thorne, Tanis. *The Many Hands of My Relations: French and Indians on the Lower Missouri*. Columbia: University of Missouri Press, 1996.

Thornton, K. P. "Symbolism at Ole Miss and the Crisis of Southern Identity." Master's thesis, University of Virginia, 1983.

Toll, Robert C. *Blacking Up: The Minstrel Show in Nineteenth-Century America*. New York: Oxford University Press, 1974.

Torry, J. *Endless Summers: The Fall and Rise of the Cleveland Indians*. South Bend, Ind.: Diamond Communications, 1995.

Tourdot, W. "Changing a High School Mascot." Ph.D. diss., Edgewood College, 2007.

Tovares, R. "Mascot Matters: Race, History, and the University of North Dakota's 'Fighting Sioux' Logo." *Journal of Communication Inquiry* 26, no. 1 (2002): 76–94.

Trachtenberg, Alan. *The Incorporation of America: Culture and Society in the Gilded Age*. New York: Hill and Wang, 1982.

———. *Shades of Hiawatha: Staging Indians, Making Americans: 1880–1930*. New York: Hill and Wang, 2005.

Turner, Frederick Jackson. *The Frontier in American History*. New York: Henry Holt, 1921.

University of Florida. "About UF." *About UF*. http://www.ufl.edu/aboutUF/.

University of Illinois. *Repertoire, 1948–1970*. Urbana: University of Illinois at Urbana-Champaign, 1970.

———. *Oskee Wow Wow Illinois Football: The First Century*. Directed by Lawrence Miller. Champaign: University of Illinois, 1990.

———. *Chief Illiniwek*. Urbana, Ill.: Students for Chief Illiniwek, 1998.

University of Mississippi. "Ole Miss Traditions." *OleMissSports*. http://www.olemisssports .com/ViewArticle.dbml?DB_OEM_ID=2600&ATCLID=541582.

University of North Dakota. "1904." http://125.und.edu/this_year.html.

University of Wisconsin. "The University of Wisconsin Marching Band History: Dvorak Era." *University of Wisconsin Marching Band History*. http://www.badgerband.com/history/ dvorak.php.

U.S. Congress. Journal of the Continental Congress. *An Ordinance for the Government of the Territory of the United States North West of the River Ohio*, 1787.

U.S. Department of Commerce, Bureau of the Census. *Census*, 1860. http://www2.census .gov/prod2/decennial/documents/1860a-14.pdf.

———. *Census*, 1870. http://www2.census.gov/prod2/decennial/documents/1870a-03.pdf.

———. *Census*, 1880. http://www2.census.gov/prod2/decennial/documents/1870a-03.pdf.

U.S. Department of State. *A Treaty of Peace between the United States of America and the Tribes of Indians called Wyandots, Delawares, Shawanoes, Ottawas, Chipewas, Putawatimes, Miamis, Eel-River, Weeas, Kickapoos, Piankashaws and Kaskaskias* or *Treaty of Greenville*, August 3, 1795. George Washington Papers at the Library of Congress, 1741–1799: Series 4. General Correspondence, 1697–1799.

Utley, Robert Marshall. *Cavalier in Buckskin: George Armstrong Custer and the Western Military Frontier*. Norman: University of Oklahoma Press, 1988.

Vane, Cullen. *College Nicknames: The Ultimate Guide*. San Jose, Calif.: Strike Three, 2011.

Van Kirk, Silvia. *Many Tender Ties: Women in Fur Trade Society, 1670–1780*. Norman: University of Oklahoma Press, 1980.

Verbrugge, Martha H. *Able-Bodied Womanhood: Personal Health and Social Change in Nineteenth-Century Boston*. Oxford: Oxford University Press, 1988.

Vesey, Laurence R. *The Emergence of the Modern University*. Chicago: University of Chicago Press, 1965.

Wakefield, Wanda Ellen. *Playing to Win: Sports and the American Military, 1898–1945*. Albany: State University of New York Press, 1997.

Walsh, George. *A Bill for an Act Locating the University of North Dakota at Grand Forks*, 1883. http://www.und.nodak.edu/history/.

Warfield, Patrick Robert. "'Salesman of Americanism, Globetrotter, and Musician': The Nineteenth-Century John Philip Sousa, 1854–1893." Ph.D. diss., Indiana University, 2003.

Warren, Louis S. *Buffalo Bill's America: William Cody and the Wild West Show*. New York: Knopf, 2005.

Watterson, John Sayle. *College Football: History, Spectacle, Controversy*. Baltimore: Johns Hopkins University Press, 2000.

———. "The Gridiron Crisis of 1905: Was It Really a Crisis?" *Journal of Sport History* 27, no. 2 (Summer 2000): 291–298.

———. *The Games Presidents Play: Sports and the Presidency*. Baltimore: Johns Hopkins University Press, 2006.

Weber, Calvin Earl. *The Contribution of Albert Austin Harding and His Influence on the Development of School and College Bands*. Urbana, Ill.: Weber, 1963.

Weber, Max, P. R. Baehr, and G. C. Wells. *The Protestant Ethic and the "Spirit" of Capitalism.* New York: Penguin Classics, 2002.

Weisman, Brent Richards. *Like Beads on a String: A Culture History of the Seminole Indians in Northern Peninsular Florida.* Tuscaloosa: University of Alabama Press, 1989.

————. *Unconquered People: Florida's Seminole and Miccosukee Indians.* Gainesville: University Press of Florida, 1999.

Welsh, Clarence. "University of Illinois Memorial Stadium." Stadium Drive Publications, University of Illinois, University of Illinois Archives.

Weston, Mary Ann. *Native Americans in the News: Images of Indians in the Twentieth Century Press.* Westport, Conn.: Greenwood Press, 1996.

Wheeler, Robert W. *Jim Thorpe: World's Greatest Athlete.* Norman: University of Oklahoma Press, 1979.

White, Richard. *The Middle Ground: Indians, Empires, and Republics in the Great Lakes Region, 1650–1815.* Cambridge: Cambridge University Press, 1991.

Wickman, Patricia R. *Osceola's Legacy.* Rev. ed. Tuscaloosa: University of Alabama Press, 2006.

Wiebe, Robert H. *The Search for Order, 1877–1920.* New York: Hill and Wang, 1967.

Wiggins, David Kenneth. *Sport in America: From Wicked Amusement to National Obsession.* Champaign, Ill.: Human Kinetics, 1995.

Wiley, B. I. *The Life of Johnny Reb: The Common Soldier of the Confederacy.* Baton Rouge: Louisiana State University Press, 1978.

Williams, Patrick, and Laura Chrisman, eds. *Colonial Discourse and Post-Colonial Theory: A Reader.* New York: Columbia University Press, 1994.

Willman, Fred. *Why Mascots Have Tales: The Illinois High School Mascot Manual from Appleknockers to Zippers.* Addison, Ill.: Mascots Publishing, 2005.

Wills, M., and J. P. Morris. *Seminole History: A Pictorial History of Florida State University.* Jacksonville, Fla.: South Star, 1987.

Winter, Thomas. *Making Men, Making Class: The YMCA and Workingmen, 1877–1920.* Chicago: University of Chicago Press, 2002.

Yale University Athletic Department. "Yale University Bulldog Tradition." *Yale Bulldogs: The Official Site of Yale University Athletics.* Bulldog Tradition. http://www.yalebulldogs.com/information/mascot/handsome_dan/index.

Yarbaugh, Roy E. *Mascots: The History of Senior College and University Mascots Nicknames.* Philadelphia: Bluff University Communications, 1998.

Yoder, P. "The Early History of the American Bandmasters Association." *Journal of Band Research* 1, Part I (1964).

Yost, Nellie Irene Snyder. *A Man as Big as the West.* Boulder, Colo: Pruett, 1979.

Young, Linda. *Hail to the Orange and Blue! 100 Years of Illinois Football Tradition.* Champaign, Ill.: Sagamore, 1990.

Zeitler, E. "Geographies of Indigenous-based Team Name and Mascot Use in American Secondary Schools." Ph.D. diss., University of Nebraska, 2008.

Zimbalist, Andrew. *Unpaid Professionals.* Princeton, N.J.: Princeton University Press, 2010.

Zinn, Howard. *A People's History of the United States: 1492–Present.* Rev. and updated ed. New York: Harper Perennial, 1995.

INDEX

Page references followed by an "f" indicate a figure.

coaches: AFCA, 23; and commercialization of football, 19; role of professional, 22; salaries of, 22; and white masculine middle-class values, 5

Cody, William "Buffalo Bill," 51. *See also* Wild West show

Cold War, universities during, 88–89

college bands: directors, training for, 54; growth of, 55; influence of, 54–55; ROTC, 54. *See also* marching bands; university bands

colleges: changing demographics at, 21, 118n30; identities for, 106; Indian athletes' access to, 9–10, 114n29; as middle-class domain, 31; role of twentieth-century, 9. *See also* higher education; universities

Collegiate Division 1A, 109

Collier's magazine, 18

"Colonel Reb," 84, 138n61

colonialism: effects of, 41; reenacted at halftime performances, 40–43

colonial period: cultural cosmopolitanism of, 136n35; Florida during, 80

colonial tropes, 5; in early twentieth century, 57; Indian men stealing white women, 98; Indians, 79; violence, 70, 108

comical performances, racialized overtones of, 34

comic strips, 96

commercialism: convergence of football with, 258; impact on American universities of, 10–11; in modern stadiums, 27; of sport, 109

commodity fetishism, 115n33

communal identity, 94

community: building white middle-class, 101; identity, boundaries of, 105; meaning, and college football, 4; role of stadium in, 30

competition, encouragement of, 19, 20

conquest: narratives of, 133n37; racialized language of, 57–63

cosmopolitanism: and modernity, 115n32; theories of, 115n31

cowboys, in Wild West show, 50

Cowell, William, 23

Crabtree, Jim, 78

"cracker," 77; rehabilitation of term, 86; signifiers for, 85; stereotypes of, 85–86; as student identity, 85

Crane, Stephen, 38

"Crane People," 130n19

Crazy Horse, 64

Creek, 57, 80; nonviolent resistance of, 136n35; settlement of, 80

critical sport studies, 114–115n30

Curtis, Edward, 103, 104; The smelt fisher— Trinidad Yurok, 104f

Custer, Gen. George Armstrong, 63–64, 68

Dacotah yearbook, 61, 68, 100; comic representation of Sioux in, 99; Indian imagery in, 66

Daily Illini (student newspaper), 21, 89, 92

Dakota Sioux, 131n29

Dakota Student (student newspaper), 133n51

Dakota Territory, 61

Daly, Maj. Charles, 23

dance, Indian, 37–40; at city jamborees, 39–40; at Olympic games, 39; of "Prince Lightfoot," 101–102, 102f; Yurok, 103

Darrow, Clarence, 38

Dartmouth College, 107

Debord, Guy, 116n35

Debs, Eugene, 38

Deland Crackers, 86

Deloria, Philip J., 7, 12, 50; *Indians in Unexpected Places*, 12; *Playing Indian*, 12

D'Emilio, John, 98

Dempsey, William Harrison "Jack," 112n11

Derrida, Jacques, 11, 114–115n30

de Soto, Hernando, 57

difference, relationship of, 11

"Disappearing Illini," 89

Dobie, Gil, 23

"Dollies," Stanford University, 101

Dreuilettes, Father Gabriel, 130n19

Duval, Clarence, 34

DuVal, Gov. William P., 80

Dvorak, Ray, 41, 52, 55

economic class: and access to higher education, 12. *See also* class

economy, post–Civil War, 3

education, biological categorization in, 58. *See also* higher education

ethnicity, "sounds" of, 50, 94

faculty, university, and white masculine middle-class values, 5

fans, football: factory workers compared
with, 25–26; of H. E. "Red" Grange, 26–27;
and white masculine middle-class values, 5
female bodies: conquest of, 99; male control
over, 98
feminist movement, and higher education,
106
Field, Eugene, 38
Fields, W. C., 96
"Fighting Sioux" identity, of UND, 8, 14,
99, 107
Fillmore, Henry, 54
Fisher, Robert, 23
Florida: during colonial era, 80; settlement
of, 80
Florida Female College, 49, 82–83
Florida Flambeau (newspaper), 78
Florida State College, 82; identity politics for,
86; racialized identities for, 85; "Rebels"
mascot of, 84; Seminole mascot of, 107;
women of, 87
Florida State College for Women, 83
Florida State University (FSU), 5, 8, 83;
athletic identity of, 77, 78–79, 88, 111;
naming of football team, 77; "Seminole"
identity of, 9, 15, 63, 86–87; spectacle for,
87; university identity for, 70
football: associations, professional, 18; college
vs. professional, 27; creation of modern, 70;
growth of popularity of, 125n7; lower- and
middle-class ethnic bodies in, 6; and mass
media, 4, 113n16; as middle-class domain,
31. *See also* king football
football, college: autonomy of, 27; business
of, 17–18, 21; commercialism of, 21; early
years, 4–5; growth of, 2–3; meaning of, 31;
as moralizing force, 18; need for, 16; origins
of, 16; people engaged in, 5; in popular
culture, 3–4; racial and cultural boundaries
for, 9; recruitment for, 17; rhetoric of, 4–5;
ritual of, 97; studying, 10
football attendance: growth of, 20; meaning
of, 31
football players: and commercialization
of football, 19; Harold E. "Red" Grange,
26–27, 26f; role of professional, 22
Forsythe, Jack "Pee Wee," 82
Fort Gibson, Treaty of (1833), 81
Fort Laramie, Treaty of (1851), 63, 64

Fort Yates, 100
Foucault, Michel, 114–115n30
4-F designation, 91–92
Franklin, Benjamin: narrative of, 120n1,
124n59; as UPenn founder, 124n59; as
UPenn mascot, 41, 124n57
Freedman, Estelle, 98
FSU. *See* Florida State University

Gadsden, James, 81
gambling, and college players, 22
Games, Frank S., 59
"Gator," as University of Florida mascot, 82,
137n49
gender: in American middle-class life,
106; in cultural history, 10; and halftime
performance, 101; norms, and sexualization
of female bodies, 98
Georgia, settlement of, 80
Ghost Dance movement, Wovoka's, 64
Giddens, Anthony, 113n17
Glassberg, David, *American Historical
Pageantry*, 106
global culture, 39, 123n49
"Golden Axe," 72
Goldman, Dr. Edwin Franko, 54
Grabel, Victor J., 54
Grable, John, 92–93, 103
Graham, Charlie, 48–49
Grange, Harold E. "Red," 26–27, 26f
Grant, Don, 86
Great Depression, 9, 76
Great Sioux Uprising (1862), 63
Great War. *See* World War I
Greeley, Horace, 3
Green, Howard R., 48, 49, 126n16
Guider, Judge Ben, 84
Guild, Thatcher Howland, 46, 47, 126n11
Gulick, Luther, 35

"Hail to the Orange," 48, 49, 52, 127n19
halftime performance, 2; changing
conception of, 55; counternarrative of
Indian performance in, 103; formalizing,
49–54; growing appeal of, 54; Indian-
themed, 6–7; limits of, 89–90; mascots
introduced into, 32; meaning of, 88; and
modern anxiety, 106; nationalism in, 88;
origins of, 41; and potential donors, 50;

racialized bodies in, 101; and settler
colonial imagination, 40–43; support for,
70; on television, 110; university bands in,
44, 49; during World War II, 92. *See also*
spectacle
Hanks, Kenneth O., 92
Harding, Albert Austin, 45, 46, 47, 49, 50, 52,
53, 55, 125n7, 126n11; formal conferences
of, 54
Harris, Joel Chandler, 38
Harris, Reed, 21–22, 118–119n34
Harvard University: early football at, 16; John
Orangeman at, 32, 33, 37, 121n9; modern
stadium built by, 27
Haskell Institute, 7, 68, 70, 76
Hatton, Thomas, 50
"Hawkeye Glory," 55
Haynie, Jerry Thomas, 45
Hearst Music of New York, 52
Heidigger, Martin, 114–115n30
Heisman, John, 23
Henderson, E. C., 23
Hennepin, Louis, 40
heterosexual behavior, *vs.* homosexual
behavior, 99
"Hiawabop," Miami University, 97
higher education: access to, 5–6; athletics
in, 117–118n18; and commercialization of
college football, 21–22; competitive world
of, 61; economic class and access to, 12;
value of, 4. *See also* colleges; universities
Hill, Howard, 48, 49, 126n16
history, retelling and reconfiguring of, 42.
See also narratives
Holthaus, Glenn, 90, 92
homosexual behavior, *vs.* heterosexual
behavior, 99
Howard, John, 67
Howard, Oliver Otis, 85
Hubbard, Bertha, 37
Hubbard, Elbert Green, 37, 38
Hubbard, Ralph, 37, 38, 43, 44, 92, 135n20
Hug, William "Bill," 106
Hurons, 58

IAA. *See* Intercollegiate Athletic Association
identity: and football, 5; middle-class, 88;
university-created, 70; white middle-class
male, 14

identity politics, 15
"Illinois Loyalty," 46–47, 47, 48, 49, 52, 126n16;
premiere of, 46
"Illinois model," 47, 54, 55
Illio yearbook, 89
immigration, 41; concerns about, 35; and
marketing of football, 6
inclusiveness, and college football, 4
Indian bodies: American fascination
with, 96; and assimilationist policies,
7–8; color descriptor for, 57, 129n7;
faux, 57; in halftime performances, 42;
hypermasculine, 62; narratives about,
13–14; national consciousness about, 13;
structured, 58; and white middle-class
identity, 9. *See also* bodies
Indian Country Today (media network), 108
Indian identity: interpretations of, 12; support
for, 108; for UND, 66. *See also* identity
Indian mascots. *See* mascots, Indian
"Indian music formula," 128n34
Indianness: colonial representations of,
97; comedic representations of, 96; and
creation of community, 100; and national
issues about gender, 101; performing, 13;
popular perceptions of, 59; and university
band identity, 52; for white middle-class
men, 9
Indian Removal Policy, of A. Jackson, 81
Indians: America's cultural fascination with,
68; athletes, discrimination against, 108;
in Boy Scout movement, 39–40, 123n53;
as contrast to white American society, 53;
and higher education, 106; knowledge
about, 43; learning about, 44; and modern
masculinity, 34–37; and narratives of
conquest, 65–66; nonviolent resistance
of, 136n35; in popular culture, 34–35; in
racial hierarchy, 71; in silent film era, 51, 52;
stereotypes of, 52; trope of disappearing,
102; in Wild West show, 50, 51f, 73–74.
See also "Indian" spectacles
"Indian" spectacles: controlled by white men,
8–9; making of, 9–14. *See also* halftime
performances; spectacle
indigenous history, 120n62
industrialization, 14; impact on American
universities of, 10–11; post–Civil War, 111n6
Industrial Revolution, 4

ABOUT THE AUTHOR

JENNIFER GUILIANO earned a Ph.D. in history at the University of Illinois at Urbana-Champaign. She is coauthor of *DevDH.org*, a digital humanities resource guide, and currently works at Indiana University–Purdue University Indianapolis, where she is a tenure-track scholar in the Department of History.

CPSIA information can be obtained at www.ICGtesting.com
Printed in the USA
BVOW07s0257220515

401426BV00001B/4/P